THE TRIUMPH, TRAGEDY AND LOST LEGACY OF JAMES M LANDIS

James M Landis—scholar, administrator, advocate and political adviser—is known for his seminal contribution to the creation of the modern system of market regulation in the United States. As a highly influential participant in the politics of the New Deal, he drafted the statute which was to become the foundation for securities regulation in the US, and by extension the founding principle of financial market regulation across the world. He was also a complex and in some ways tragic figure, whose glittering career collapsed following the revelation that he had failed to pay tax for a five-year period in the 1950s. The oversight was to cost possible elevation to the Supreme Court, forced prosecution and sentencing in 1963 to one month's imprisonment, commuted to forced hospitalization, and subsequent suspension of licence to practice. This candid and revealing book sets his life in the context of his work as an academic, legislative draftsman, administrator and Dean of Harvard Law School. In rescuing from history Landis' battles and achievements in regulatory design, theory and practice, it speaks directly to the perennial problems in financial market regulation—how to deal with institutions deemed too big to fail, how to regulate the sale of complex financial instruments and the role that the professions can play as gatekeepers of market integrity. It argues that in failing to learn from the lessons of history we limit the capacity of regulatory intervention to facilitate cultural change, without which contemporary responses to financial crises are destined to fail.

The Triumph, Tragedy and Lost Legacy of James M Landis

A Life on Fire

Justin O'Brien

·HART·
PUBLISHING

OXFORD AND PORTLAND, OREGON
2017

Hart Publishing
An imprint of Bloomsbury Publishing Plc

Hart Publishing Ltd	Bloomsbury Publishing Plc
Kemp House	50 Bedford Square
Chawley Park	London
Cumnor Hill	WC1B 3DP
Oxford OX2 9PH	UK
UK	

www.hartpub.co.uk
www.bloomsbury.com

Published in North America (US and Canada) by
Hart Publishing
c/o International Specialized Book Services
920 NE 58th Avenue, Suite 300
Portland, OR 97213-3786
USA

www.isbs.com

**HART PUBLISHING, the Hart/Stag logo, BLOOMSBURY and the
Diana logo are trademarks of Bloomsbury Publishing Plc**

First published in hardback, 2014
Paperback edition, 2017

British Library Cataloguing-in-Publication Data
A catalogue record for this book is available from the British Library.

ISBN: PB: 978-1-50991-301-5
HB: 978-1-84946-617-2

Typeset by Compuscript Ltd, Shannon
Printed and bound in Great Britain by
Lightning Source UK Ltd

To find out more about our authors and books visit www.hartpublishing.co.uk. Here you will
find extracts, author information, details of forthcoming events and the option to sign up for our
newsletters.

For Mon Anguille

A wisp, a wick that is
its own taper and light
through the weltering dark.

Seamus Heaney, 'A Lough Neagh Sequence'[1]

---

[1] S Heaney, *A Door into the Dark* (London, Faber and Faber, 1969).

PREFACE

On Wednesday 29 September 2010 the *Financial Times* published a radical pledge. Seventeen senior financiers based in the City of London committed to subjugating the profit motive of trading floors to what was termed 'a larger social and moral purpose which governs and limits how they behave.'[1] Corporate responsibility to society, it was argued, could not be shirked nor delegated by the board and senior management: 'Ultimately, it is the responsibility of the leaders of financial institutions—not their regulators, shareholders or other stakeholders—to create, oversee and imbue their organizations with an enlightened culture based on professionalism and integrity. As leaders of financial institutions we recognize and accept this personal responsibility.'[2] The pledge, coming in the immediate aftermath of the global financial crisis (GFC), provided what appeared to be a demonstrable commitment to higher ethical standards. The public commitment was underscored by a major conference the following week at the Mansion House, the official residence of the Lord Mayor of the City of London. The incumbent, Nick Anstee, termed the pledge a 'manifesto.' It had, he claimed the capacity to 'silence the cynics and the pessimists who doubt the ability of the City to put its house in order.'[3]

The symbolic power of both the pledge and the conference derived from the articulation of a tangible corporate responsibility to society. Both were predicated on an acknowledgment that external oversight, no matter how invasive, could not vouchsafe societal protection. This could only be secured through 'the culture of organizations, and what they see themselves as existing to do, and how they ensure this culture is promoted and strengthened.'[4] The formulation appeared to transcend narrow legal obligation. It repositioned the corporation, particularly one based on financial services, as an agent of societal preferences. This, the signatories agreed, was the foundation stone of trust, without which no sustainable market could function. Nick Anstee warned with prescience, however, that failure would lead, inevitably and necessarily, to external monitoring. Four years later, the initiative lies in tatters. It is both ironic and (perhaps) fitting that the originator of the pledge should have been Marcus Agius, the former chairman of Barclays. He was forced to resign in August 2012 because

---

[1] M Agius et al, 'Financial Leaders Pledge Excellence and Integrity,' *Financial Times*, 29 September 2010, www.ft.com/intl/cms/s/0/eb26484e-cb2d-11df-95c0-00144feab49a.html#axzz2C8HKL1jb.

[2] Ibid.

[3] For background to conference, see A Hill, 'City's Ethics Awareness Lessons Must Percolate Down,' *Financial Times*, 4 October 2010, www.ft.com/intl/cms/s/0/87bd776e-cfec-11df-bb9e-00144feab49a.html#axzz3EcQP1rMb.

[4] Agius et al, above n 1.

of the bank's complicity in the still burgeoning London Interbank Offered Rate (Libor) manipulation scandal. The implications of the reputational demise of the Barclays chairman extend far beyond personal humiliation. International investigations at the time of writing (September 2014) are demonstrating the existence of a cartel operating at the highest echelons of finance that does much to undermine the coherence and efficacy of the crisis-management procedures put in place in the aftermath of the GFC.

Post-crisis there is always an incentive, if not necessity, for regulators to create new rules to rebuild trust and confidence. Ill-considered in design or implementation they can generate high compliance costs if not necessarily reducing risk. They can also exacerbate adversarial tensions. The current deadlock in Washington over implementation of the Wall Street Reform and Consumer Protection Act of 2010 (Dodd–Frank) replicates (and indeed speeds up) contestation over authority and legitimacy that is depressingly familiar to students of regulatory dynamics. The Public Company Accounting Reform and Investor Protection Act of 2002 (Sarbanes–Oxley), for example, passed in the aftermath of the collapse of Enron and WorldCom, was explicitly designed to embed 'corporate conscience'.[5] In implementation it transmogrified into a huge rent-seeking opportunity for the audit profession. Market conduct regulators saw authority progressively diminished and legitimacy questioned unless delivering an agenda geared towards the facilitation of risk. This risk we were told, repeatedly, had been diversified. It made the system more resilient than at any other time in history. It was indicative that the then chief executive of Citigroup, Chuck Prince, could tell the *Financial Times* in July 2007 that 'when the music stops, in terms of liquidity, things will be complicated. But as long as the music is playing, you've got to get up and dance. We're still dancing'.[6]

The scale of the crisis triggered by the vaporization of the US sub-prime securitization market in August 2007 demonstrated the fragility of a global architecture based on such an exceptionally emaciated conception of responsibility. That mistake was equally apparent in the City of London, where the vaunted risk-based principles-driven regulatory system was shown to be equally dysfunctional. From the perspective of this book, and policy formulation more generally, it is essential to emphasize that, irrespective of whether a rules- or principles-based approach was used to interpret regulatory purpose globally post Sarbanes–Oxley, neither proved capable of embedding restraint or effective risk management. This then raises the question of why?

In part the answer lies in the social mores of global finance. All markets are socially constructed. Their sustainability depends on the strength of the underpinning ecosystem that conditions practice. If through design or unintended consequences that system becomes corrupted there can be no long-term

---

[5] C Glassman, 'Sarbanes–Oxley and the Idea of "Good" Governance' (speech delivered at the American Society of Corporate Secretaries, Washington, DC, 27 September, 2002).

[6] M Nakamoto and D Wighton, 'Citigroup Chief Stays Bullish on Buy-outs,' *Financial Times*, 9 July 2007, www.ft.com/intl/cms/s/0/80e2987a-2e50-11dc-821c-0000779fd2ac.html#axzz2a0eeMBJF.

solution. The mistake was primarily an ideological one, based on the illusion of free markets and informed by the efficient capital market hypothesis. This controversial theory informed regulatory strategies globally. Its falsification has prompted a veritable avalanche of regulatory reform initiatives. Six years on, however, we remain mired in crisis management. This reflects, in part, the power of the financial services lobby. The stasis is also informed by ongoing contestation over what caused the crisis, degree of responsibility and what constitutes or should constitute the balance between rights and duties in the creation and maintenance of market integrity.

The risks have been intensified by the emergence of a new series of scandals, most notably the manipulation of key financial benchmarks. Critically, the manipulation post-dates the onset of the GFC and the bailouts it prompted of major financial institutions. That traders within the leading UK bank RBS, for example, which was effectively made a ward of state because of prior failure, could be allowed to attempt to manipulate Libor demonstrates all too clearly how pernicious banking culture had become and how disconnected from societal obligation contemporary practice within the industry had become. It is in this context that one must evaluate the reform agenda against the stated purpose of capital markets. Does the emphasis on creating safety nets divert attention from an ongoing malaise that misallocates capital? Can corporate culture be changed, and, if so, how? Crucially, what is or should be the role of the state? Answering these questions necessitates historical and comparative analysis. In this we have no better case study than the New Deal, the last major attempt to change the paradigm governing capital market regulation.

The initial success of the New Deal experiment can be traced to the combination of five ideational and political economy factors. First, the policy imperatives of the initial Roosevelt administration (1933–37) advanced the necessity and legitimacy of state intervention. Second, the policy imperatives were predicated on a rebalancing of private rights and public duties, a strategy that was subsequently overwhelmingly endorsed at the ballot box in 1936. Third, initial judicial skepticism that rendered legislative action unconstitutional was overcome by a progressive whittling away of the influential freedom of contract model, the growing institutionalization of judicial restraint and, in part, through an unconsummated but nevertheless real threat in 1937 to 'pack the court' unless the judiciary accepted political will. Fourth, the nascent administrative agencies, in particular the Securities and Exchange Commission (SEC), placed a 'cop on the beat,' doing much to restore public confidence. Fifth, the initial emphasis was not on direct enforcement but changing industry practice through an associational model of governance. It clearly specified purpose and sought to enroll market actors within a regulatory paradigm that replaced caveat emptor with a disclosure philosophy.

At its core was a belief that sustainable reform could only be achieved at an industry-wide level in which there was an internalization of responsibility. The tragedy is that there remains very little acceptance of that responsibility. Attempts by business today to limit the remit of the SEC over the granularity of regulation covering internal control mechanisms mirror the charged atmosphere pertaining as Landis was drawing up the legislation that established the agency. Writing in 1934 just before the bill was debated in the US Congress, Landis complained: 'The Stock Exchange Bill is receiving a terrific beating. All the corporate wealth of this country has gone into the attack and carried it all the way to the White House.'[7] Although the legislation was passed that year and the SEC established, its remit and authority waned incrementally at first and dramatically in the 1990s. The reduction in power has consistently failed to ignite public controversy.

In the absence of the kind of catastrophic crisis witnessed in the Great Crash of 1929 or the extent of corporate scandal revisited at the cusp of the millennium, again in 2008 and most recently the exposure of the Libor scandal, battles over financial regulation take piecemeal form through refinements in interpretation of legislative clauses. The fragmented and technical nature of this glacial process masks the cumulative effect of technical change. It can leave an outer shell of protection lacking the structural substance to withstand systemic shocks. Unfortunately, until the exposure of the Libor scandal, we were stuck in this dispiriting rut. In this sense the failure to deliver on the pledge for restraint by the erstwhile chairman of Barclays to the *Financial Times* is talismanic of the sector's bad faith. Society has a right to expect better. Regulators have a duty to ensure protection is offered and political actors an obligation to ensure the lessons of history are learnt.

In the course of writing this book I have amassed a number of intellectual debts, as well as an inordinate amount of air miles. I gratefully acknowledge the substantial financial support provided by the Australian Research Council. Its provision of a Future Fellowship has provided the freedom to engage in sustained research. My colleagues at the Centre for Law, Markets and Regulation (CLMR) at the University of New South Wales have put up with frequent absences and maintained the quality and quantity of analysis that has made our online portal such a significant resource in tracking regulatory policy. In particular I wish to thank my close friend and colleague George Gilligan as well as Scott Donald, Rob Nicholls and Megan Bowman as well as my sparring partner, Dimity Kingsford Smith. Beyond the CLMR, I wish to acknowledge the support of my Dean, David Dixon, who recognized the strategic importance of engaging with industry. This work also necessitated engagement with regulatory authorities and I would particularly like to thank the Australian Securities and Investments Commission for its continued support, in particular Greg Medcraft and Peter Kell. At international level I have learned enormously from interaction with Ashley Alder (Hong Kong), Leonardo Periera (Brazil), Howard Wetston (Ontario), Martin Wheatley (United Kingdom) and David Wright (Secretary General of the International Organization of Securities Commissions). At a practitioner level, I have also benefited greatly from the insights provided by leading

---

[7] T McCraw, *Prophets of Regulation* (Cambridge, MA, Harvard University Press, 1984) 178.

lawyers Greg Golding, Andrew Lumsden and John Morgan. The chief executive of the Professional Standards Authority, Deen Sanders, has been gracious in his interrogation of how regulatory theory can advance practice, the sine qua non of effective knowledge transfer. Senior academic colleagues in Australia engaged throughout the writing process, in particular John Braithwaite, Thomas Clarke, Olivia Dixon, Pamela Hanrahan, Ian Ramsay, Seumas Miller and Veronica Taylor. I have been exceptionally fortunate in the international network of scholars I interacted with on a regular basis. Charles O'Kelley has been a gracious host in Seattle, providing a refuge to sketch out the structure of this book. Lawrence Lessig and the team at the Edmond J Safra Center for Ethics at Harvard University, in particular Mark Somos, Bill English and Gregg Fields, provided an exceptionally enriching environment to tease out some of the themes in this book, while Colin Scott at University College Dublin provided the space to complete it. Eric Talley at Berkeley and Mel Dubnick at the University of New Hampshire provided much food for thought, as did the exceptionally erudite Dan Coquilette, author of a forthcoming history of Harvard Law School. Judge Jed Rakoff and his brother, Professor Todd Rakoff, were exceptionally helpful and I also wish to acknowledge Robert Morgenthau for agreeing to revisit the events associated with Landis' fall from grace. Sally Wheeler at Queen's University, Belfast, has long been a source of unparalleled knowledge, support, kindness and empathy at both professional and personal level for which I am humbly grateful. All authors require guidance and support from their publishers and Hart Publishing could not have provided more effective stewardship of this manuscript, from commissioning to publication.

As the loci of my research turns once again to present and future trajectories of regulation, I leave the past enriched by the process of historical investigation. The book could not have been completed without the generous support of friends and family and the inspiration provided by my children Elise, Jack, Justin and Saoirse. It is for them and for broader society that this book is designed. Without learning from history we risk repeating it. At its core, financial regulation is a normative exercise. We lose sight of its purpose at our peril. Tracing the lost history of the Landis experiment reminds one of the eel making its journey back to the fathoms of the Sargasso Sea, an image captured so vividly by Seamus Heaney in the epigram that informs this book. Returning to the origins of financial regulation, with Landis as our guide, we can see clearly how the past informs the present and how learning its lessons open up possibilities. They just need to be illuminated, as Elizabeth Headon, *mon anguille*, knows only too well.

Justin O'Brien
Cambridge, MA and Sydney
September 2014

CONTENTS

Preface   vii

Introduction – The Trials of James M Landis   1

1   The Draftsman: The Normative Underpinnings of the Disclosure
    Paradigm   13

2   The Administrator: Codes of Conduct and the Dynamics of
    Regulatory Politics   37

3   The Activist: Institutionalizing the New Deal   61

4   The Firefighter: The Existential Choice   81

5   The Transformational Dean: Law, Lawyers and Society   93

6   The Advisor: Revitalizing and Losing Regulatory Authority   113

7   The Fall: Hubris and the Making of a Greek Tragedy   135

Conclusion – The Lost Legacy: James M Landis and the
Future of Regulatory Capitalism   163

Index   189

Introduction

The Trials of James M Landis

'One grasps for shadows the better to comprehend sunlight. One reaches into the past, more clearly to know today and tomorrow. It is the privilege of all who care about education to test the depth and quality of that shadow for there, perhaps more than anywhere, one must try to pierce the brilliance of continuing dawns,' noted James M Landis, the Chairman of the Securities and Exchange Commission (SEC), in a speech delivered at the Catholic University of America in March 1937.[1] Landis, one of the most pivotal figures in establishing and legitimating external oversight of the capital markets, was at the time ruminating whether to return to the academy.

An outsider, born in Tokyo in 1899, Landis had risen to the apex of bureaucratic power. There he had put into practice the ideas that animated the progressive jurist Louis Brandeis, for whom he had clerked after graduating from Harvard Law School. His public service for the Roosevelt administration, his connections in both Washington and New York, and his preference for evidence over unsubstantiated assumption, had guided initial success, including at Harvard itself, where he became a tenured professor in 1929. Not surprisingly, Harvard's law faculty as well as the university itself was keen to see his return to Cambridge to navigate the relationship between Washington and the country's pre-eminent legal educational establishment, not least because of the rapid expansion of the federal bureaucracy.

As a legislative scholar, draftsman and regulator Landis knew few equals, then or since. While other prominent members of the informal Brains Trust that provided advice to Roosevelt were better known at the time, none with the exception of William O Douglas—a mercurial self-promoter who inveigled his way to the SEC and from there to the Supreme Court though the patronage of Landis—had such pronounced influence on regulatory policy. Four years on the frontline of at times vicious battles over whether and how to impose restrictions on freedom to contract in capital markets had, however, taken its toll. The SEC, the agency Landis had been instrumental in designing, had survived Supreme Court challenge, notwithstanding criticism from the bench that its methods risked application of unaccountable and arbitrary power.[2] It was an accusation that Landis treated with barely disguised contempt when in a major speech

---

[1] JM Landis, 'Address to the Third Annual Eastern Students Conference' (speech delivered at the Catholic University of America, 20 March 1937).
[2] *Jones v Securities and Exchange Commission*, 298 US 1, 24–25 (1936).

1

in Chicago just ten days before the Catholic University address he accused a majority of the Supreme Court of 'writing their own individual economic prejudices and predilections into the fabric of constitutional law.'[3] Such trenchant criticism of the highest court in the land reflected intellectual bravery. It showed willingness to engage in partisan disputes in equal measure. It also reflected a personal commitment to the praxis between cutting-edge academic research and policy development. For Landis in 1937 a further tactical and strategic challenge remained unresolved: how and through what mechanism to institutionalize the ideational gains of the New Deal?

The challenge consumed him as he oscillated between the academy and regulatory and private practice over the next three decades. It was a quest that was to prove his personal undoing. In 1963 Landis was publicly humiliated in the Federal Court of the Southern District of New York, where he was convicted and sentenced to one month's imprisonment for failing to file income tax returns. Commuted to forced hospitalization on the orders of Chief Justice Sylvester Ryan, the ruling sent an unambiguous message that none could be held above the law.[4] The case and its handling had profound political implications for the Kennedy administration, which had mandated a substantial reorganization of regulatory agencies as a result of specific recommendations made by Landis to the president-elect in December 1960. In prosecuting the architect of the New Deal for what amounted to a misdemeanor, the Department of Justice felt it had little choice. Landis was to become a victim of political expediency.[5] An already brittle personality cracked under the strain. Landis entered a downward spiral into alcoholism and depression. His personal and professional life disintegrated. Despite the suggestion by Chief Justice Ryan that Landis could once more aspire to greatness, the judge was no doubt aware that the defendant would probably never recover. He never did. A year later he was dead, found floating in his swimming pool three weeks after being suspended from legal practice. The tragedy was complete.

On his death in July 1964 the *New York Times* noted that Landis had 'achieved the rare distinction of being regarded as a conservative by liberals and as an extreme liberal by conservatives.'[6] What drove him remained elusive throughout his life. As an early extended profile in *Fortune* magazine put it following his nomination to the SEC in 1933, the 'gaunt, hawk-like, scholarly' professor 'had one talent lacking in certain of his conferees when he came to Washington, he

---

[3] JM Landis, 'The Power the Court has Appropriated' (speech delivered at Fourth Annual Woman Conference, Chicago, 10 March 1937), reprinted in *Vital Speeches of the Day* (1 April 1937) 358, http://web.ebscohost.com/ehost/pdfviewer/pdfviewer?sid=ea9e0eb3-63db-41a9-bfdd-2960ba8ffd95%40sessionmgr4&vid=2&hid=17. For a full discussion of the speech and its significance, see Chapter 3.

[4] *United States of America v James McCauley Landis*, 63 Cr 654 (1963).

[5] As late as the 1980s, non-payment of income taxes was 'rampant' among law partners in New York City: see D Seligman, 'Middle Age Delinquents,' *Fortune*, 18 December 1989, http://money.cnn.com/magazines/fortune/fortune_archive/1989/12/18/72857/index.htm.

[6] 'James M Landis Found Dead in Swimming Pool of Home,' *New York Times*, 31 July 1964, 1, 21 at 21

knew how to keep his mouth shut. So he remains the unknown that he was the day he stepped off the train from Boston.'[7] He was to remain socially distant throughout his career. He continually sacrificed friendships for the allure and transformative capacity of power to effect social change. Notwithstanding the social awkwardness and somewhat abrasive personality, in his lifetime Landis garnered personal admiration from within his narrow circle of social friends and broad professional respect in equal measure. 'I loved the man dearly. He had a most unusual mind. I mean yes, was he self-destructive? Did he drink too much? Did he? Yes. ... [A] remarkable mind and a good human being. Just destroyed himself,' was the plaintive assessment of close colleague and partner in a legal practice, Justin Feldman.[8] A more distant appreciation in the *Harvard Law Review* noted that Landis was 'on fire' as a student.[9] It also epitomized an illustrious public career primarily informed by but not limited to his stewardship of the disclosure paradigm that underpins securities regulation.

Landis was the critical architect of the Securities Act (1933), governing new issuance, and the Securities Exchange Act (1934), which extended regulatory oversight to existing securities and mandated associational governance with the exchanges through the establishment of the SEC.[10] He served on the agency's inaugural board, becoming its second chairman with the public endorsement of his predecessor.[11] As Joe Kennedy left the SEC headquarters he interrupted the first Landis press conference by calling out 'Good-bye Jim. Good luck to you. Knock 'em over.'[12] It was to be the start of a lifelong collaboration with the Kennedy family.[13] By the time of Landis' death three decades later, Joe Kennedy was incapacitated by a serious stroke. The president, groomed for office under

[7] 'Legend of Superman Surrounds James Landis,' *Milwaukee Journal*, 29 July 1934, 5 (extracting *Fortune Magazine*, August 1934 profile).

[8] Interview with Justin Feldman, SEC Historical Society, 22 June 2004, 83, http://3197d6d14b5f19f2f440-5e13d29c4c016cf96cbbfd197c579b45.r81.cf1.rackcdn.com/collection/oral-histories/feldman062204Transcript.pdf; see also *The Reminiscences of Justin Feldman* (Columbia University Oral History Project, 1973) 181 (describing Landis as 'one of the greatest human beings I have ever known').

[9] E Griswold, 'James McCauley Landis 1899–1964' (1964) 78 *Harvard Law Review* 313, 316 ('Surely a man who has done so much should be judged by the best that he can do; and Landis at his best was a great lawyer and legal scholar').

[10] For biographies of Landis, see D Ritchie, *James M Landis, Dean of Regulators* (Cambridge, MA, Harvard University Press, 1980); T McCraw, *Prophets of Regulation* (Cambridge, MA, Harvard University Press, 1984); see also J Braithwaite and P Drahos, 'Globalization of Corporate Regulation and Corporate Citizenship', in F MacMillan (ed), *International Corporate Law Annual* (2003) 26 (describing Landis as a seminal scholar of regulatory strategy).

[11] 'Landis Heads SEC; Succeeds Kennedy,' *New York Times*, 24 September 1935, 1, 37 (quoting Kennedy saying: 'I see no reason in the world why any business interests need have the slightest misgiving that he will not give them the fairest and squarest deal a man can get. I would deem it an honor to have him as a trustee of anything I owned. He is thoroughly cognizant of the importance of the successful administration of these acts in helping to revive the business of the country': 1).

[12] Ibid, 37.

[13] D Nasaw, *The Patriarch: The Remarkable Life and Turbulent Times of Joseph P Kennedy* (New York, Penguin Books, 2012) 769 (noting the appointment of Landis as special advisor to John F Kennedy, the president-elect, in 1960 and articulating that next to family Joseph Kennedy 'trusted no one to watch out for his son as he did Jim Landis').

the watchful direction of Landis, was also dead, victim of assassination in Dallas the previous November. Robert Kennedy, who as Attorney General bore ultimate responsibility for the Landis prosecution, represented the contemporary House of Camelot. Visibly moved by the tragedy that had befallen the key engineer of the administrative process, Robert Kennedy openly wept at Landis' funeral service.[14] It was indicative of wider political remorse that the then Deputy Attorney General, Nicholas Katzenbach, gave the eulogy. Given the inherent conflict of interest associated with Landis' relationship with the Kennedy family, Katzenbach had overseen the investigation and prosecution on the tax charges. Notwithstanding his calculation of the political necessity of prosecution, Katzenbach viewed the Ryan judgment as an 'outrageous demonstration of judicial ego.'[15] Reviewing the evidence it is hard to disagree with the somewhat partial assessment of Arthur Schlesinger that for all concerned the case was 'an unhappy business.'[16] The extent to which it is so is fully revealed in the final chapter of this book, based on remarkable testimony from Robert Morgenthau, the prosecutor in the case and sole surviving participant.

Before evaluating the fall and its impact on regulatory design, it is necessary to reconstruct Landis' importance as a regulatory theorist and practitioner. In so doing the arc of his life and its relevance to contemporary debate on financial regulation can be more accurately presented. Of critical importance in this respect is the integration of technical and normative considerations in regulatory design. The creation of the SEC allowed Landis to experiment with a framework he had first articulated in 1931.[17] Integrating enforcement with attempts to guide industry towards socially beneficial outcomes, Landis never saw the regulatory agency's role as solely that of policing. He maintained that administrative law could, should and did perform a crucial task in operationalizing initial democratic choices and subsequent political mandates. At the same time, he was profoundly aware of the challenge of ensuring appropriate accountability mechanisms, the failure to attend to which would leave the entire project subject to judicial criticism.

Through a combination of tactics and strategy there can be no questioning his mercurial shrewdness in establishing and legitimizing the regulatory state. A

---

[14] Ritchie, above n 10, 202.

[15] N Katzenbach, *Some of It Was Fun: Working With RFK and LBJ* (New York, WW Norton & Co, 2008) 102 (describing the case of one of the hardest things had to do in the Department of Justice). In a promotional interview for the book, Katzenbach describes the case as 'something that had to be done,' which he argued Landis himself was aware of and accepted but which 'did not amount to a row of beans,' see http://bigthink.com/users/nicholaskatzenbach#!video_idea_id=5612.

[16] A Schlesinger, *Robert Kennedy and his Times* [1978] (New York, Mariner Books, 2002) 391.

[17] JM Landis, 'The Study of Legislation at Law Schools: An Imaginary Inaugural Lecture' (1931) 39 *Harvard Graduates Magazine* 433 ('The criminal penalty, the civil penalty, the resort to the injunctive side of equity, the tripling of damage claims, the informers share, the penalizing force of pure publicity, the licence as a condition of pursuing certain conduct, the confiscation of offending property—these are the samples of the thousand and one devices that the ingenuity of many legislatures has produced. Their effectiveness to control one field and their ineffectiveness to control others remains yet to be explored': 437).

review of his writings and experience demonstrates that throughout his public life Landis had not sought power for material benefit. Instead, the critical animating purpose was to direct progress, address real social needs and face down vested interests, which by virtue of their power had the capacity and resources to subvert democratic will in favor of what he saw as outmoded claims to authority. It was this belief system that informed his extraordinary attack on the Supreme Court in Chicago referenced above.[18] This belief system itself cannot be understood in a vacuum. It was forged as a consequence of his upbringing as a child of missionary parents and further scarified by the horror and carnage of World War One, during which he served as a volunteer for the YMCA. In academic terms, it was honed in the febrile atmosphere of the 1920s, in which the parameters of normal science were stretched as never before, and put into practice as a consequence of Roosevelt's landslide election in 1932.

James McCauley Landis was born in Tokyo on the cusp of the twentieth century. He spent his formative years in Japan, where his parents had dedicated their lives as Presbyterian missionaries. The young Landis was initially educated in what he later reflected was 'one of the most extraordinary schools I ever attended.'[19] By the age of thirteen he had been taught the Greek and Roman classics, including Horace and Cicero, by an 'Irish schoolmaster whose standards were equivalent to those of Harrow and Eton.'[20] It was an experience that was to inform Landis' commitment to educational excellence as he progressed to Princeton and then Harvard, where he secured the highest marks of his class, and one of the best academic records in the history of the law school. As Erwin Griswold, the Dean of Harvard Law School pointed out in an appreciation published after his death

> Landis had a brilliant mind. But it was a restless mind, too. He did not know how to relax. He was always reaching out, seeking new fields, new tasks, new challenges. Perhaps his missionary background had something to do with his constant search for new releases of his energy.[21]

A more personal assessment came from Justin Feldman, his law firm partner, who detected an inner loneliness in Landis informed by his separation from an austere but happy family life at the age of 13 to return to the United States.[22]

Both assessments are reflected in a series of taped interviews Landis gave to Columbia University's Oral History Project in 1963 and 1964. The interviews, conducted as Landis faced prosecution for tax violations, shed considerable light on the forces that forged his driven personality. What becomes clear is the profound presence and absence of his father. 'He was an extraordinary

---

[18] Landis, above n 3.

[19] *The Reminiscences of James M Landis* (New York, Oral History Collection, Columbia University, 1964) 2.

[20] Ibid.

[21] Griswold, above n 9, 316.

[22] Interview with Justin Feldman, above n 8, 83.

man. I never appreciated him until perhaps it was too late,' Landis reflected.[23] The voice noticeably softens as he recalls growing up in Tokyo. His father had dedicated his life to the development of Japan, assimilating rather than living an expatriate life. His father's life was, according to Landis, one well lived. It was a life to which his German-born mother adapted, teaching Sunday school and working as a volunteer in a leprosy hospital. The combination of 'considerable Biblical indoctrination in childhood' with its focus on leprosy and a fear of contagion terrified the young Landis, who was brought by his mother along with his sister to the hospital to give a violin recital.[24] The incident was, however, talismanic of how values were instilled in the household. For the Landis family, it was not enough to preach religious certainty. The faith had to be lived:

> It was part of the routine of life, and you took that, just as you take any routine that is imposed by family life. I didn't resent it at all. I had no feeling of resentment about it whatever. Just like having coffee for breakfast or something of that nature.[25]

For Landis, the critical influence his father imposed was, therefore, a code of living:

> My father never believed … that you had to take every word of the Bible for literal truth. He was too intelligent a man to do that. But he did believe in certain fundamental truths of it. He was a little strict about it, a little stricter than my mother. My mother liked to play cards, for example. He wouldn't play, but she taught us. He had no objection to it. My mother used to live to have a drink of beer on occasion. Being a German she liked it. Well, he wouldn't. He was strict about things like that. But he had enough sense not to impose personal restrictions upon other people. He had certain ethical restrictions that he imposed upon the family as a whole.[26]

The ethical code, combined with many years spent outside the United States, meant that the family was cast as perennial outsiders. When forced to leave Japan in the aftermath of World War One, Landis' father was distraught:

> He was unhappy here [in the United States]. You take a man of 55 who has spent all of his life in Japan, unfamiliar with this country when he comes back, he can't really get a good teaching job or something of that nature and his friends are all out there

reflected Landis.[27] By that stage, Landis was ensconced in Princeton. His connections with important Presbyterian laymen facilitated his father's return to his beloved Japan:

> With a bit of organization, we put together these laymen and got them to exert some pressure on the church, and the church in turn, succeeded in putting a little pressure on the government. So he went back. Well, he really went back to die, which he did

---

[23] *The Reminiscences of James M Landis*, above n 19, 4.
[24] Ibid, 11.
[25] Ibid, 11.
[26] Ibid, 12. William Jennings Bryan was an influential Democrat politician who unsuccessfully ran for president on three separate occasions between 1896 and 1908. A devout Christian, he opposed Darwinism on religious grounds.
[27] Ibid, 7.

within three years of that time. I think I knew that, but it was better that he die there than that he die here.[28]

By that time Landis' own religious faith had eroded, in large part as a consequence of his own experiences on the western front. Like many of his generation, World War One was to change Landis in a profound manner. Too young to enlist, he became a medical volunteer in 1917 with the British Young Men's Christian Association, later transferring to the American division when he reached the age of eighteen. Dispatched to the frontline in Ypres, he witnessed at first hand the carnage of trench warfare. It was to destroy belief in a charitable God if not in the need for social order:

> I didn't lose my faith in say, Woodrow Wilsons's concept of social justice and I don't say I became an atheist. That isn't so. But to assume that there is a good God—I don't assume that there isn't any God—but to assume there is as good God, all of my experiences fail to engender any basis for an inference of that type. I've seen too much tragedy in my life.[29]

In an environment of senseless slaughter he found active attempts to recruit to the faith bordering on the obscene:

> They had a lot of ministers or guys who wanted to see ministers come in there and they wanted to do the job of conversion. Well, I certainly have no objection to honest-to-god padres, who know their business and know when they should talk religion and when they should not. But this business of trying to get hymn singing going every night at 7 o' clock or 8 o'clock or something of that nature is just nonsense.[30]

On his return to the United States he embarked on a different course. 'I abjured the idea of the ministry after my experiences in World War One. I knew I could have no faith in preaching something which I didn't believe.' He returned to Princeton, where he toyed with the idea of being a writer 'but there did not seem to be much opportunity along that line, because I had no resources to keep myself going.'[31] He applied for and won a scholarship at Harvard Law School:

> The legal profession sort of interested me and I went there but I made up my mind that if after the first year I didn't like it or I didn't do well, hell, I'd go somewhere else, get some other job or something of that nature. Fortunately or unfortunately, at the end of the first year I headed the class. Well, I had to go on. I moved from 75—which is nothing today—75 was then a great mark. I moved from 75 to 82, which was extraordinary.[32]

The person who made the most lasting impression on Landis at Harvard was Felix Frankfurter, with whom he worked, initially as a research assistant and then as a co-author:

---

[28] Ibid, 7.
[29] Ibid, 13.
[30] Ibid, 23–24.
[31] Ibid, 31.
[32] Ibid 32.

He was a time-consuming man to work with. In other words if you worked with him he could spent two or three hours talking around the subject before he either got down to the point of going over a memorandum that you had written or dictating anything on it himself.

The following year he went to Washington to clerk with Louis Brandeis, a job brokered by Frankfurter, a year Landis described as 'one of the best years I ever spent in my life.'[33]

[Brandeis] was a great man, a far greater man than most men I have had the opportunity to meet. ... He was a pretty generous man too—I mean generous from an intellectual standpoint. He had the habit of getting a new secretary every year, which in a way was an exhibition of his own humility, because he felt that after one year he'd taught them all that he could teach them. But once you proved yourself with him, and that would take maybe two, three weeks, namely that you were trained, he was extremely generous to you. He took you in, substantially as a junior partner of his firm. Of course he had ultimate responsibility, no question about that. Again and again, I can recall where he would hold up a majority opinion or a dissent just because I disagreed. We would resolve the ultimate disagreement either by my agreeing with him, or by our understanding as to what we disagreed about.[34]

What Landis was taught primarily, however, was a belief in social justice and the critical role to be played by government in advancing it. A brief visit to the Soviet Union gave the young lawyer a lifelong sympathy for the goals of communism but a belief that incremental change through social democracy offered a more humane as well as productive alternative. In the existential conflict between capitalism, socialism and democracy, Landis was very much influenced by the vision articulated by Joseph Schumpeter, the former Austrian Finance Minister, who also taught at Harvard. As with Schumpeter he was aware of the power of the 'creative destruction' of capitalism, recognizing with his fellow academic that the stock market was a poor substitute for the Holy Grail. Where he departed from the economist was a lifelong belief in the view that law was made not given and that those choices, inherently political in nature, were best delivered under the guise of neutral experts insulated from the vagaries of the electoral cycle.

On his return to Harvard, in one of his first public lectures, for example, Landis noted that the development of health and safety legislation, 'a response to a very real need, was enacted in the face of bitter opposition, and represented a growing consciousness on the part of society that there were limits upon what trade could demand of society.'[35] Ten years later, following his tenure at the SEC, he delivered essentially the same message arguing that:

[S]tatutory mechanisms can be looked at in terms of creating liberties or rights of

---

[33] Ibid, 37.

[34] Ibid, 37–38.

[35] See eg JM Landis, 'Restrictive Legislation as a Social Benefit' (speech delivered at the Conference on the Problems of the New England Textile Industry under the Auspices of the Committee on Women in Industry of the Cambridge League of Women Voters, Harvard Business School, 28 May 1929) 7.

groups of people, the liberty to be protected against market manipulation, the creation of a right of continuity in radio programs, or of a right of reasonable safety in one's bank deposits. … To view departures from a nineteenth century economy as an encroachment upon the democratic idea, is to insist that democracy and a laissez-faire philosophy of government must go hand in hand.[36]

He recognized from the beginning, therefore, that tactical success at the regulatory level was subject to shifting political priorities. Strategic success required shaping the trajectory of the legal profession as a whole. In Landis's worldview, a lasting transformation of American political and legal discourse could only be achieved through the praxis between regulatory practice, academic thought leadership and, critically, a sense of professional obligation that put service ahead of client interest. Such an integrated approach to legal theory and practice made him one of the leading policy entrepreneurs of his time.[37]

There was no better place to effect such a transformation than through stewarding the strategic direction of Harvard Law School, the alma mater from which he, along with Felix Frankfurter, built up the field of administrative law. It was no surprise then that later in 1937 Landis accepted the position to lead Harvard Law School. As only the fifth dean in its history, he took over from his professional nemesis, Roscoe Pound. Although drawn increasingly to a succession of government assignments as the university operated on a skeletal basis during the war years, he was to lay the foundations of a transformative academic agenda that encompassed but extended far beyond regulatory politics.

Just one year after his appointment as Dean of Harvard Law School he was to pen *The Administrative Process*. This retrospective theoretical justification of the regulatory state remains his abiding public legacy.[38] It is less remarked upon how Landis was forced to manage and (at times fall foul of) the existential conflict between political calculation and administrative integrity. Nowhere was this conflict more evident than in his appointment as the deportation examiner in a 1939 case that transfixed the United States.

The ruling and its rationale, which was subsequently overturned in 1942 on overt political grounds,[39] gives granular articulation of the ideas that shape *The Administrative Process*, a book that Landis always meant as a preamble rather than a definitive text. 'Some day,' he wrote to a colleague at the University of Iowa in 1939, 'I hope I can get time to really explore and extend some of the ideas that were there advanced in a rather tentative manner, or better, I hope that someone

---

[36] JM Landis, 'Law and New Liberties' (1939) 4 *Missouri Law Review* 105, 107–08.

[37] R Shamir, *Managing Legal Uncertainty: Elite Lawyers and the New Deal* (Durham, NC, Duke University Press, 1995) 152.

[38] JM Landis, *The Administrative Process* (New Haven, Yale University Press, 1938).

[39] *The Reminiscences of James M Landis*, above n 19, 59. The Supreme Court eventually found that decision unconstitutional in a ruling that referenced favorably Landis' adjudication: see *Bridges v Wixon* 326 US 135 (1945). This did not stop ongoing prosecution. The issue was finally resolved in Bridges' favor in 1953, see *Bridges v United States*, 346 US 209 (1953), which again referenced Landis, arguing that 'only a weak yielding to extra-judicial clamor would excuse acceptance of the testimony of witnesses to this case as proof of the allegations of the complaint': see *United States v Bridges*, 133 F Supp 638, 643.

else will do it.'[40] The book derives from a series of lectures given at Yale and is widely regarded, with justification, as a classic. As the then Dean of Yale Law School, Charles Clark, put it to Landis, 'I have been reading over your lectures, and think they are fine. They state positively, with force and reasoned argument, what to date has been so generally said only by way of defense from attacks. I think they well might prove a Bible for the Washington departments.'[41] The political damage caused by the Bridges hearing, however, had blunted Landis's capacity to engage at the highest levels of the political establishment. The death of Roosevelt in 1945 meant he lost critical political support that was only truly re-established with the presidential election of John F Kennedy in 1960.

For the neophyte president, lacking in executive expertise, Landis was a critical resource, whose long association with the family provided a basis for trust. The subsequent Landis report for Kennedy on how to rejuvenate the administrative process reflected just how far from the ideal the regulatory agencies he was so instrumental in midwifing had deteriorated from original purpose.[42] In so doing he suggested concrete measures to deal with what his colleague Louis Jaffe had termed the regulatory disease of 'arteriosclerosis.'[43] It was, however, a challenge that Landis was unable to implement in practice. In part this can be traced to the rise in professional lobbying, which had significantly reduced Landis' capacity when serving as the chair of the Civil Aeronautics Board in the Truman administration, a post he lost in 1947 (by voluntarily resigning before

---

[40] JM Landis to Professor Paul Sayre, University of Iowa Law School, 14 February 1939, Harvard University Archive, Dean's Office UAV512.20 1937–39, Correspondence Box 5. Remarkably, however, some of Landis' colleagues continued to present a manifesto drawn up in 1938 as a complete, unchanging, program: see also L Jaffe, 'James Landis and the Administrative Process' (1964) 78 *Harvard Law Review* 319 ('We must recall that our generation—that of Landis and myself—judged the administrative process in terms of its stunning performance under the New Deal. We did not in our estimate take into account the unique concatenation of circumstance which made for that performance: the desperate panic of the people, the terrible shock to the confidence and prestige of those who had held power; the rush into the vacuum of a whole phalanx of talented, passionate, exasperated, deprived men, those who for years had been clamoring for reform, and those who were their disciples. ... These were the galvanic forces that brought the New Deal legislation and stoked the high fires of its administration': 323).

[41] Charles Clark to James Landis, 27 January 1938, Dean's Office UAV.512.20 1940–47 Correspondence Claflin–Del Box 9, Harvard University Archives.

[42] JM Landis, *Report on Regulatory Agencies to the President-Elect* (21 December 1960), available at: http://c0403731.cdn.cloudfiles.rackspacecloud.com/collection/papers/1960/1960_1221_Landis_report.pdf; see also *The Reminiscences of James M Landis*, above n 19, 638 (noting that '[R]outine business before these administrative agencies was much too heavy to permit them to do the broad kind of policymaking that was essential. They didn't have the power to delegate enough of their duties, so that they could keep, in a sense, their desks clean and their minds free to think about the major problems they faced'). The arguments foreshadowed many made by regulatory capture theorists: see G Stigler, 'Public Regulation of the Securities Markets' (1964) 37 *Journal of Business* 117.

[43] L Jaffe, 'The Effective Limits of the Administrative Process: A Reevaluation' (1954) 67 *Harvard Law Review* 1105 (describing how agencies had become rigidified, a process he terms rather vividly 'arteriosclerosis': 1109. Jaffe concluded '[W]e have evolved our administrative system. We have worked out a great variety of basic forms and doctrines, which have determined its structure and its relation to the other organs of government. But its operation in some respects has not been clearly foreseen. It is to these aspects of the system that we must now direct our energies': 1135).

being pushed) because of vehement industry opposition.[44] In part it was also compromised as a consequence of the secret investigation into his tax affairs, which forced a progressive removal from public office. His fall from grace lost the academy and the policy community a vital voice as political discourse began to conceive government as the problem of, but not the solution to, the complexities of contemporary life.

There is much historical and contemporary value in revisiting these pivotal conflicts. Indeed, the issues they raise of regulatory authority, legitimacy and accountability continue to resonate. They remain some of the defining if intractable problems of our time. What are the appropriate limits of government? Can or should administrative agencies displace the judiciary? Is the relationship between executive agencies and government truly independent or interdependent? What constitutes or should constitute expertise? What accountability mechanisms should be put in place to guard against arbitrary exercise of power? These issues are explored thematically in successive chapters.

From the design of the disclosure paradigm (1933) through the Angel Island deportation hearing (1939) to his report two decades later to president-elect Kennedy (1960), the book discusses the centrality of Landis and his vision to the formulation and implementation of regulatory theory and practice. Critical to that process is the critical question of purpose. For Landis, the question of why one regulates is of paramount importance. Of necessity, this requires an ongoing dialogue between the regulator and the regulated and subservience of vested interests to the public good, which, in turn, has to be politically mediated. How to secure the legitimacy of such intervention remains foundational to regulatory authority. As with Banquo's ghost in Shakespeare's *Macbeth*, however, Landis has himself all but disappeared from public view. It is indicative, for example, that Landis' portrait does not adorn the walls of the imposing library at Langdell Hall, the centerpiece of the Harvard Law School campus. He is the only former dean of Harvard Law School not accorded such professional courtesy. The only public recognition at Harvard is a bronze sculpture, hidden from public view just down the aisle from the Elihu Root Special Collection Room, an addition to the library Landis himself had commissioned to facilitate historical research.

The failure to hang the commissioned portrait is, I argue, unfortunate. There is much for Harvard as an institution to be proud of in celebrating the life and times of one of its most illustrious students and academic leaders. This is not in any way to downplay Landis's own responsibility for his downfall. The tragedy— the result of hubris, willful blindness and procrastination in equal measure—was avoidable. More importantly, however, we have in the process lost sight of the normative underpinnings of the disclosure paradigm he was so instrumental in building. It is time once again, as Landis admonished, to grasp 'in the shadows

---

[44] 'Chairman Landis of CAB Ousted by Truman,' *St Petersburg Times*, 31 December 1947, 2; 'Firing Jim Landis Stirs Biggest Fuss in Years,' *St Petersburg Times*, 10 January 1948, 7 (noting that Landis had antagonized both the airlines and the influential Secretary of Commerce, Averill Harriman, whom the regulator treated as 'a not too bright law student').

the better to comprehend sunlight.'[45] 2014 marks the eightieth anniversary of the creation of the SEC, the federal agency that most completely reflects Landis' distinct approach to regulatory design. It also marks the fiftieth anniversary of his passing. In exploring the triumph, tragedy and lost legacy of James M Landis, the book asks a fundamental question: what are the contemporary consequences of failing to incorporate the lessons of history into the design and ongoing evaluation of sustainable capital markets?

The book draws on a series of interviews provided to the Columbia University Oral History Project.[46] It is also informed by a review of additional personal papers relating to Landis' tenure as dean at Harvard Law School. These papers were made available to scholars for the first time in January 2013. They detail how Landis used the position to transform the form, content and purpose of legal education and the responsibility of the academic as a public intellectual. They also make clear that in design and application, the normative question of why one regulates trumps the technical considerations of how one regulates. As such they provide a particularly illuminating lens through which to explore the contemporary problems of regulatory design. In large measure, the problems are remarkably similar. In exploring the reasons for his triumph and explaining (but not condoning) the factors that led to his fall from grace, this book seeks to reconnect contemporary regulatory politics with its normative roots. In so doing it also provides a rationale for the hanging of portrait still held in storage at Harvard Law School of one of the most illustrious, if flawed, students, scholars and citizens it has ever produced.

---

[45] Landis, above n 1.
[46] See *The Reminiscences of James M Landis*, above n 29.

1

The Draftsman: The Normative Underpinnings of the Disclosure Paradigm

The New Deal remains the paradigmatic and most sophisticated, holistic attempt to shift cultural mores by imposing external restraints on capital market governance. As with the contemporary manifestation of financial crisis, the architects of the New Deal were forced to confront questions associated with opacity and complexity in the design and marketing of financial products, how to embed restraint, and how to define and limit systemic risk. Despite the similarities in terms of scale and societal impact, there is one fundamental difference. In sharp contrast to the piecemeal reforms of today, the New Deal was based on a fundamental, if at times conflicting, reshaping of corporate and regulatory purpose. The eventual result, to be sure, was haphazard and, at times, chaotic. Rendering private corporate interests—if only temporarily—subservient to societal obligation did, however, lead to a profound recalibration of American society. Moreover, the erosion of that compact has, in large part, brought us a successively damaging series of interlinked corporate and regulatory scandals. Seen in this context, the global financial crisis of 2007 onwards is not a failure of culture. Rather, it is what happens when the needs and self-referential cultural framing of specific communities of practice gain broader ideational support. Critical in this regard has been the intermediating power of Wall Street and other prominent financial centers to shift social, cultural and, crucially, political norms. The emphasis on the welfare-enhancing impact of light-touch regulation, the privileging of freedom and innovation over security and stewardship were purported to advance communal virtues. More accurately they reflected unsustainable (and ultimately failed) self-serving commercial values. Not for the first time in regulatory design, the search for credible reform necessitates going back to the future in order to reclaim a lost institutional memory.

For the progenitors of the original administrative state in the 1930s the aim was not to operate within accepted paradigms—legal, economic, political, institutional or theoretical. The objective was to destabilize them by creating an alternative reality. It was one informed by direct federal intervention across large swathes of industrial society. The critical objective was not the overthrow of capitalism but rather credible ongoing sustainable reform in which regulatory authority could guide a given industry as a whole towards socially beneficial outcomes. The unresolved question was on what basis such an approach could or should be legitimated.

The scale of the ambition in addressing this conundrum, as outlined in Franklin D Roosevelt's presidential nomination speech at the Democratic convention in 1932, remains as breathtaking in its audacity as eerily apposite to contemporary problems of regulatory design in capital markets:

> Out of every crisis, every tribulation, every disaster, mankind rises with some share of greater knowledge, of higher decency, of purer purpose. Today we shall have come through a period of loose thinking, descending morals, an era of selfishness, among individual men and women and among Nations. Blame not Governments alone for this. Blame ourselves in equal share. Let us be frank in acknowledgment of the truth that many amongst us have made obeisance to Mammon, that the profits of specula-tion, the easy road without toil, have lured us from the old barricades. To return to higher standards we must abandon the false prophets and seek new leaders of our own choosing.[1]

By the time of his inauguration the following March, Roosevelt's rhetoric had soared still further. The *ancien régime*, already discredited by the economic and social calamity of the Wall Street crash and its immediate aftermath, crumbled. It lost all remaining credibility as targeted hearings in Congress found in banking executives a series of villains that appeared recruited direct from central casting. Roosevelt ruthlessly exploited the hearings, which were conceived by his prede-cessor, Herbert Hoover, while retaining a distance form policy calibration in the interregnum between election and attaining power in March 1933. He quietly suggested the expansion of the hearings on the cusp of inauguration, seeing in them the strands to be weaved into a compelling narrative for the articulation of an as yet to be conceived vision.[2] It provided the backdrop for a political screenplay directed by a politician who retained an adroit understanding of the possibilities and limitations associated with the integration of technical and normative dimensions in public policy formulation and implementation. Criti-cally, as Roosevelt understood perfectly, the moral laxity of Wall Street financiers provided an unprecedented, if contingent, window of opportunity to advocate and implement federal controls on both business and the capital markets. This was a crisis the president was determined not to waste, political currents permit-ting. While his inaugural speech is best remembered for the soaring admonition to a cowed people that 'the only thing to fear is fear itself,' the historical signifi-cance lies in the call to reorder social norms:

---

[1] FD Roosevelt, 'The New Deal' (speech delivered at the Democratic National Convention, 2 July 1932). For contemporary disputation over whether market ordering reflects rationality, see R Shiller, 'A Debate Simmers in Stockholm,' *New York Times*, 18 January 2014, BU6.

[2] For background to the hearings, see M Perino, *The Hellhound of Wall Street: How Ferdinand Pecora's Investigation of the Great Crash Forever Changed American Finance* (New York, Penguin Press, 2010); see also J Burk, 'The Origins of Federal Securities Regulation: A Case Study in the Social Control of Finance' (1985) 63 *Social Forces* 1010 (noting the critical, if neglected, impacts of a 'series of politically contingent events beyond the power of financiers (or anyone else) to foresee or to control': 1027).

The moneychangers have fled from their high seats in the temple of our civilization. We may now restore that temple to the ancient truths. The measure of the restoration lies in the extent to which we apply social values more noble than mere monetary profit. … There must be an end to a conduct in banking and in business, which too often has given to a sacred trust the likeness of callous and selfish wrongdoing. Small wonder that confidence languishes, for it thrives only on honesty, on honor, on the sacredness of obligations, on faithful protection, on unselfish performance; without them it cannot live. Restoration calls, however, not for changes in ethics alone. This Nation asks for action, and action now.[3]

This emphasis on action, however, flatters to deceive. It presupposes that Roosevelt came to office with a predetermined integrated program. Finding discrete mechanisms to operationalize political change remained frustratingly elusive. This applied at both micro- and macro-levels. As a consequence, policy veered drastically.[4] Irrespective of potential utility, the application of innovative policy proposals to kickstart stalled industrial and agricultural production had enormous implications for the balance of power across many dimensions of American political, social and economic life. An exceptionally weak economic recovery fueled unease at the level and potential consequences of experimentation on such a scale. Comfortable majorities in both houses of Congress provided the illusion of unified control. American political parties, however, are exceptionally weak facsimiles of their Western European counterparts. Considerable divisions existed within the coalition of forces that swept Roosevelt to power. These tensions were further exacerbated by open conflict between the administration and powerful interest groups from industry as well as intermediating firms and associations servicing the capital markets. Many of these saw in the judiciary the last bastion of protection against what they deemed to be the aggressive pursuit of executive power. They had traditionally relied upon Congress to stave off activist agendas. Denied veto power by unassailable electoral majorities, they complained instead of the importation of totalitarian tendencies. They now combined legal challenge that the administration was violating cardinal precepts governing the operation of state-federal relations with the suggestion that such moves, underpinned by a rapid expansion of federal administrative agencies, also violated the separation of powers at the federal level itself. For good measure, this was further leavened by aggressive congressional lobbying that such an approach to governance limited the capacity of individual members to mediate the effect of federal action within their local constituencies, as well as ability to secure financial backing for re-election campaigns.

[3] FD Roosevelt, 'Inaugural Address' (speech delivered at Capitol Hill, Washington, DC, 7 March 1933).

[4] The definitive account of the first Roosevelt administration remains Arthur Schlesinger's trilogy, *The Crisis of the Old Order, 1919–1933* (New York, Mariner Books, 2003); *The Coming of the New Deal, 1933–35* (New York, Mariner Books, 2003), *The Politics of Upheaval 1935–36* (New York, Mariner Books, 2003); for specific evaluation of policy towards banking institutions and securities markets, see J Seligman, *The Transformation of Wall Street* (New York, Wolters Kluwer, 2003) 1–38; see also M Parrish, *Securities Regulation and the New Deal* (New Haven, Yale University Press, 1970).

The administration found itself further buffeted from forces on the left. Domestic industrial and financial failure fanned labor unrest, which in turn, raised worker expectations and fear from employer groups as well as conservative religious commentators of social dislocation in equal measure. The union movement, emboldened by the scale of the crisis, demanded the protection of collective wage bargaining in return for quiescence in major northern urban centers. Its leveraging power was enhanced by an albeit weak commitment to support Roosevelt's political agenda against more aggressive moves advocated by populist figures such as Huey Long of Louisiana. The approach served a dual purpose. First, it ensured ongoing relevance at a time in which unemployment decimated union membership. Second, it provided a direct, if not necessarily dominant, voice in the shaping of new governance arrangements now enshrined by actual or proposed legislative change. An already shrill political atmosphere was further amplified by the growth of mass communications. In particular, radio performed a key transformative function on the form and content of political debate. It brought into the American home news of a world in which stability and order were being fundamentally challenged by change and chaos. As never before, international developments challenged the perception that the United States could, somehow, remain immune from international geopolitics. The rise of the Soviet Union, the emergence of fascism in Italy and the electoral triumph of Nazi Germany, and looming conflagration in Europe provided populist demagogues with diametrically opposed argumentation that both catastrophe and the possibility of inculcating meaningful change was within sight.

Re-reading the primary sources from the 1930s evokes a sense of *fin de siècle*. The old order had buckled under both the strain of its internal contradictions along with changing conceptions of the nature of democracy itself. These competing forces provided the intellectual space for the articulation of a very different vision of American society and the role of business within it. At stake, therefore, was an existential question. Would the reform agenda be informed by symbolic or substantive considerations? Reformers had reason to hope that this time things would be different. First, the magnitude of the crisis suggested that evidence-based reform proposals might generate sufficient traction to breach existing political, judicial and academic paradigms. Second, the paucity of talent within the political party machines as well as limited capacity or willingness with the federal bureaucracy in Washington DC itself, opened significant space for external policy entrepreneurs to mold history. 'I was willing to talk to anybody in those days who would listen, about doing something because the situation in the country was rapidly approaching the kind of climax that we know about now,' explained Rexford Tugwell, an agricultural economist at Columbia.[5] A strenuous advocate of central planning, Tugwell was instrumental in assembling the 'Brains Trust', a high-profile group of academics informally

---

[5] *The Reminiscences of Rexford G Tugwell* (Columbia University Oral History Archive, December 1950) 5.

advising the Roosevelt campaign. Impressed by the success of the mobilization of the economy under federal oversight during World War One, Tugwell believed only such a coordinated approach could deal with the most serious peacetime catastrophe facing the country since independence. It was a view that found resonance in a range of disciplines. Experience, experiment and avowed faith in the rule of academic experts to solve the complexity of modern society had already combined to drive a powerful if inchoate interdisciplinary intellectual movement, increasingly concerned at the trajectory of US politics. Anchored in the elite citadels of learning, most notably Harvard, Yale and Columbia, these academics were now given an unparalleled opportunity simultaneously to translate theory into practice and generate theory from practice. Personal and professional rivalry interweaved with a sense of destiny delivered through intermittent access to the political inner circle.

In Roosevelt himself, the academics found a receptive if uncommitted listener. Adroitness in mollifying critics, flattering advisors, managing factional politics and exploiting oppositional weakness was critical in his securing party nomination. It demonstrated, primarily, tactical rather than strategic acumen. He knew when and how hard to push. Of equal importance, he was cognizant of the exact political percentage to be gained or lost in translating rhetorical flourishes into concrete measures. Separating investment and commercial banking and dealing with the urgent crisis in the countryside were immediate and achievable policy objectives. Regulating the markets through initial stock issuance and the exchanges themselves, however, could not be effectively tackled without revisiting the form and purpose of the corporation. This facilitated a major debate on both the technical nature and substantive purpose of corporate law that in many ways was a microcosm of the tensions within the New Deal as a whole.

The scale of the economic crisis allowed renewed deliberation on whether corporations owed substantive public duties that limited freedom to contract and that transcended the confines of academic conflict. If the dominance of state-level chartering facilitated a race to the bottom in terms of business obligation, to what extent had the federal government both a right and a duty to change the dynamics, particularly if accompanied by what appeared to be an overwhelming popular mandate?[6] The challenge for the administration was to translate the theoretical if contested justification for change into practical advances capable of withstanding political suspicion and judicial skepticism. Here the enlisted academics (almost all of whom espoused progressive thinking) were on less secure grounds. Adolf Berle, the Columbia University law professor and member of Tugwell's Brains Trust, for example, candidly admitted of a policy platform provided to the president-elect that aspiration trumped detail. 'I ought to say

---

[6] EM Dodd, 'Statutory Developments in Business Corporation Law, 1886–1936' (1936) 50 *Harvard Law Review* 27, 53 (noting that the 'tendency towards federal regulation of business corporations has proceeded at a greatly accelerated pace [that] indicates a widespread feeling that a larger measure of control over corporations than the states have achieved, including a larger measure of control over the relations between the management and the investor, is desirable').

that today I would give a student of mine who worked out that memorandum a complimentary B minus for effort, because judged by today's standards it is amateurish in the extreme; he recalled.[7] The naïvety reflected, primarily, as Berle conceded, a failure to read the political currents. Charting a course through treacherous political and judicial eddies necessitated an exceptional firm grasp on the political tiller that, arguably, only a politician as shrewd as Roosevelt could deliver. There could be no doubting the magnitude of the intellectual prize on offer. Success would, Berle believed, lead to truly transformative outcomes:

> The then revolutionary conception was simply this: for the first time in its history the federal government had to assume responsibility for the economic condition of the country. Today we take that for granted, but in 1932 this was a revolutionary and dangerous conception. The federal government was there to keep order, do certain reform work, assist from time to time, but the normal processes of laissez-faire economics were supposed to provide the results. This memorandum flew squarely in the face of that. That, I suppose, is its principal significance.[8]

In many ways, Berle's emphasis was neither surprising nor, on the face of it, unreasonable. The governance and accountability issues associated with the separation of ownership and control in publicly listed corporations had been the focus of Berle's landmark treatise, co-authored by Gardiner Means, *The Modern Corporation and Private Property*, published in time to inform debate in the lead-up to the November election.[9] In that book, one of the most influential on corporate governance ever published, they had famously argued with prescience that 'the law of corporations might well be considered as a potential constitutional law for the new economic state, while business practice is increasingly assuming the aspect of economic statesmanship.'[10] Reflecting on the animating purpose of the reform as articulated to Roosevelt in 1932, Berle noted that 'the freewheeling corporation that could do anything it pleased with more motivation from the stockholdings of directors and promoters than any consideration for either production or the public seemed to me impossible.'[11] The challenge was both intoxicating and, for academics long cloistered from the reality of Congressional politics, exceptionally complex to deliver, even for those such as Berle whose scholarship had a deserved reputation for excellence:

> This was a situation in which any reasonable idea could be presented. You stood a fair chance of having it adopted, usually modified as indeed it should be. For an intellec-

[7] *The Reminiscences of Adolf A Berle* (Columbia University Oral History Project, 1974) 170; see also J Schwarz, *Liberal: Adolf A Berle and the Vision of an American Era* (New York, Free Press, 1987) 70–75.

[8] *The Reminiscences of Adolf A Berle*, above n 7, 173–74 (ever the social scientist, Berle noted 'empirically this anticipated Keynes. We didn't have any theoretical justification for this until Keynes published his general theory in 1934': 177).

[9] W Bratton and M Wachter, 'Shareholder Primacy's Corporatist Origins' (2008) 34 *Journal of Corporation Law* 99, 103–04.

[10] A Berle and G Means, *The Modern Corporation and Private Property* (New York, Macmillan, 1932) 357.

[11] *The Reminiscences of Adolf A Berle*, above n 7, 121.

tual this was the golden period. ... On the other hand, I learned something. General theory is of no use in a political campaign or indeed in government generally. The men who are going to have to act have to have very specific recommendations—do this or do that—or have to have some ways of hammering theoretical considerations into a program for practical action.[12]

The consultative approach generated the admiration and loyalty of his closest advisors, many of whom had temporarily left academic positions to assist the campaign. Raymond Moley, a professor of criminal law at Columbia who became the first chief of staff, opined of Roosevelt:

> [W]hat seemed likely to distinguish him was his moderation, his smiling indifference to extravagant criticism, his instinctive response to the nuances of public opinion, his desire to persuade and to win over people, his tentative and un-dogmatic approach to public problems, his complete freedom from that sense of personal destiny that makes rulers confuse their own triumph with the exaltation of principle.[13]

Roosevelt's strategy, which was to remain constant throughout his tenure, was to use academic insight as a tactical rather than a strategic weapon. It was an approach Roosevelt articulated most clearly to Berle himself, who, in turn, saw it as a compact worthy of entering into. Berle recalled Roosevelt telling him:

> You go and do the work. You tell me what you think and what you think I ought to do. Leave the politics to me. That's a dirty business. Your business is to try to find the line that you think is what should be done. I'll have to decide later how much of it can be done or whether it can't be done at all. That's politics. But you tell me what you think. Those were our terms of reference, I know of nothing more luxurious than that, for intellectuals.[14]

As the decade unfolded, academics from the fields of political science, economics, public administration and law were, therefore, to play pivotal, if at times competing, roles in the design and justification of new frameworks of governance across areas as diverse as industrial relations, securities regulation and agricultural reform, and, critically, political governance itself. Public administration scholars, for example, were instrumental in providing justification for an expansion of executive power on the grounds of administrative coherence and cohesion.[15] This would lead to accusations that they were handmaidens to the

---

[12] Ibid, 185–86.

[13] R Moley, *After Seven Years* (New York, Harper & Brothers, 1939) 396. Others saw Roosevelt as a political dilettante, see R Shamir, *Managing Legal Uncertainty: Elite Lawyers and the New Deal* (Durham, NC, Duke University Press, 1995) 152. In a revealing quotation in the Shamir book, a veteran Washington correspondent for the *New York Times* noted that the academics on the whole 'had a tremendous influence on [Roosevelt] because he had no strong convictions except that he wished well for his country. He wanted the American people to be strong and fine and he wanted to go down in history as the benevolent—not dictator because he never thought of it that way— but as the great American President, who pulled his country out of a Depression, saved its system, saved business, saved capitalism. And at the same time put everybody in his place and prevented all the groups of the people from pursuing their particular sins': 28–29.

[14] *The Reminiscences of Adolf B Berle*, above n 7, 187–88.

[15] *Report of the President's Committee on Administrative Management* (Washington, DC, Govern-

creation of an 'imperial presidency'.[16] Some political scientists thought a degree of centralized planning could create 'a concert of interests' but found that their diagnosis questioned on grounds of ego as much as on principle.[17] In this heady atmosphere, discipline, institution and diagnosis of the root problem divided academic opinion. In the context of the first Roosevelt administration, Washington DC was also a place, if not the place, to secure advancement of personal or political interest, if necessary by traducing the reputation of others. Roosevelt showed brilliance in handling the disputatious academics, as concerned with protecting their professional positions vis-à-vis rivals as advancing meaningful policy change. Personal rivalries and ego constrained effectiveness as much as academic and political disagreement. This can be seen in the somewhat jaundiced opinion Berle had of William O Douglas, a former colleague at Columbia and, at that time, a prominent Yale law professor. In a cutting assessment Berle described Douglas as:

> A moody man, regurgitating thoughts and ideas and I think not wholly easy with his own ego at that time. Ambitious, first rate head. A bit intolerant of other people's different views; able to maintain his own with great effectiveness. And, it seems to me, a little too slashing in his public attitudes, in dismissing the opposition.[18]

Berle himself was not immune to such criticism. 'Berle's personal relationships were never very good. He always had difficulty. Berle was kind of a "walking mind" and not a modest one,' concluded Rex Tugwell.[19]

Intellectual brilliance alone, however, was not enough to ensure ongoing access to a presidency determined to make its mark and acutely aware that innovation brought its own risks. A further set of skills was required to turn policy aspiration into concrete outcomes. This, in turn, privileged the elevation of pragmatism over principle. In the negotiation over what should constitute the appropriate balance between the executive, the legislature and the judiciary it was, therefore, not surprising lawyers sympathetic to the goals and operation of the New Deal would eventually rise to dominate the Washington bureaucratic establishment.[20] In summary, a triple-lock had to be unpicked for which

---

ment Printing Office, 1937) 53 ('Strong executive leadership is essential to democratic government today').

[16] J Fesler, 'The Brownlow Committee Fifty Years Later' (1987) 47 *Public Administration Review* 291 (Fesler, who served on the taskforce, notes 'the charge that the Brownlow Committee set in train the development of the "imperial presidency" can be advanced only by those who have not read the Committee's report' given the fact that it had stated categorically that 'the preservation of the full accountability of the Executive to the Congress is an essential part of our republican system': 292, citing *Report of the President's Committee*, above n 15, 48.

[17] For discussion of the academic research that informed the final report, see S Newbold and L Terry, 'The President's Committee on Administrative Management: The Untold Story and the Federalist Connection' (2006) 38 *Administration and Society* 522.

[18] *The Reminiscences of Adolf A Berle*, above n 7, 141–42.

[19] *The Reminiscences of Rexford G Tugwell*, above n 5, 19; see also J Srodes, *On Dupont Circle: Franklin and Eleanor Roosevelt and the Progressives Who Shaped Our World* (Berkeley, CA, Counterpoint, 2012) 198.

[20] See J Auerbach, *Unequal Justice: Lawyers and Social Change in Modern America* (Oxford, Oxford

those with legal training had an innate advantage. Firstly, legislation needed couching in turns ambiguous or unthreatening enough to secure initial congressional assent. Secondly, it needed to be sufficiently flexible to cover unforeseen outcomes. Thirdly, it had to be robust enough to withstand judicial scrutiny. As the federal government expanded dramatically, a new nexus was created linking the administration and the country's leading law schools, in particular Harvard. The broader the agenda became, the less emphasis was placed on sectoral expertise, even in areas as technical as corporate law and finance. While Berle was a highly influential adviser, Professor Felix Frankfurter of Harvard gradually eclipsed him to become, by far, the most influential academic policy entrepreneur in terms of setting strategy.[21]

Even before the election of Roosevelt, Frankfurter had recognized that the complexity of contemporary life necessitated managing an ongoing conflict between partisan politics and independent expertise. 'In a democracy,' he wrote,

> politics is a process of popular education—the task of adjusting the conflicting interests of diverse groups in the community, and bending the hostility and suspicion and ignorance engendered by group interests towards a comprehension of mutual understanding. For these ends expertise is indispensible. But politicians must enlist popular support for the technical means by which alone social policies can be realized.[22]

Frankfurter's importance derived from his capacity to provide precisely that expertise. The source of that influence could, in part, be traced to a long-standing personal relationship with the president that dated back to the Wilson administration. Government service during World War One demonstrated to Frankfurter the strength and limitations of political action. Absent ongoing support from the apex of executive power, all influence risked waning on the foot of populist opposition, competing priorities and transient political attention.

Denied immediate elevation to the Supreme Court by Roosevelt, in part because anti-Semitic bigotry threatened confirmation, Frankfurter preferred to work behind the scenes, if not manipulating then certainly influencing policy choices. It was indicative of his standing that he could turn down a consolation offer to become Solicitor General. Frankfurter explained that he could provide more substantial service by acting as external counsel from his base in

---

University Press, 1976) 226; see also P Irons, *The New Deal Lawyers* (Princeton, Princeton University Press, 1982) 14.

[21] See 'The Wonder Boys in Washington,' *Fortune*, July 1933, 119. It is indicative of Frankfurter's standing that his elevation to the Supreme Court could be deemed a demotion: see 'Profile: Felix Frankfurter,' *New Yorker*, 30 November 1940. For those in his orbit, the nomination to the highest court in the land was a foregone conclusion, 'It goes to show that a man cannot escape his destiny. Besides it is better to make the business of the Supreme Court rather than write about it,' wrote an admiring Milton Katz, see M Katz to Felix Frankfurter, 5 January 1939, *Papers of Milton Katz*, Box 27, Harry S Truman Library, Never one to hide his own influence Frankfurter replied, six months later, with a handwritten addendum expressing thanks for the congratulation that 'PS You can make the business of the Supreme Court by writing about it,' see Felix Frankfurter to Milton Katz, 25 July 1939, *Papers of Milton Katz*, Box 27, Harry S Truman Library.

[22] F Frankfurter, *The Public and its Government* (New Haven, Yale University Press, 1930) 161.

Cambridge. In so doing he elevated obsequiousness to a political art form. This is in no way to undermine his importance as a policy entrepreneur. As one of the leading constitutional lawyers in the country, he was exceptionally well placed to evaluate the legality of political innovation and indeed advance his interpretations through the pages of the country's most prestigious legal journals. Moreover, as a popular professor he was capable of steering the trajectory of administrative politics through strategic placement of top graduates at the base of the bureaucratic pyramid. Capable of forging and sustaining deeply loyal relationships, Frankfurter was to conduct his orchestra of administrators with gusto.

For Frankfurter 'the interplay of circumstance, the environment in which people play, is important, just as they, in part, predominantly create the environment.'[23] The mercurial professor viewed the symbiotic relationship essential to how Washington operated and indeed the source of its perennial attraction, and later recalled of his own experience as an administrator in the following terms:

> It's an interesting place if you have got anything to do, but it is also a dreary place, made so [by how] many dreary people who are here because there are interesting people here and who themselves are not interesting. The people who professionally pursue interesting people tend to make the place less interesting.[24]

During World War One and in its immediate aftermath, Frankfurter had been a regular visitor to what became known as the 'House of Truth,' a home at 1727 19th Street owned by Robert Valentine, the Commissioner of Indian Affairs, about which Frankfurter gleefully reported:

> Everybody who was interesting in Washington sooner or later passed through that house. The magnet of the house was exciting talk and it was exciting because talk was free and provocative, intellectually provocative. We were all young, as it were, in our late twenties or early thirties and all desirable, available young men for dinner parties where we met young women. So a gay time was had.[25]

By 1933, Washington had become the most interesting city in the nation. Frankfurter was exceptionally well placed to render it more so. In the process he vindicated (if not lionized) his own career choices, his perception of the role of the lawyer in society and crucially his calculation of the elevation of merit over ethnic background.[26] Through his amassed cadre of like-minded acolytes,

---

[23] *Conversations with Justice Frankfurter* (Columbia University Oral History Project, 1956) 221; for discussion of excitement of New Deal era itself by participants themselves, see K Louchheim (ed), *The Making of the New Deal: The Insiders Speak* (Cambridge, MA, Harvard University Press, 1983).
[24] *Conversations with Justice Frankfurter*, above n 23, 206.
[25] Ibid, 202.
[26] GE White, 'Felix Frankfurter, the Old Boy Network and the New Deal: The Placement of Elite Lawyers in Public Service in the 1930s' (1985) 39 *Arkansas Law Review* 631, 634; see also M Parrish, *Felix Frankfurter and His Times: The Reform Years* (New York, Free Press, 1982); for more critical account, see HN Hirsch, *The Enigma of Felix Frankfurter* (New York, Basic Books, 1981).

Frankfurter thus facilitated a policy agenda informed by Justice Oliver Wendell Holmes' pithy comment that 'the life of law is not logic but experience.'[27]

As with their counterparts in political science, public administration and economics, but to a far greater extent, the lawyers recruited into Washington-based agencies used the institutions created by the New Deal as a laboratory to explore how an alliance between government and business could best institutionalize corporate restraint. In a detailed empirical study, for example, Peter Irons found that 60 percent of the litigation lawyers involved in just three New Deal regulatory agencies—the National Recovery Administration, the Agricultural Adjustment Agency and the National Labor Relations Board—were products of Harvard, Yale and Columbia, with Harvard alone accounting for 40 percent of the total.[28] Critical to Frankfurter's influence was the lobbying skill of Harvard Law School alumnus Thomas 'Tommy the Cork' Corcoran. Corcoran facilitated the placement of Harvard graduates across the bureaucracy. As he recalled, unsentimentally, in a 1977 interview:

> The town was full of people trying to make the world over and others just trying to make it work. I was one of the ones trying to make it work. We had the best of the Republicans and the Democrats. There was no partisanship in town. There was incredible ability. A first-class government isn't just ten men in the Cabinet; you need a thousand first-class men. In those days we had them, partly because nobody else could pay them. Everybody else was broke.[29]

While financial necessity was of critical importance, it is also the case that federal service provided a mechanism to break through an artificial glass ceiling. As such, it is not surprising that a majority of the elite recruits came from Irish and Jewish backgrounds, most notably Corcoran himself and his long-term associate, Benjamin Cohen. Each was to play a pivotal role to steering legislation through Congress and subsequently, in the case of Cohen, defending it before the Supreme Court.[30] These key battles are explored in detail in subsequent chapters. The key point to underscore at this stage is the inevitability of the

---

[27] OW Holmes, *The Common Law* (Cambridge, MA, Harvard University Press, 1881) 1, 89 (for Holmes, 'state interference is an evil, where it cannot be shown to be a good').

[28] See Irons, above n 20, 6–8.

[29] See C Crawford, 'New Dealer Tommy the Cork Recalls FDR, and Justice Holmes and Has a Warning for Jimmy Carter,' *People*, 18 April 1977, www.people.com/people/archive/article/0,,20067658,00.html. For discussion of the rise of the lobbyist, see M Janeway, *The Fall of the House of Roosevelt: Brokers of Ideas from FDR to LBJ* (New York, Columbia University Press, 2004) 5–6 (noting the strength of the networks developed by Corcoran).

[30] The Cohen–Corcoran partnership was to become a long-lasting one: see Moley, above n 13, 285 ('Those who interpreted their association as that of "front" man and scholar missed its inner reality. It was a combination of a man who loved life, gloried in manipulating people, and of a man who feared life, despised compromise with reality'); see also Janeway, above n 29, 6–7 (noting that Corcoran and Cohen, 'operating without formal designation as two of the most significant White House aides in history, held nominal positions in other government agencies down the line. They personified the fact that the intellectual and policy-making force of all these men was of greater note than their actual job titles'); for recent biographies, see W Lasser, *Benjamin V Cohen: Architect of the New Deal* (New Haven, Yale University Press, 2002); D McKean, *Tommy the Cork: Washington's Ultimate Insider from Roosevelt to Reagan* (Stearforth, 2003).

immediate and repeated conflict over what constituted or should constitute the appropriate balance between individual rights and public duties.[31] Given the fact that the federal judiciary was itself heavily dominated by Republican appointees, the legal argument took on overt political implications. These, in turn, further solidified the pre-eminence of and reliance on legal advisors.

Nowhere was the conflict as intense as in the nascent field of administrative law, a field dominated by the unparalleled status of Frankfurter as both academic and consummate insider.[32] Following the publication in 1968 of selected correspondence between Frankfurter and Roosevelt, Raymond Moley noted sardonically that the book 'may not enhance the reputation of its two principal characters but will be immensely useful as a text for people interested in the wiles and ways of palace politics.'[33] In this Frankfurter knew few equals. Writing in 1948 without a trace of irony to Frankfurter, then elevated to the Supreme Court, Professor Milton Katz of Harvard, a former combatant himself, bemoaned the infusion of politics into academic, and in particular, legal thought:

> It sometimes seems to me that administrative law needs protection from some of its 'champions' almost as much as it does from its challengers. It may perhaps have been appropriate for a while to treat administrative law as if were a projection into the law schools and law journals of the political controversies of the Roosevelt administration. On net balance, this attitude may or may not have served a useful purpose; at any rate it was understandable for a time. But the attitude seems to me to have outlived whatever justification it may have had. … Although the mentality 'for administrative law' (in the sense of a kind of juristic emanation from general political support of various regulatory and tax measures) offends in a less obvious way than the mentality 'against administrative law', it seems to me that legal education and scholarship could dispense with both. Perhaps administrative law could then be examined earnestly, objectively and respectfully as an intricate and profoundly significant organic growth within the continuous life processes of the legal system.[34]

Frankfurter recognized in his self-deprecating reply that the debate was and would remain politically charged. Using, rather self-consciously, a musical

---

[31] The most radical of these innovations, the National Recovery Administration imposed a series of production codes (for full discussion of the NRA, see Chapter 2). The enabling legislation, the National Industrial Recovery Act (1933) was deemed unconstitutional in 1935, see *ALR Schechler Poultry v US* 295 US 495 (1935); for background to the NRA and its notoriously erratic first director, General Hugh Johnson, see J Whitman, 'Of Corporatism, Fascism and the First New Deal' (1991) 39 *American Journal of Comparative Law* 749, 751–52. The Supreme Court also invalidated the Agricultural Adjustment Act (1933) in *United States v Butler*, 297 US 1 (1936); for a balanced review of the literature, see GE White, *The Constitution and the New Deal* (Cambridge, MA, Harvard University Press, 2000) 16–32.

[32] M Horwitz, *The Transformation of American Law 1870-1960* (New York, Oxford University Press, 1992) 213–46 (noting 'disputes over questions of administrative law became thoroughly intertwined with raging political struggles over the legitimacy of the regulatory state itself': 231).

[33] See R Moley, 'Frankfurter and Flattery,' *Sarasota Herald Tribune*, 1 February 1968, 5; see, more generally, M Freedman, *Roosevelt and Frankfurter: Their Correspondence 1928-1945* (Boston, MA, Little, Brown, 1968); for history of the animosity between Moley and Frankfurter, see Auerbach, above n 20, 171 (noting a 'deliberate strategy of private support and public distancing').

[34] Milton Katz to Felix Frankfurter, 13 February 1948, *Papers of Milton Katz*, Box 27, Harry S Truman Library.

metaphor, he had no doubt that he would be given credit for conceiving the 'libretto for the song':

> In the meantime the music without words conveys not wholly clear sounds. As someone who has enjoyed verbal combat all of his life, who am I to tell anyone else that he is wasting his time to indulge in it? But I sometimes wonder what profit there is in discussing matters with people who are so sure that wisdom on the whole began with them or, at all events, that disinterested scholarship is founded on the thought that no good can come out of Nazareth—the Harvard Law School being Nazareth.[35]

If, however, there was indeed to be a prophet of regulation and a new dispensation for regulatory authority based on evidence it was, however, not to be played by Frankfurter himself, but his most successful protégé, James M Landis. Through political and academic acumen, Landis was to be instrumental in building what prominent gossip columnists at the time termed the 'greatest nest of New Dealers in Washington.'[36] While his success necessitated the initial patronage provided by Frankfurter and the ongoing (if, at times, unwanted) provision of strategic advice, Landis was to become the single most influential figure in stewarding and legitimating the administrative process.[37] In so doing, he eclipsed in practical terms all of the other academics involved in recalibrating American society. His opportunity to do so derived from four interlinked factors: the failure of credible and sustainable alternatives (including those put forward by academic colleagues); a willingness to engage in the administration of created entities; the provision of a retrospective theoretical justification for the administrative process; and the subsequent institutionalization of that vision through his ongoing scholarship and stewardship of Harvard Law School.

The primary mechanism for achieving this position in the pantheon of regulatory theory was the invitation by Frankfurter to create a legislative framework governing new issuances of securities. 'When I think of what you did to me my making me, overnight, an authority on finance, I am not sure whether you acted wisely or not,' Landis wrote playfully to Frankfurter in March 1934.[38] History would record that the decision was one of Frankfurter's most prescient in managing the politics of Roosevelt's court.

Primary responsibility for the 1932 electoral promise to introduce securities reform was initially provided to Houston Thompson, the Federal Trade Commis-

---

[35] Felix Frankfurter to Milton Katz, 17 February 1948, *Papers of Milton Katz*, Box 27, Harry S Truman Library. In an interview conducted in 1953, Frankfurter complained that 'my wife says that there can be few people who know as little about themselves as I do. There can be still fewer people who reflect upon themselves as little as I have in the past. Therefore, when you ask me how to account for myself, you are asking me, as it were, suddenly to speak a foreign language that I haven't been instructed in': see *Conversations with Justice Frankfurter*, above n 23, 35.

[36] J Alsop and R Kinter, *Men Around the President* (New York, Doubleday, 1939) 70.

[37] Seligman, above n 4, 62 ('In time, Landis would be responsible for the most memorable articulation of Frankfurter's view of government-by-administrative agency,' citing JM Landis, *The Administrative Process* (New Haven, Yale University Press, 1938)).

[38] James M Landis to Felix Frankfurter, 6 March 1934, *James Landis Papers*, Special Collections Department, Harvard Law School Library, Box 16-7.

sioner. Thompson, an early Roosevelt supporter, had written the initial campaign pledge. Immediately after the election he sought a conference with Roosevelt but was disappointed to see the task placed in the hands of Samuel Untermeyer, whose involvement in securities regulation dated back to the 1912 House Committee of Banks and Currency (the Pujo Hearings). The Pujo investigation, for which Untermeyer had served as general counsel, had determined the existence of a banking cartel, which had facilitated 'a vast and growing concentration of control of money and credit in the hands of a comparatively few men.'[39] Notwithstanding claims by John Pierpont Morgan that the first law of credit is 'character,'[40] and the conclusion of the investigation that no law had been broken, the hearings were instrumental in raising political and popular unease about the intersection of power between Wall Street and the industrial complex that controlled the rail, oil and steel industries.[41] In a critical exchange, which did much to undermine the credibility of the legendary banker, Untermeyer extracted a remarkable statement from the legendary banker:

> Mr Untermyer: Does Wall Street speculation, Mr Morgan, draw a great deal of money from the country?
> Mr Morgan: I think so; yes.
> Mr Untermyer: Would you favor any legislation that would reduce the volume of speculation?
> Mr Morgan: No.
> Mr Untermyer: You would let speculation run riot?
> Mr Morgan: Yes.[42]

In its final report, the Pujo Committee outlined the manner in which unregulated securities offerings could cause a calamity, which itself drew heavily from a state-level investigation in New York in 1909:

> A real distinction exists between speculation which is carried on by persons of means and experience, and based on an intelligent forecast, and that which is carried on by persons without these qualifications. The former is associated with regular business. While not unaccompanied by waste and loss, this speculation accomplishes an amount of good which offsets much of its cost. The latter does but a small amount of good and

---

[39] *Report of the Committee Appointed Pursuant to Sections 429 and 504 to Investigate the Concentration of Control of Money and Credit, Report No 1593* (62nd Congress, 28 February 1913).

[40] *Money Trust Investigation of Financial and Monetary Conditions in the United States Under House Resolutions Nos 429 and 504*, Part 15, 19 December 1912, 1084.

[41] See C Lindbergh, *Banking and Currency and the Money Trust* (Washington, DC, National Capital Press, 1913) 53 (demonstrating the way in which the major banks, particularly JP Morgan, adroitly used public relations to skew newspaper coverage). Lindbergh, a member of the House of Representatives who was instrumental in establishing the Pujo Hearings, had justified the process on the grounds that Congress itself had been corrupted: 'Are *we* satisfied that the bankers to whom *we* pay enormous tributes from our very life's necessities ... should control financial legislation? Shall the people supinely pay the constantly increasing usury, and still cheer their popularly elected representatives for permitting bankers to control the bills that are to be reported to the House, as well as the debates on them? ... Are the people to have no hearing on the questions of banking, currency, and usury' (78).

[42] *Money Trust Investigation*, above n 40, 1090.

an almost incalculable amount of evil. In its nature it is in the same class with gambling upon the racetrack or at the roulette table, but is practiced on a vastly larger scale. Its ramifications extend to all parts of the country. It involves a practical certainty of loss to those who engage in it. A continuous stream of wealth, taken from the actual capital of innumerable persons of relatively small means, swells the income of brokers and operators dependent on this class of business; and in so far as it is consumed, like most income, it represents a waste of capital. ... But for a continuous influx of new customers, replacing those whose losses force them out of the 'street,' this costly mechanism of speculation could not be maintained on anything like its present scale.[43]

As the Pujo report demonstrated all too clearly, the passage of time did not improve matters. A lack of political will and extensive lobbying power had stymied any capacity at state or federal level to introduce any credible restraint. Untermeyer's investigation concluded that while the province of federal government to directly regulate the stock exchanges was constitutionally questionable, it did have a responsibility to use existing power over interstate commerce to limit socially damaging behavior:

It has appeared that sales of stocks on the New York Stock Exchange average $15,500,000,000 annually; that but a small part of these transactions is of an investment character; that whilst another part represents wholesome speculation, a far greater part represents speculation indistinguishable in effect from wagering and more hurtful than lotteries or gambling at the race track or the roulette table because practiced on a vastly wider scale and withdrawing from productive industry vastly more capital; that as an adjunct of such speculation quotations of securities are manipulated without regard to real values and false appearances of demand or supply are created, and this not only without hindrance from but with the approval of the authorities of the exchange, provided only the transactions are not purely fictitious. In other words, the facilities of the New York Stock Exchange are employed largely for transactions producing moral and economic waste and corruption; and it is fair to assume that in lesser and varying degree this is true or may come to be true of other institutions throughout the country similarly organized and conducted. Your committee believes, therefore, that Congress has power unconditionally to prohibit the mails, the interstate telegraph and telephone, the national banks, and all other instrumentalities under its control, from being used in executing, negotiating, promoting, increasing or otherwise aiding transactions on such stock exchanges.[44]

As with the failure of the New York investigation the Pujo probe achieved little more than highlighting the structural problem. The critical difference in 1932–33 was that the crisis in the financial markets was not contained to those who lost money through speculation. Untermeyer remained convinced, however, that the same constitutional barriers existed to limit direct federal regulation over securities and the exchanges on which they were traded. He advocated, therefore, to

---

[43] *Report of the Committee Appointed Pursuant to Sections 429 and 504 to Investigate the Concentration of Control of Money and Credit, Report No 1593* (62nd Congress, 28 February 1913) 42–43 (citing favorably the findings of a 1909 investigation into speculation at the New York Stock Exchange commissioned by Governor Hughes, which is appended in full as Exhibit 27).

[44] Ibid, 116.

Roosevelt a scheme involving the use of the post office as primary regulator.[45] The suggestion alarmed the president's closest advisors. They saw logistical as well as competency problems in entrusting such a complex task to what was essentially a utility provider.[46] The search for a solution was rendered more acute because of what the administration saw as a unique opportunity to capitalize on favorable media coverage to Roosevelt's resolute action in closing the banks to prevent a run on deposits just days after his inauguration. Requiring urgent action, Roosevelt once again turned to Hunter Thompson. Thompson was delegated to develop the legislation with the help of the Attorney General, Homer Cummings. Untermeyer was partially mollified by the suggestion that his work could form the basis of subsequent regulation of the exchanges in the event that credible proposals for self-regulation were unforthcoming. Thompson's draft was hurriedly introduced in Congress, accompanied by a much-cited two-paragraph message from the president:

> The federal government cannot and should not take any action which might be construed as approving or guaranteeing that newly issued securities are sound in the sense that their value will be maintained or that the properties which they represent will earn profit.
>
> There is, however, an obligation upon us to insist that every issue of new securities to be sold in interstate commerce shall be accompanied by full publicity and information, and that no essentially important element attending the issue shall be concealed from the buying public. This proposal adds to the ancient rule of caveat emptor the further doctrine: 'Let the seller also beware.' It puts the burden of telling the whole truth on the seller. It should also give impetus to honest dealing in securities and thereby bring back public confidence.'[47]

Almost from the start, however, it was clear that the proposed legislation could lead to insurmountable problems in practice. The draft provided the Federal Trade Commission (FTC) with authority to preclude issuance from entities it deemed 'not based on sound principles, and the revocation ... is in the interests of the public welfare.'[48] The application of such authority prompted significant misgivings on the part of Representative Sam Rayburn, whose stewardship of the House Committee on Interstate and Foreign Commerce proved essential in guiding debate on securities reform. As Rayburn noted caustically:

> [I]t is mighty easy when you go to write a stature, if you want to delegate absolute authority; you can write that in a very short statute; but the question that this

---

[45] Ibid.

[46] Seligman, above n 4, 52 (quoting Raymond Moley, who was in charge of implementing the legislative agenda, as saying that 'the Post Office Department was essentially as service organization. The idea of sticking an immense regulatory machine into it horrified my sense of the administrative proprieties').

[47] *House of Representatives Report No 85* (73rd Congress, 29 March 1933); cited in, for example, JM Landis, 'The Legislative History of the Securities Act of 1933' (1959) 28 *George Washington Law Review* 29, 30; Seligman, above n 4, 53–54.

[48] Ibid, 54; see also R Moley, *First New Deal* (Harcourt, Brace & World, 1966) 312 (describing the draft as 'a hopeless and unintelligible confection').

committee has got to determine is whether or not you want to give anybody that kind of authority.[49]

The need to address that core deficiency, which Rayburn communicated to Moley at the conclusion of the hearings on 4 April 1933, was to prove pivotal for the future trajectory of securities regulation in the United States. Moley immediately telegrammed Frankfurter, who replied: 'Three of us will arrive at the Carlton [a landmark hotel in Washington, DC] Friday morning.'[50] The three included an invitation to James Landis, the young professor of legislation at Harvard, whose career Frankfurter had been so instrumental in advancing. Landis later recalled the moment his career was to change: 'I can recall well the morning of that request. It was a Thursday in early April and my next classes were scheduled for the following Monday. Frankfurter thought, however, that the job could be done over that weekend. We consequently left on the night train for Washington.'[51]

Landis had begun a commute from Cambridge to the capital that was to transform the governance of Wall Street through the auspices and example of the Securities and Exchange Commission (SEC). Putting into practice the ideas developed in his innovative course on legislation at Harvard, he became one of the most significant policy actors of his generation (and arguably in the history of regulatory design). Landis stewarded the agency through early legitimacy and accountability firefights with the financial sector, showing as much acumen in navigating the complexity of political contingency and judicial gamesmanship as in legislative drafting.[52] It began with a Friday morning conference Frankfurter convened with Ben Cohen, bringing into the discussions Thomas Corcoran, arguably, as noted above, the most effective lobbyist to emerge from the New Deal.

Although the relationship was tense, there could be no doubting the intelligence on offer. As Landis recalled, 'it was a strange team—Corcoran ebullient, moving easily with the new forces in the administration; Cohen reserved and almost shy; but both brilliant and indefatigable workers.'[53] Their first task was to deconstruct the failings of the Thompson draft. Landis dismissed it as nothing less than 'a complete debacle.'[54] The primary problem was a lack of specificity. Rather than implementing

---

[49] Ibid, 56.

[50] See Moley, above n 13, 180 ('It's interesting to look back at that simple breakfast as a moment of transition in the lives of those men. It was Cohen's first contact with the New Deal, his entrance into national affairs. For Landis, it was the step onto the escalator that was to carry him to the chairmanship of the SEC and, shortly afterward, to the deanship of the Harvard Law School. And it was to make inevitable Felix's appointment to the Supreme Court of the United States by Franklin Roosevelt').

[51] Landis, above n 47, 33.

[52] J Burk, *Values in the Marketplace: The American Stock Market Under Federal Securities Law* (Piscataway, NJ, Transaction Publishers, 1988) 43.

[53] Landis, above n 47, 34.

[54] *The Reminiscences of James M Landis* (New York, Oral History Collection, Columbia University, 1964) 158.

what Mr Roosevelt had set forth in his message [his electoral pledge], Thompson sought to introduce a standard of qualification. By qualification I mean that some federal agency would determine whether securities themselves, no matter how truthfully they might be described, could nevertheless not be sold on the basis that they didn't meet certain standards of qualification. These standards were never well described.[55]

For Landis such an approach was doomed to fail:

It was a terribly poorly drafted piece of legislation. In the first place it didn't carry out the President's ideas. In the second place, it introduced sanctions and responsibilities on the federal government for the quality of securities that were being sold, which even today [1963] I don't believe the federal government and I don't believe even a state agency ought to exercise.[56]

Moreover the litigation risk associated with such a provision would have had the effect of essentially closing the securities industry in its entirety.[57] This calculation represented a clear limit to what regulators could or should do. Landis had imbibed well the warning from Frankfurter that experts administering legislative directives required ongoing political support, something that could only be vouchsafed by minimizing suspicion that their determinations were based on arbitrary and unaccountable judgments. As Landis explained it:

My fundamental belief is that if the truth is told about these things, then it is up to the parties to decide whether they want to buy them or not. If they want to buy them, and speculate, well, let them go ahead and speculate. I've always felt that the furthest that practical administration could go was to call for a statement of the truth about any enterprise; but that some governmental agency should say you shouldn't buy stock in ABC company—I don't know who can decide a thing like that.[58]

---

[55] Ibid, 157 ('Brandeis said to me, "Houston Thompson has every great quality that makes a great lawyer, except one. He's got a great bearing, he's got a good presence." I said, "What quality does he lack, Mr Justice?" Brandeis replied, "Brains."').

[56] Ibid, 157.

[57] Landis, above n 47, 32 ('This device operated only to lock the barn door after the horse had been stolen, but at the same time it held an incalculable threat over the sellers of securities, so dire and yet so unpredictable that it is doubtful whether responsible investment bankers would have willingly chosen to subject themselves to the possibility of its exercise').

[58] *The Reminiscences of James M Landis*, above n 54, 158. It was a formulation that was to stand the test of time; see *Securities and Exchange Commission v Capital Gains Research Bureau* 375 US 180 (Goldberg J) (1963) ('A fundamental purpose common to these statues, was to substitute a philosophy of full disclosure for the philosophy of *caveat emptor* and thus to achieve a high standard of business ethics in the securities industry': 186). This necessitates, however, balancing valid and spurious claims, see J O'Brien, *Redesigning Financial Regulation* (Chichester, John Wiley & Sons, 2007) 66–67 (citing Judge Milton Pollack's argument that the federal securities laws are not meant 'to underwrite, subsidize and encourage ... rash speculation in joining a free-wheeling casino that lured thousands obsessed with the fantasy of Olympian riches but which delivered such riches to only a scant handful of lucky winners'). See generally, CE Fletcher, 'Sophisticated Investors Under the Federal Securities Laws' (1998) 1998 *Duke Law Journal* 1081, 1100 (noting US Eighth Circuit precedent that 'there is no duty to disclose information to one who reasonably should already be aware of it' beyond the basic facts so that outsiders may 'draw upon their own evaluative expertise in reaching their own investment decisions'). Such an approach, in which sophistication is gauged on financial resources, has been questioned in recent litigation in Australia: see *Wingecarribee Shire*

None of this is to suggest that Landis was in any way either enamored by or trustful of Wall Street. He was a realist. His strategy was based on explicit enrolment and sustained attempt to leverage the restraining power of reputation, a commodity devalued because of how sections of the industry had previously operated. Reliance on truth and reputation were narrower and more easily communicable frameworks to both guide the legislation through Congress and protect it from future constitutional challenge. In an early indication of tactical prowess the Landis–Cohen–Corcoran trio 'knocked this thing out in two days.'[59] This thing was to be the initial draft for the Securities Act (1933). The initial draft, modeled heavily on England's Companies Act, limited regulatory requirements 'to full and fair disclosure of the nature of the security being offered and that there should no authority to pass upon the investment quality of the security,' thus eradicating, in part, concern over the exercise of arbitrary power.[60] In addition a waiting period was to be instituted with the onus for delay in processing the security placed on the regulatory authority.

In Landis' estimation the delay served a number of interlocking functions. First, it would ameliorate retail susceptibility to invest in speculative or manipulative schemes in case the opportunity was missed. Second, it would allow for more considered wholesale evaluation. Third, it gave the regulatory authority time to consider market practice and emerging trends. Fourth, it provided partial assurance that the FTC would operate under prescribed limitations, which specified only the registration requirements and penalties associated with non-compliance. 'We were particularly anxious through the imposition of adequate civil liabilities to assure the performance by corporate directors and officers of their fiduciary obligations and to impress upon accountants the necessity for independence and a through professional approach,' Landis reasoned.[61] This

---

Council v Lehman Brothers Australia (in liq) [2012] FCA 1028 ('Grange was, and held itself out as, an expert on financial products and in the giving of financial advice to local government councils. The Council officers were, in contrast, not expert in either field. Rather they were reliant on Grange for information and advice about the SCDO [Synthetic Collateralized Debt Obligation] products it was seeking to sell or buy. ... Each occasion was a serious one involving the possible investment of significant sums of public money by a person that Grange appreciated, or ought to have realized, was financially uninformed or, at the very least, far less informed than it about the nature of those products': 786). Increasingly, in the United States there are suggestions that the SEC should be given the power to ban either specific products or access to them: see S Omarova, 'From Reaction to Prevention: Product Approval as a Model of Derivatives Regulation' (2013) 3 *Harvard Business Law Review* 98; id, 'License to Deal: Mandatory Approval of Complex Financial Products' (2012) 90 *Washington University Law Review* 63. For comparative review of how this is achieved with pharmaceutical products, see Daniel Carpenter, *Reputation and Power: Organizational Image and Pharmaceutical Regulation at the FDA* (Princeton, Princeton University Press, 2010).

[59] *The Reminiscences of James M Landis*, above n 54, 160.

[60] Landis, above n 47, 34.

[61] Ibid, 35. In a scathing footnote Landis observes that '[D]espite the fact now generally recognized that the registration requirements of the Securities Act have introduced into the accounting profession ethical and professional standards comparable to those of other professions, the then dean of the accounting profession, George May of Price Waterhouse & Co was strangely oppose to our proposed requirements for independent accountants' (ibid, fn 12); see also T McCraw, *Prophets of Regulation* (Cambridge, MA, Harvard University Press, 1984) 172 (noting that Landis 'persistently

emphasis on recruiting the professions as gatekeepers of market integrity was essential in legitimating what amounted to a radical departure from current practice. There were further tactical and strategic reasons for adopting such an approach. Within this framework, the specific forms of disclosure were designed to inform the investing public of actual practice. So doing, it was argued, made it possible to incrementally change the boundaries of acceptable behavior. The design was further predicated on an acceptance by industry of the deleterious effect of past excesses and a concomitant mindfulness moving forward in the exercise of responsible leadership. In its original formulation, therefore, the legislation was always conceived as a means to an end, rather than an end in itself. As Baldwin Bane, who was to serve as one of Landis' key lieutenants put it, in its final iteration, the Securities Act was explicitly designed as a moral instrument:

> Its aim was to restore to a numbed national conscience some semblance of sensitivity. It was of a spirit such as this that the Securities Act was born, free of vindictiveness that might easily have been attached to it, reasonable in its demands and build upon tried experience in their formulation. It would be idle to pretend that it does not ask something of the security world, but it also promises much in return—the opportunity of creating a true and honorable profession by the assumption and adequate discharge of public responsibilities.[62]

Critical in this process was how the ongoing Pecora investigation into banking practices provided a justification for action. Landis was to trace the origins of the Securities Act to the 'spectacularly illuminating' Pecora hearings, which, he argued, went far beyond the 'peccadillos of groups of men involved in the issuance and marketing of securities':[63]

> It indicted a system as a whole that had failed miserably in imposing those essential fiduciary standards that should govern persons whose function is to handle other people's money. Investment bankers, brokers and dealers, corporate directors, accountants, all found themselves the object of criticism so severe that the American public lost much of its faith in professions that had theretofore been regard with a respect that had approached awe.[64]

Demonstrating an acute awareness of political sensitivities, the drafting team met with Thompson. This was designed to assure him that the proposed legislation

emphasized the necessity of using all the incentives potentially inherent in the industry to give every person involved—executive, accountant, broker, banker—a stake in helping to enforce the law').

[62] See BB Bane, 'The Securities Act of 1933' (1933) 1 *Certified Public Accountant* 587, 592; see also *The Reminiscences of Adolf Berle*, above n 7, 184 ('The Stock Market in reality is the paying and receiving teller's window of a great savings bank, and it is the measure of value of the savings held by individuals, also by institutions, To allows these appraisals to vary from day to day and allow the actual values in exchange to be manipulated, especially by the individuals in charge of the industries in question, violates the underlying function of these markets in the present system. This seems to me to be practical sentiment that even the financial community generally favors. That was a mistake. It didn't').

[63] Landis, above n 47, 30.

[64] Ibid. For a personal account of the hearings and its impact, see F Pecora, *Wall Street Under Oath* (New York, Simon & Schuster, 1939).

represented little more than refinements to his original draft.[65] The formulation had the added advantage of sparing the president any embarrassment associated with appearing to resile from the initial message (and apparent endorsement) to Congress in late March. The draft proposal was then presented to Rayburn's committee. It was a further indication of Frankfurter's standing that once the case had been made all but the Harvard professor were asked to leave the room as a decision on how to proceed was taken. The House Committee mollified, Cohen and Landis were then asked to serve as consultants on the final draft, under the direction of the legislative draftsman of the House of Representatives, Middleton Beaman. Landis' taped interviews provide a revealing insight into how the process unfolded:

> For two days, Beaman wouldn't allow you to put a pencil to paper. He wanted you to know just exactly what you wanted to do, before you started writing. I know that both Cohen and I were a little suspicious of him, as to whether he didn't want to kill this whole thing, with all these dilatory tactics. But within four or five days, we began to appreciate his work and his method of approach. I guess we worked for three or four weeks perfecting the draft, and with his help ... we put this thing together. In my opinion and the opinions of a great many other people, it's about as good a piece of legislative draftsmanship as you can find in federal legislation.[66]

A critical innovation was to place the detail of the registration process in accompanying schedules rather than in the main text of the bill. It was a move designed explicitly to reduce contestation at congressional hearings, and one that Landis attributes to Beaman.[67] The revisions that Landis and the other drafters introduced, however, did little to mollify Wall Street. Still smarting over the severity of the Thompson draft and uneasy about the direction in which the House might take, the financial world actively lobbied Roosevelt's most senior aides, including Raymond Moley. Amid conditions of great secrecy the team assembled by Frankfurter continued refining the text, occasionally falling out with each other, sometimes to such an extent that it required external mediation.[68]

---

[65] Landis reports that Frankfurter himself did not attend the breakfast meeting, which is discretely explained as a consequence of 'preoccupation with other political matters': see Landis above n 47, 36.

[66] *The Reminiscences of James M Landis*, above n 54, 162–63. Landis later admitted that he initially viewed Beaman with suspicion, recalling that: 'It was exasperating to Cohen and myself. We would meet Corcoran in the evenings, inasmuch as his duties prevented him from giving his full time to the project, and give vent to our suspicions that this delay bore symptoms of sinister Wall Street plotting. We were wrong. It was these discussions that first evolved the exact scope that we wanted the Securities Act to cover. "Public offerings" as distinguished from "private offerings" proved to be the answer': see Landis, above n 40, 37. This bifurcation between sophisticated and unsophisticated investors remains at the heart of securities regulation.

[67] Landis, above n 47, 38 ('I do recall his comment that, handled as a schedule, it would probably be glossed over by the committee after that committee had exhausted its patience on the bill itself. In this he proved to be right. I believe that he knew as well as we that the core of the registration requirements lay in those schedules')

[68] See D Ritchie, *James M Landis: Dean of Regulators* (Cambridge, MA, Harvard University Press, 1980) 47 (noting that Frankfurter, in turn, had enlisted the support of Moley to 'keep an eye on Landis, "who in his intensity has not been wholly wise in his relations with Ben [Cohen]"'); Moley, above n 13, 181 ('I had to ease things up between Landis and Cohen, whose intensity, sensitive-

Notwithstanding ongoing political support, Moley was concerned that the lack of communication with external stakeholders was unnecessarily creating tension with Wall Street, which, if unaddressed risked the much broader program of reform. As a consequence Wall Street delegation was provided limited access to a closed meeting of the House Committee.[69] The failure of preparation and hyperbole convinced Rayburn that any further amendments would only be considered with his explicit approval. This prerogative gave Rayburn, as Landis noted with admiration 'complete control of the situation. The bill passed with scarcely a murmur of dissent.'[70]

The bill then went to a full conference committee of Congress, where again careful preparation privileged the framing advanced by the House of Representatives. Rayburn used procedural tactics to facilitate a vote on which version of the bill should form the basis of the final draft. Allowing the Senate to put forward its text forced a tied vote. As a consequence, the motion was denied and the House bill emerged as the working document by default.[71] The dominance of the House of Representatives was reinforced as the conference proceeded. 'Representatives of the House were assiduous in their attendance, the Senate members less so,' recalled Landis.[72] This along with the tact of Sam Rayburn in handling disputatious Senate colleagues secured easy passage and on 27 May 1933 it became law. It was a bruising experience for the drafting team. The decision not to entertain voluble criticism from Wall Street, both before and after its passage, was, however, to prove fateful. A prominent business commentary, for example, had the following complaint:

> The moment was obviously not propitious for deliberate, impartial lawmaking and that the Act shows the influence, probably unconscious, of the emotional bias of the time, seems quite clear. Its effect is to be seen in the unreasonable liabilities and excessive penalties that the law creates. ... The law by its excessive penalties, by defining inadequately the standard of care required of directors and others, by leaving in doubt in

ness, and twenty-four-hour-a-day exposure to each other occasionally induced those blow-ups that explorers recognize as unavoidable when any two men are isolated under conditions of strain'); see also Lasser, above n 30, 78 (noting how Corcoran was often called to mollify disputes, earning the admiration of Frankfurter, who opined 'Tom is a prince and one day will be king'). The placing of the registration requirements was the core strategic dispute. Cohen (and Frankfurter) advocated placing it in the main text. As we have seen, intervention by Beaman placed it in an accompanying schedule, see above n 65.

[69] Landis, above n 47, 40. Landis reports that the failure by the Wall Street delegation to substantiate assertions backfired: 'Rayburn, who is an expert in judging experts, exhibited considerable annoyance at these accusations, not only on our account, but also [John Foster] Dulles' allegations that Rayburn was sponsoring legislation that would undermine our financial system. Rayburn insisted that all that was being demanded was that the system should live up to its pretensions.'

[70] Ibid, 41. In a letter to Landis, Cohen remarked that '[T]he debate was rather dry and much of it off point but the votes were there. When it was all over Rayburn remarked he did not know whether the bill passed so readily because it was so damned good or so damned incomprehensible,' cited in Lasser, above n 30, 79.

[71] As Moley candidly explained, '[E]veryone agreed that, whatever the defects of the Frankfurter–Cohen– Landis–Rayburn bill, they were as nothing compared with the Thompson bill's. The question was how to inter the Thompson bill quietly and decently': see Moley, above n 13, 182.

[72] Landis, above n 47, 45.

some cases who may be held liable, and in general by encouraging unjustified litigation, is making many corporation executives afraid to proceed with any plans calling for the registration of securities, and is thus retarding business.[73]

Within the academic community, opinion was mixed. The complete reliance of the investor on the free functioning of the market makes vital the outlawry of any tampering with its mechanics, opined George Feldman.[74] The administration, itself, had little doubt about its efficacy but worried whether the negotiating process made strategic sense. It was a view expressed with characteristic bluntness by Moley himself:

> I agreed that, as a long-time measure, the Act was a fine job. Yet I believed it overlooked the fundamental reality of the situation. That reality was that the corporation lawyers of the country sincerely felt that the Act was excessively cumbersome. Whether or not this was true was of less moment than the fact that corporations and bankers believed that it was and consequently hesitated to float new issues. By so much, recovery was retarded. It's my opinion (and this is an issue no one can ever decide definitively) that a little less perfectionism in April and May, 1933, a little less conviction of rectitude, a little less pooh-poohing of the 'hysterical outcries of the Wall Street boys,' and a little more of the appearance of sympathy and reasonableness would have gone a long way toward serving the ends of both recovery and reform. The draftsmen of the Act argue that there'd have been no flotations anyhow in 1933. But that's like a mother who doesn't stop her little boy from reading ghost stories before he goes to bed on the ground that he'd have nightmares anyway.[75]

Once the Securities Act had been enacted, Landis was soon called upon to return to Washington as a consultant to the FTC, where he found the agency 'had no conception about how to administer this act. ... They had no sympathy with this legislation. It was pretty much dammed by Wall Street and regarded as one of these crackpot New Deal measures.'[76] The decision to appoint Landis was broadly welcomed in the media.[77] It was viewed with suspicion by those on the right,

---

[73] 'Business Recovery and the Securities Act,' (1933) 13 *Guaranty Survey* 1, 3.

[74] GA Feldman, 'The New Federal Securities Act' (1934) 14 *Boston University Law Review* 1, 3 (noting that the Securities Act did not suffer the mark of impermanence that effected other New Deal legislation). This is not to say, however, that the legislation was immune from constitutional challenge: see N Isaacs, 'The Securities Act and the Constitution' (1933) 43 *Yale Law Journal* 218 ('In the case of the Securities Act it may be that the die-hards of the old School will fail to find the necessary words of negation in traditional constitutional law, while reluctantly granting the elasticity of the enabling clauses than have ben relied upon. On the other hand, in spite of the general tendency of the realists, or whatever they call themselves, to align themselves with the new legislation, it may well be that their own principles stop them short of their goal. The idea of transferring this branch of police law from the states to the federal government strains traditions and principles more than it does words').

[75] Moley, above n 13, 183.

[76] *The Reminiscences of James M Landis*, above n 54, 173; see also J Frank, *If Men Were Angels* (Harper & Brothers, 1942) 9 ('What we, in a democracy, must insist upon is a *government of laws well administered a by the right kind of men*' [italics in original]).

[77] See L Parton, 'The Mastermind Back of the National Securities Act,' *New York Sun*, 17 October 1933 ('Young Prof James M Landis of Harvard enjoys a distinction somewhat like that of Albert Einstein. It is said that only three men understand his national securities act—his act because he wrote most of it. Just how it seems that act is in for some overhauling and Prof Landis, recently

who saw in the growing power of young lawyers congregating in the home of Corcoran and Cohen a deliberate throwback to the House of Truth made famous by Frankfurter and his associates two decades earlier.[78] Along with the implementation came the much more arduous task of extending its operation to the exchanges. It was to generate a deep-seated and intense conflict over regulatory authority and legitimacy, which to this day remains unresolved.

appointed Federal Trade Commissioner, is again the master plumber'). The most detailed profile of Landis, again largely complimentary, was published the following year, see 'The Legend of Landis,' *Fortune*, August 1934, 46.

[78] 'Britten Says 'College Boys' Plot Red Rule, *Washington Herald*, 21 April 1934, quoting Rep Fred Britten (R) Illinois: 'This little red house down in Georgetown is occupied by Mr Cohen, Mr Corcoran and Mr Guthrie (Reconstruction Finance Corporation) and almost every night men like Ferdinand Pecora, Frederick C Howe (AAA) and James MacCauley Landis and the men who wrote the Fletcher–Rayburn bill meet there. It is this little red house in Georgetown where every night of the week young men of communistic mind meet, so-called young students. They call them Felix Frankfurter's hot dogs'; for discussion of the house as a meeting place, see Lasser, above n 30, 84; for comparison with Frankfurter's own experience, see above n 25, and accompanying text.

2

The Administrator: Codes of Conduct and the Dynamics of Regulatory Politics

The disjunction between stated and lived values, linked to the failure of internal compliance or disclosure to counteract it, underpins episodic demands for an oversight design for capital market governance that better institutionalizes restraint. Unfortunately the intensity of those demands is variable. This is a further disconnect between political and regulatory cycles. Short-termism is as powerful a dynamic in political as well as financial markets. This makes it essential, therefore, to manage contingency. The occurrence of further scandal and the need to manage this helps translate initial political promise to concrete regulatory reality. The emphasis on intervention transcends the hoary bifurcation of whether prescriptive 'rules' or more granular articulation of 'principles' are more effective in guiding market behavior. As we have seen in the global financial crisis, both approaches failed to address what is now widely acknowledged to be a systemic ethical deficit.[1] Moreover, the moral deficit revealed most recently in the financial benchmark scandals scandal underscores how ineffective the normative capacity of compliance alone is in embedding cultural change if perceived to be little more than a necessary minimal legal and mechanistic response to external restraints. A more holistic approach to risk management is required that links private rights to public duties. In this regard the professions play a pivotal mediating role and it was their enrollment that informed the early (and now partially lost) agenda of both the FTC and the SEC under James M Landis. Unless these lessons are remembered and understood, it is far from certain that sustainable reform of financial markets is possible.

From the beginning, Landis sought to enroll the professions, in particular lawyers and accountants, in the attempt to build market integrity. The role Landis conceived for the legal profession in shaping societal preferences is explored more fully in Chapter 6. Given its role in the preparation of financial statements the initial emphasis of the FTC and the SEC on audit quality and the distinct contributions that the accountancy profession could make to safeguard market

---

[1] H Sants, 'Delivering Intensive Supervision and Credible Deterrence' (speech delivered at the Reuters Newsmaker Event, London, 12 March, 2009) 2 ('The limitation of a pure principles-based regime have to be recognized. I continue to believe the majority of market participants are decent people; however a principles-based approach does not work with people who have no principles').

integrity made tactical and strategic sense. Typical was a late 1933 address by Landis to the Chartered Public Accountants Association in New York on how it was in the association's own interests to support the normative change in political direction. The Securities Act, he argued in one of his first public addresses as a Federal Trade Commissioner, was to be welcomed rather than fought over. 'Studied and colorless consideration of the Act and the character of its effects has, in the main, been lacking. Such intemperate attitudes to this most complex problem of the control of corporate financing are nothing short of a tragedy,' he noted.[2] Emboldened by his critical implementation role, for Landis the issue was not simply one of personal pique. He saw how ongoing contestation could rent asunder already fragile social bonds. Given public hostility, a failure by the financial services industry to accept responsibility posed ongoing risks not only to the banking community but also, critically, to those providing professional advisory services to it. Landis issued the following warning:

> And if the issue develops, as it now threatens to develop, into one of the public against the bankers, instead of that of a consideration of the best interests of the public—a concept which still includes the banking group—what legislation will evolve out of such an emotional tempest is certain to be both unwise and impractical. With that kind of an attitude it would be difficult and dangerous to prophecy what legislation might develop. I cite these facts merely as illustrative of a Congress with its emotions un-aroused but deeply conscious of the evils which unrestrained exploitation of our capital resources had brought into existence.[3]

The stark message was part of a determined campaign. It combined an implicit threat with explicit incentives to those with, or who aspired to have, professional status. The plea to accept the political mandate for change, and the threatened opprobrium against those determined to flout it, was accompanied by a more nuanced suggestion that a warranted commitment to professionalism could pay material and reputational dividends. A month earlier Landis' key lieutenant at the FTC, Baldwin Bane, traveled to the World Fair, staged in Milwaukee, to make a similar argument to the broader business community. 'If half of the energy expended upon propaganda for amendments to the Act were enlisted in an effort to advise the [Federal Trade] Commission in the wise exercise of its powers, the Government and issuers, bankers, lawyers, accountants, and other experts would be far nearer to a solution of their problems,' he admonished his listeners.[4] Each speech was predicated on convincing the professions that the rules of the game had changed: the reform agenda, delivered through adaptive and particularized administrative oversight, was both necessary and permanent. Landis was forced to find some mechanism to make the legislation work, developing detailed rules governing the extent of information required and how the FTC would adjudi-

---

[2] JM Landis, 'The Federal Securities Act and Regulations Relating to the Work and Responsibility of the CPA' (speech delivered to New York State Society of Certified Public Accountants, New York City, 30 October 1933) 5–6.

[3] Ibid.

[4] BB Bane, 'The Federal Securities Act of 1933' (1934) 14 *Boston University Law Review* 35, 45–46.

cate whether compliance was substantive or technical in nature. In so doing, he recalled an early meeting with Roosevelt, in which the president recounted 'the Republicans never want to do anything, so they're always united. But we Democrats want to do things, and we get disunited in wanting to do things.'[5] Thereafter, according to Landis, he assumed leadership. 'I didn't bother him. I mean I assumed the responsibility of deciding things that I felt I had the right to decide.'[6] To achieve progress, Landis was to set out a durable framework. It compartmentalized legislation and administration into two discrete phases. Legislation would determine what policies to pursue. Administration, on the other hand focused on the discovery of how to make chosen policies effective. As Bane put it, 'along this road [to more effective governance] lies a better understanding between Government and finance of their common problem, remembering always that the public interest and the protection of investors must be the guiding consideration.'[7] This formulation, however, left unresolved what constituted the public interest, the role professions could or should play, and how the administrative agencies charged with oversight would divine compliance with still vague statutory objectives. In what remained an exceptionally volatile economic environment, it was by no means certain which route would be taken by an administration still grappling with how to govern in the face of acute policy contradictions. It remains a perennially vexed problem in regulatory design and one in which the CPA like other professional associations has a critical role to play.

The CPA itself was exceptionally reticent about the wisdom of the restrictions on new issuance. In particular, it questioned the efficacy of the disclosure paradigm. The principal argument, which remains a constant refrain, focuses on the superficially plausible claim that disclosure would, in the main, be ignored even if understood by investors privileging the search for yield over prudent risk management. Moreover, it would also impose unnecessary expense on promoters, thus limiting new issuance.[8] As such, the auditors positioned themselves as neutral observers in the fraught political debate over implementation of the Securities Act and what appeared to be its inevitable expansion to the governance of the capital markets themselves. Indeed reform of the stock market underpinned the initial work of Samuel Untermeyer for the administration until

---

[5] *The Reminiscences of James M Landis* (Columbia University Oral History Project, 1963–64) 178.

[6] Ibid, 187.

[7] Ibid.

[8] Statement by WA Staub, President of the NY State Society of CPA (a large part printed in *New York World Telegram*, 27 March 1934) on file in *The Papers of James M Landis*, Box 2-2, Harvard Law School Special Collections Department ('The volume of detail required in a registration statement for a proposed security offering, and the amount of matter required to be put in a prospectus for the offering, is in many cases so great that very few investors can understand it, let alone take the time to study it. In such a case, it may be believed that the investor has been protected when the only practical result is that he has been overwhelmed with data which he is unable to comprehend; at the same time a very heavy and uneconomic expense has been imposed upon the issuer of the security'); for contemporary debate, see H Hu, 'Too Complex to Depict: Innovation "Pure Information" and the SEC Disclosure Paradigm' (2012) 90 *Texas Law Review* 1601.

his displacement by the Frankfurter team. Moreover, the ongoing revelations of the Pecora investigation for the Senate Banking Commission suggested that the problems were structural.[9] Nonetheless, the CPA also displayed an early appreciation of how competing dynamics within the administration over the role of government in fashioning the future of entire industries offered opportunities for itself. 'The part that the certified public accountant will play in the drama of the New Deal is yet to be clearly written but we do know it is a big part, a part that as it unfolds must key the performance and add greatly to the success of that drama,' the CPA reported in a widely circulated bulletin.[10]

Enrollment provided industry associations such as the CPA with a mechanism to give credibility and authority to their status as a profession. In so doing it also cemented the CPA's own intermediating position. As the CPA concluded, without irony:

> What the trade association has so strikingly become to an industry—the hub in the wheel around which the effects of its members must revolve and be synchronously activated—so your Society with increasing force and influence must occupy the same position in the practice of public accountancy in this State. Unless the members of a trade association cooperate whole-heartedly, pull together and present a united front, the industry suffers in prestige and in power.[11]

The critical question for the CPA and for the wider financial services industry was whether that agenda could be best delivered through the auspices of an agency established to curtail cartels or one formed to allow it in the name of social progress (and political expediency). While the CPA had been polite to Landis, it was immediately clear that the National Recovery Administration (NRA) offered a more malleable partnership than the FTC. The two agencies were involved in an irreconcilable conflict over the design, function and implementation of voluntary codes of conduct as a replacement to directed legislative action. There was agreement that such codes could articulate some common purpose. There was also considerable contestation over what would be constrained in the process. Would it be governmental capacity? Could the codes be effective if governed self-referentially or was external oversight a necessary precondition for changes in market practice? If the former, would symbolism be privileged over substantive reform? Intelligence and practitioner advice at the time suggested it could work in both ways.

Writing to Landis in November 1933, for example, a prominent West Coast corporate lawyer included a newspaper article in which he advocated industry cooperation. As with the CPA, the lawyer saw in the reform agenda the repositioning of discourse on corporate and professional purpose. The existence of

---

[9] J Seligman, *The Transformation of Wall Street: A History of the Securities and Exchange Commission and Modern Corporate Finance* (New York, Wolters Kluwer, 2003) 76.

[10] 'CPA and the New Deal,' *Monthly Bulletin*, New York State Society of CPA, October 1933, 3.

[11] Ibid.

the NRA offered an opportunity not to be squandered he had publicly argued. According to the lawyer Ben Ehrlichmann:

> It is inconceivable that the NRA should give way to the old condition of destructive competition. The only possible outcome of such a situation would be a revival of the old anti-trust law in even more rigid form. I believe businessmen generally would much prefer the NRA to such a state of affairs. The fact must be recognized that this administration in Washington is a reformist group. The President wants to make changes in the national interest. He is seeking to expose that vague entity, the general public, as a human factor in our affairs. His ideas are new but they are intensely practical and his theories and plans, I believe in the main, are workable.[12]

Here was evidence that some leading lawyers saw in the NRA an opportunity to change rather than game the system. In further correspondence, Ehrichmann noted to Landis that:

> [The] securities men, and bankers too, are rather enjoying martyrdom. ... As far myself, I am more impressed than ever with the need for strict regulation, aimed not only at the practical conduct of securities distribution, but also bearing on the character of the individuals and companies engaged in brokerage and securities activities.[13]

Such an approach chimed with the normative approach of truth in securities that animated the Landis approach to regulatory intervention.[14] Acutely aware of the machinations at play, Landis was, however, circumspect in his reply. 'One gets rather pessimistic here about the attitude of our larger financial centers,' he wrote,

> for they seem to regard any attempt to compel them to do business in a different manner than has hitherto been their wont as not only impracticable but closely approaching something unholy. But the chief difficulty is an intrinsic unwillingness to look squarely at matters that are confessedly experimental in their application though permanent in their objectives.[15]

It was precisely this fear of permanence that animated the response of the New York Stock Exchange, the epicenter of the financial services industry, to the changed regulatory dynamics made manifest by Landis' appointment to the FTC.

---

[12] Ben B Ehrlichmann to James Landis, 15 November 1933, *The Papers of James M Landis*, Harvard Law School Special Collections Department, Box 6-6 (enclosing newspaper clipping, 'NRA Is Here to Stay, Asserts BB Ehrlichmann,' *Seattle Times*, 14 November 1933).

[13] Ben Ehrlichmann to James Landis, 15 November 1933, *The Papers of James M Landis*, Harvard Law School Special Collections Department, Box 6-6.

[14] See also Bane, above n 4 (arguing the only legislation that 'is founded upon a moral background that has been passed in the past twenty years, is the Securities Act. Its aim was to restore to a numbed national conscience some semblance of sensitivity. It was of a spirit such as this that the Securities Act was born, free of vindictiveness that might easily have been attached to it, reasonable in its demands and build upon tried experience in their formulation. It would be idle to pretend that it does not ask something of the security world, but it also promises much in return-the opportunity of creating a true and honorable profession by the assumption and adequate discharge of public responsibilities').

[15] James Landis to Ben Ehrlichmann, 18 November 1933, *The Papers of James M Landis*, Harvard Law School Special Collections Department, Box 6-6.

The Exchange was determined to ensure the viability and legitimacy of self-regulation. It was an indication of its power that its president, Richard Whitney, could secure a meeting with Roosevelt immediately after the passage of the Securities Act. For Whitney, governmental control was both unnecessary and anathema to the American spirit of free enterprise.[16] Nonetheless, Whitney was also cognizant of the strength of shifting political currents and the need to at least appear to be tacking towards compromise. Bombastic refusal to engage was no longer possible. He stressed the value in cooperation with the NRA as it provided the vehicle for articulating and managing an emasculated conception of common purpose. What he needed, however, was evidence of the administration's overreach to give the Exchange leverage in the negotiations. The leverage was provided by the acquittal of the prominent banker, Charles Mitchell, on charges of tax evasion. These charges derived from a devastating appearance before the Pecora investigation the previous spring. The past failure to combat the perception of illegality and moral laxity had done much to shift the political narrative, made manifest in the prosecution of Mitchell, and facilitated the passage of emergency legislation including the separation of investment and retail banking as well as the Securities Act itself. The acquittal provided the first real opportunity to challenge that narrative. In a pattern that was to become deeply engrained, the failure of the prosecution opened the door for impassioned resistance, which combined tactical guile and strategic dissemblance.[17] Belated and minor nods towards structural change, including limits on conflicted remuneration, were accompanied by an open courting of the NRA. If change was to be countenanced, Whitney surmised, it would be on the investment industry's own terms. Experimentalism would indeed work in both directions.

While belief in experimentalism animated Landis' approach to the administrative process, there were, however, limits to what he was prepared to countenance. If intrinsic flaws were identified or gamesmanship uncovered, policy refinement and transparent choices would be necessary. Notwithstanding his inexperience in Washington power politics, he had seen enough to be concerned. The NRA, itself established as a consequence of an attempt by Roosevelt to neutralize attempts to legislatively impose a maximum working week and minimum wage, had the unintended effect of galvanizing industry to use it as a mechanism to subvert the administration's goals. In particular, its emphasis on coordination posed an existential threat to the settled policy framework underpinning the FTC. Across a whole swathe of industries, there was early recognition within the commission that far from weakening power, governmental endorsements of codes of conduct provided industry with an opportunity to retain it.[18]

---

[16] Seligman, above n 9, 75–76.

[17] Ibid.

[18] K Finegold and T Skocpol, *State and Party in America's New Deal* (Madison, University of Wisconsin Press, 1995) 10 (noting that 'business control was a hollow victory, however, because the same lack of state capacity that allowed business to dominate the NRA made the program an economic and political disaster.' Finegold and Thackpol conclude that the ultimate failure of the NRA

The notoriously erratic General Hugh Johnson, the head of the NRA, swept aside any objections that engagement risked capture.[19] For Johnson, the NRA, unrestrained from past restrictions on coordinated industry responses on an anti-trust basis, marked the advent of an innovative 'sociological experiment.' The NRA, he claimed, was not only nimbler than pre-existing commissions. It could and should become a vital partner in securing economic recovery, something he deemed the FTC incapable of. By January 1934, the conflict had become close to unbridgeable. Faced with that reality, Roosevelt continued to publicly hedge. Johnson would be constrained but not sacked despite a remarkable public assault on the FTC, couched in his characteristically colorful prose:

> There was—and there is about as much cooperation between the Federal Trade Commission and the Industry as there is between a lion tamer with a black-snake whip a revolver and a strong-backed chair, standing in a cage with six great jungle cats snapping and snarling on six star-spangled hassocks—that is their version of economic planning and industrial self-government.[20]

The speech was a rearguard action against not only the FTC, which had increasingly come to see as the NRA itself as a failed experiment, but also key governmental advisors, including early influential members of the Brains Trust.[21] Early alliances crumbled in the face of a determined, financially well-resourced lobby much more adroit at reading complex political currents. While the concerns about the NRA and its courting of industry spanned a number of sectors, it was most problematic in the securities field. Argumentation over the mandate, governance processes and level of discretion provided to the NRA

'imposed limitations on future policymakers by encouraging the disaggregation of business organization and the mobilization of a larger and more militant labor movement': 223); see also M Hiltzik, *The New Deal: A Modern History* (New York, Simon & Schuster, 2011) 274 (noting 'the regimentation of industry into cartels mocked progressive ideals and failed to achieve recovery in practice').

[19] For a biography of Johnson, see J Kennedy Ohl, *Hugh Johnson and the New Deal* (DeKalb, IL, Northern Illinois University Press, 1985).

[20] H Johnson (speech delivered at the National Retail Dry Goods Association, New York City, 24 January 1934).

[21] Rex Tugwell, for example, had begun to voice considerable unease about the irascible General Johnson; Raymond Moley, now back in New York, remained sanguine. For opposing views on Johnson, see *The Reminiscences of Rexford G Tugwell* (Columbia University Oral History Archive, December 1950) 62 (describing Johnson as 'a man of enormous energy but not enough thought to carry through, and he had a good many loyalties, which didn't jibe with the New Deal. He was very much an emotional type of man and he couldn't stand any direction.' Tugwell recalls going to Roosevelt in 1935 and arguing, '[T]his thing's going wrong. You are doing this thing wrong. You are going to get into trouble and it's sure to bust in your face. You're going to be very embarrassed and not only that, its hampering recovery and it's making us ridiculous. It's one of those things which you ought to take hold of and crack': 60); for a more sympathetic account, see R Moley, *After Seven Years* (New York, Harper & Brothers, 1939) 190 (noting that 'I blame myself for not seeing that this intertwining of jumbling of emergency and long-time policies was unsound and for not protesting it.' The decision by the Supreme Court to render the NRA unconstitutional in 1935 'delivered Roosevelt from one of the most desperate administrative muddles he ever confronted and gave him the opportunity to start over, in this field, with a fairly clean slate. Unfortunately, once the slate had been cleaned, Roosevelt seemed unable to make up his mind what to write on it': 306).

was critical in the fight over the implementation of the Securities Act and the battle over proposed regulation of the stock exchanges throughout the winter of 1933–34. The stage was set with the promulgation of a Code of Fair Competition for Investment Bankers.[22] Endorsed by the industry on 27 November 1933, its defining feature was the centralization of industry power. Capacity to frame the operation and determine compliance remained with the banks themselves. The code established a management committee comprising 21 voting members. Fifteen were to be appointed by the president of the Investment Banking Association of America, a further 6 through a 'fair [but not defined] method to represent employers not members of the IBA and [in addition] a [further] representative [would be] appointed without vote by the President of the United States of America.' Having a representative on the management board but precluding that representative from the exercise of power (including the right to dissent) presented enormous risks to the administration. It provided a patina of endorsement and, therefore, legitimacy. It also preordained the emasculation of government authority, cutting against the entire stated rationale of the NRA.[23] The intervention was viewed with suspicion in the academic community. One pertinent example came from George Feldman in the pages of *Boston University Law Review*, who saw in the creation of the NRA an unprecedented opportunity to demonstrate good faith:

> Certainly if a desire existed among stock exchanges and underwriting firms to place upon themselves, self imposed regulations in the interest of the public, a glorious opportunity was presented in drawing up codes of fair competition under the National Recovery Administration. Yet strangely enough the codes submitted by the two industries are singularly barren of any regulatory provisions. The codes contain nothing but the usual provisions concerning the hours and wages of labor. The Investment Banking Code presents a promise of rules on unfair trade practices within ninety days. The result must be awaited with hope rather than confidence.[24]

The promulgation coincided with the convening of a panel established by the Treasury Department to evaluate the impact of the Securities Act on the functioning of the capital markets. The mere existence of the panel demonstrated the growing sophistication of the campaign against further reform. It also highlighted the lack of coordination between regulatory agencies. The leading corporate lawyer, Arthur Dean, and influential lobbyist, Henry Davidson, were drafted in to represent Wall Street. Dean had been a vocal critic of the initial legislation. In August 1933 he had publicly maintained that legislative complexity and the severity of the liability provisions closed off the capacity of major corporations to raise finance. Unless amended, he claimed, the initiative would hamper economic recovery and, inevitably, lead to a rise in unemployment. Surely, he had then concluded, 'it seems hardly necessary to burn down the house to exter-

---

[22] Investment Banking Association of America, *Code of Fair Competition for Investment Bankers* (New York, IBA, 1933).

[23] For a strident defense of the rationale, see Moley, above n 21, 184.

[24] GA Feldman, 'The New Federal Securities Act' (1934) 14 *Boston University Law Review* 1, 33.

minate vermin.'[25] In order to balance the committee, Adolf Berle from Columbia was seconded to provide support to and (if necessary) form a restraining force on Landis, who remained adamant that no changes to the Act could be contemplated. As expected, Dean reprised the arguments made in the *Fortune* article. The conflict within the panel inevitably leached out to the White House as each side began a charm offensive, attempting to influence the drafting of what was to become the Securities Exchange Bill.[26]

Landis provided a detailed memo to the president that dismissed any weakening of the Securities Act on both technical and strategic grounds. 'Innumerable amendments to the Act have been suggested,' he explained. 'A number of them of a technical nature can be disregarded, inasmuch as from a technical standpoint the Act, as developed by administrative regulation and interpretation, is fully workable. The main pressure for amendments relates to a lessening of its liabilities provisions.'[27] The first of these was 'an attempt to limit the right to suit to those who relied on an untrue or misleading statement in the prospectus or registration statement, in conformity with a similar requirement in the British Companies Act. This suggestion, fair on its face, in reality opens up an enormous loophole for evasion.'[28] Moreover, in order to close it the federal government would have to exercise compulsion powers on brokers to deliver prospectuses across state lines, a course of action that Landis deemed potentially unconstitutional. The proposed provision was, therefore, a potential trap. Instead the neophyte administrator urged the president to commit to an evidence-based approach:

> A definite assurance that the Act will be modified only as experience dictates and that such experience is at present lacking will go far to bring about a spirit of working with the Act. The hope that the Act will be shortly modified has been responsible for the organization of 'strike' activities against the Act and the arrangement of temporary financing to tide over until financing can be done under a relaxed Act. ... Legislation of necessity highly technical and which must withstand the assaults of highly paid and competent legal advice bent on finding a way around, in order to function must be integrated as a whole. Changes seemingly innocuous may open wide opportunities for evasion, and the delegation of this task to those not wholeheartedly for the effectuation of the principles of the Act is an invitation to subversion of its major objectives. Unfortunately the pressure of the force outlined above has created a situation where the only safe course seems to be that of remaining adamant on the Securities Act.[29]

Landis informed the president that he had submitted these 'general reflections with such humility as is appropriate on the part of one untutored in the matters of politics and statesmanship, but as representations of convictions born of

---

[25] A Dean, 'The Federal Securities Act,' *Fortune*, August 1933, 104, 106.

[26] See Moley, above n 21, 284–86 (noting Moley's role in coordinating the work of Cohen and Corcoran in drafting the Securities Exchange Bill).

[27] James M Landis to Franklin Delano Roosevelt, 4 December 1933, *The Papers of James M Landis*, Harvard Law School Special Collections Unit, Box 9-5.

[28] Ibid.

[29] Ibid.

unbroken months of worrying over this situation.'[30] The anxious if not strident tone did much to reduce the power of the intervention. It is indicative that even as industry presented a united front, Adolf Berle counseled the president to accept compromise. For Berle, progress towards developing functioning and sustainable capital markets was being stymied by unrealistic demands on both sides. As he advised the president:

> Anyone in favor of reopening the Act is supposed to have sold out to the bankers. From the opposite point of view, those defending the Act in its integrity are supposed to have a narrow-minded partisanship of their own drafting. ... The theory that the Securities Act absolutely must not be touched without disloyalty to the New Deal strikes me as unduly emotional. ... The act can be, and should be, improved.[31]

As an administrator, Landis was much more cautious. Unlike Berle, he would have to implement the proposed changes, which he believed were offered in bad faith.[32] Berle, on the other hand, remained convinced that the exchange could be reformed from within, a position he later regretted.[33] The failure of Roosevelt to make a definitive decision convinced Landis of the need to enlist a broader range of political and academic allies. 'How truly despicable some of their tactics are. I really thought they were essentially decent though somewhat misguided people, but I have my doubts now,' he wrote Felix Frankfurter on 13 December 1933.[34] Those doubts were in part informed by the manner in which industry was playing one regulatory agency against another, in particular the FTC–NRA relationship. For Landis, it had become clear that the NRA was the weak link in the chain. On the same day he wrote to Roosevelt he, therefore, reached out

---

[30] Ibid.

[31] Adolf Berle to Franklin Delano Roosevelt, cited in Hiltzik, above n 18, 175; see also Moley, above n 21, 183 (noting that 'a little less perfectionism in April and May 1933, a little less conviction of rectitude, a little less pooh-poohing of the "hysterical outcries of the Wall Street boys," and a little more of the appearance of sympathy and reasonableness would have gone a long way towards serving the ends of both recovery and reform'); see also J Wang, 'Neo-Brandeisianism and the New Deal: Adolf A Berle Jnr, William O Douglas and the Problem of Corporate Finance in the 1930s' (2010) 33 *Seattle University Law Review* 1221 (noting Douglas' active support of the NRA approach in a 3 January 1934 letter to Berle, in which he argued 'The gradual drift, or better yet, the conscious direction of the United States into the investment banking business is one of the most significant contributions to the mastery of high finance which this generation has seen. Any securities act could point with pride to such an accomplishment': at 1225. A combination of the failure of the NRA and the exigencies of office forced Douglas to 'quietly abandon' this approach: 1226).

[32] JM Landis, 'The Legislative History of the 1933 Securities Act' (1959) 28 *George Washington Law Review* 20; see also *The Reminiscences of James M Landis* (Columbia University Oral History Project, 1963) 177–78.

[33] *The Reminiscences of Adolf Berle* (Columbia University Oral History Project, 1974) 184 ('The Stock Market in reality is the paying and receiving teller's window of a great savings bank, and it is the measure of value of the savings held by individuals, also by institutions. To allow these appraisals to vary from day to day and allow the actual values in exchange to be manipulated, especially by the individuals in charge of the industries in question, violates the underlying function of these markets in the present system. This seems to me to be practical sentiment that even the financial community generally favors. That was a mistake. It didn't').

[34] James M Landis to Felix Frankfurter, 13 December 1933, *The Papers of James M Landis*, Harvard Law School Special Collections Unit, Box 16-7.

to Representative Sam Rayburn, who had done so much to secure passage of the Securities Act.[35] With prescience, Landis noted that

> [T]he relationship of this Commission to the NRA is likely to present one of the most thorny problems in the near future. As you know, there has yet been no reconcilement between what appear to be somewhat different economic philosophies held by the NRA and this Commission. The reconcilement may, perhaps, be appropriately worked out through the compliance work in which this Commission will undoubtedly have a hand. As I conceive the National Recovery Act, this Commission has a distinct Congressional mandate to play an important role in that whole movement. It will be interesting to see that develop and to have a hand in it.[36]

Landis masked the sense of panic by adopting a jocular tone:

> The real tragedy of this work is that there are only 24 hours in the day. If Congress, at the next session, would only exercise the powers that Joshua exercised over the sun, it would be a great help. I suggest that a bill to command the sun to stay still should be one of the central points on the coming legislative program; but I suppose that would be in conflict with the shortening of the work day that is being sponsored elsewhere.[37]

The intimated unease was captured by an internal report prepared for Landis and the other members of the FTC on the workings of the NRA. While the report does not explicitly mention the Code for Fair Competition for Investment Bankers, its findings are directly on point. Assigned to be the chief legal liaison officer to the NRA from the FTC, the author of the report, Millard Hudson, was flabbergasted by what he termed the 'chaotic conditions' at the NRA.[38] He reported that:

> There is hardly an important form of monopolistic practices which the Federal Trade Commission and the courts have endeavored to prevent in the past, that is not authorized and more or less explicitly provided for in these codes; not of course by individuals, but what is a great deal worse, by the cooperative activities of whole industries. It would be an exaggeration to say that any remonstrances against these things have resulted in any substantial improvement.[39]

Two weeks later Hudson provided a more in-depth account. 'The industries, having got the bit in their teeth, are running amok, and are bent upon destroying the good work accomplished by the Commission in the past and to prevent its doing any more in the future.'[40]

The final report outlines four principal reasons why the 'sociological experiment' so loudly proclaimed by General Johnson had created a path-depend-

[35] See Seligman, above n 9, 78.

[36] James M Landis to Sam Rayburn, 13 December 1933, *The Papers of James M Landis*, Harvard Law School Special Collections Department, Box 9-2.

[37] Ibid.

[38] ME Hudson, 'Memorandum for the Commission: Work at the NRA,' 6 December 1933 (on file in *The Papers of James M Landis*, Harvard Law School Special Collections Unit, Box 18-8).

[39] Ibid.

[40] ME Hudson, 'Memorandum for the Federal Trade Commission,' 22 December 1933 (on file at *The Papers of James M Landis*, Harvard Law School Special Collections Unit, Box 18-8).

ency that preordained failure. First, as Landis had hinted to Rayburn, there was no procedure to adjudicate diametrically opposed conceptions of regulatory purpose. Moreover, given the disputatious if not poisonous relationship, without external intervention nor was there any real possibility of either side ceding deference to the other. A second problem—by no means limited to the FTC–NRA relationship—was how to manage the ambitions of new recruits into a fast metastasizing Washington bureaucratic establishment. The establishment of a smorgasbord of new agencies posed difficult coordination issues. The combination of inter-agency turf wars and individual ego made this as inevitable as it was intractable. As Hudson reported, many of the legal representatives within the NRA were 'young, inexperienced men, many of whom knew nothing whatever about the [Federal Trade] Commission's work. It was easy for the industries to put things over on them.'[41] More seriously, Hudson detected two structural problems associated with the operation of the NRA. 'Having given the industries in the early codes practically everything they asked for, it was difficult to refuse those which came later,' he reported.[42] The problem was exacerbated by the

> unwillingness of the Administrator to set up any effective form of control over the administration of the codes. He is leaving it, by his own statement, as far as possible to the boards set up within the industries themselves. This means that matters in which they are interested will receive attention and probably little else will.[43]

The internal report was forwarded to Roosevelt, who in turn turned over responsibility for evaluation of code operation to the FTC, effectively limiting the power of the NRA long before the Supreme Court deemed it unconstitutional the following year.[44]

The approach adopted by Landis received substantial backing from some but by no means all in the academic literature. George Feldman, writing in the *Boston University Law Review*, noted that:

> [T]o permit self-regulation by investment bankers would be little short of farce. In the past, complete immunity from any accounting to the general public, has caused the public interest to be completely disregarded. Investment banking has been a business

---

[41] Ibid.

[42] Ibid.

[43] Ibid.

[44] The loss of authority angered Johnson, who embarked on an increasingly histrionic and futile campaign to change the president's mind. In his New York address he argued, '[I]t is stated that I suppressed a report of the Federal Trade Commission to the president on the operation of the NRA. I asked the Federal Trade Commission to send a man over here to see if we were doing properly what we had to do. He came but he never said a word to me. I now understand that he did report to the Commission in a paper marked confidential—one of those X21 confidential spy reports which no one had the courtesy to discover to me. There is suppression for you. I now learn that someone has sent it to the president. But I never heard of that report until last night when a self-invited counter espionage agent told me about its subject matter. There was nothing in it but a charge that we have made mistakes. Nobody is louder in that assertion than I. Apparently the president—gentleman that he is—ignored it': see Johnson, above n 20.

without a conscience. Congress, at its last session, supplied such a conscience. That conscience is the Federal Securities Act.[45]

Landis himself entered the debate surreptitiously by forwarding an opinion piece to be published in the influential journal *Today* (edited by Moley) under the name of Sam Rayburn: 'There is more in this attack on the Act than a mere squabble over details,' Rayburn thundered on behalf of Landis.[46]

> No more impertinent campaign has ever been organized against a statute immediately after its passage. Its very impertinence would in itself be sufficient reason to refuse to yield to it. But the pressure for amendment, theoretically limited to so-called details is too clearly an attack upon the fundamentals of the Act.[47]

Landis also found himself under attack from those who charged the act had not gone far enough. The limited purpose of the initial act provoked a bitter dispute between Landis and William O Douglas of Yale Law School, which was never fully resolved. Douglas viewed the disclosure paradigm as insufficient. What was required, he argued, was a much more substantive reordering of relations between market participants.[48] Douglas explicitly wrapped his critique of the legislation in the imprimatur of others. 'As Berle has said, the Securities Act, though probably one of the most spectacular types of legislation, is of secondary importance in a comprehensive program of social control over finance,' he wrote.[49]

> There is nothing in the Act which would control the speculative craze of the American public, or which eliminate wholly unsound capital structures. There is nothing in the Act which would prevent a tyrannical management from playing wide and loose with scattered minorities, or which prevent a new pyramiding of holding companies violative of the public interest and all canons of sound finance. All the Act pretends to do is to require the 'truth about securities' at the time of issue, and to impose a penalty for failure to tell the truth. Once it is told, the matter is left to the investor.[50]

This essentially corporatist approach, advocated mainly by the Columbia-based members of the original Roosevelt 'Brains Trust', was always regarded as suspect by Landis and his colleagues at Harvard. Douglas, who at the time was angling

---

[45] Feldman, above n 24, 32.

[46] S Rayburn, 'The Federal Securities Act,' *Today*, 30 December 1933; see also Sam Rayburn to James M Landis, 20 December 1933, *The Papers of James M Landis*, Harvard Law School Special Collections Unit, Box 9-2 ('I did not have time to more than read it and Ray Moley [the editor] was waiting for it I let it go as was ... I wish to assure you that I wrote a damn good article').

[47] Rayburn, above n 46.

[48] WO Douglas and G Bates, 'The Federal Securities Act of 1933' (1933) 43 *Yale Law Journal* 171; see also, however, WO Douglas, 'Directors Who Do Not Direct' (1934) 47 *Harvard Law Review* 1305, 1324 (advocating that 'disclosure in the form of annual reports in the future should be distinguished for the unhesitant manner in which it makes disclosures and sets forth information. That simple expedient will go far as a corrective of conditions which have been constantly recurring in our corporate history. Its prophylactic effects will equal in importance any other single measure which can be adopted').

[49] Douglas and Bates, above n 48, 171.

[50] Ibid.

for opportunity, saw in the Act an opportunity to insert himself into policy debates, and demanded the creation of an agency, the powers of which he did not specify.[51]

> Its discretion to classify, interpret, impose conditions, or exempt would be exercised in light of the public interest and the protection of investors. Such an agency as finally and fully developed would be comparable to few which we know today. An agency for control in the security field would have a maze of different and diverse enterprises with which to deal. There are no simple and clear categories into which the problems fall. There are as complicated as the entire social and industrial system. They are essentially kaleidoscopic. So it is no easy task to set up an administrative agency which would adequately and effectively exercise control in this field. But if the Securities Act is a mere harbinger of additional regulation over finance the problem of administrative control will become more and more acute as years pass. It is therefore essential that the main structural features of that agency be set with a view not only to its immediate needs but also its later requirements.[52]

Landis viewed the intervention as politically loaded. 'They tell me that Bill Douglas is quite hot about the Securities Act,' he noted with sarcasm. 'Is Bill bitten by some bug or does he, like much of the New York Bar, feel like this operates as a stranglehold on the capital markets, not to speak of the banker's fee.'[53] On 6 March 1934 Landis noted to Frankfurter that 'Douglas seems to me to lack a tremendous sense of the realities that are involved in this problem and how the relentless drive for profits leads men to do things and then defend them.'[54] On 17 March 1934, Frankfurter replied that 'Douglas is trying to reflect too much the people in the big offices and the business schools, among whom he likes to appear as a sound and knowing fellow.' Frankfurter went on to comment that Douglas had privately opined to him that 'his public articles against us are a form of high strategy. Well it's too high for my eyes to scale.'[55] The correspondence reflects a growing frustration by both men towards industry opposition to and academic misunderstanding of the paradigm shift associated with the passage of the Securities Act. Most notably, this derision is directed towards Douglas himself, who, it is clear, neither Landis nor Frankfurter entirely trusted from the very beginning.[56]

At this stage, reading the political winds, Douglas, initially so dismissive of the

---

[51] *The Reminiscences of Adolf Berle*, above n 33, 142 ('Douglas believed that a high power position was the ultimate instrument by which you get things done ... I rather think that in the long run it is the intellectual positions that a man takes that get results').

[52] Ibid.

[53] James M Landis to Thurman Arnold, 2 December 1933, *The Papers of James M Landis*, Special Collections Department, Harvard Law School Library, Box 1.

[54] James M Landis to Felix Frankfurter, 6 March 1934, *The Papers of James M Landis*, Special Collections Department, Harvard Law School Library, Box 16-7.

[55] Felix Frankfurter to James M Landis, 17 March 1934, *The Papers of James M Landis*, Special Collections Department, Harvard Law School Library, Box 16-7.

[56] This suspicion of Douglas was also shared at Columbia, see Berle, above n 18, and accompanying text.

act,[57] shifted tack. He argued that the time had come for more invasive oversight. He maintained that while codes of conduct were useful, effectiveness required a comprehensive calibration of corporate governance duties and responsibilities, administrative and professional reform. This, in turn, necessitated diagnostic capacity of past and current failings as well as ongoing external oversight in order to implement corrective and therapeutic measures.[58] Douglas maintained that the primary problem to be addressed was the 'lack of social mindedness hitherto sadly lacking both among businessmen and their legal advisers.'[59] This symbiotic relationship had done much to demean both the profession and the industry it had allegedly served. Douglas noted that 'evils of the last decade' could only be addressed by moving towards federal incorporation. This structural reform would, however, only be the first stage. Critically, he saw it as a conduit for far-reaching governance change. Shareholders needed to be mobilized 'into an active and powerful group so that there may be a competent and respectable patrol of the field of finance.'[60] This would be achieved by taking control away from executive management. Shareholder representation on the board

> would be there, not for the purpose of managing the enterprise, but with the object of supervising those who do and of formulating the general commercial and financial policies under which the business is to be conducted. Such a body of men would not always be in a position to know the details of the business in such a way as to satisfy the standards, which the Securities Act, for example imposes upon them. But they would be in a position of dominance and power to serve the stockholders effectively.[61]

This in turn, he argued, required separate but interlocking codes of conduct, with 'adequate [but undefined] machinery for their enforcement.'[62] The machinery proposed included sustained external administrative control:

> And for that pervasive administrative control it means the training and development of a professionalized class skilled in the technique of business, the art of law and the skill of government. To these will fall the task not only of policing business so that the profit motive will be articulated with the public good, but also of assuring to the investor more protection against the malpractices of management than management has supplied to date on its own initiative.[63]

What remained unclear on this analysis was whether the NRA provided a threat or opportunity. What was crystal clear, however, was the extent of Douglas' ambi-

---

[57] Douglas and Bates, above n 48.

[58] Douglas, above n 48.

[59] Ibid, 1307.

[60] Ibid, see also Douglas and Bates, above n 48, 171 ('If the Securities Act is a mere harbinger of additional regulation over finance the problem of administrative control will become more and more acute as years pass. It is therefore essential that the main structural features of that agency be set with a view not only to its immediate needs but also its later requirements'); see also A Berle, 'High Finance: Master or Servant' (1933) 23 *Yale Review* 20, 42.

[61] Douglas, above n 48, 1314 (citing section 11).

[62] Ibid, 1317.

[63] Ibid, 1328

tion.[64] The measures suggested, while capable of checking malpractice, did not address a more fundamental problem, which, as Douglas recognized, derived from what he termed an 'amazing absence of social consciousness on the part of directors and business executives and by their lack of any awareness of the implications and results of many practices which flourished in recent years.'[65]These derived from a worldview that privileged technical adherence to the letter of the law but derogation from overarching spirit. For Douglas, the legal profession was singularly culpable for what he termed

> [The] almost perverted singleness of purpose with which they have championed the cause of their clients, whether it be in the drafting of a deposit agreement, the conduct of a reorganization, or the marketing of securities. It has resulted in getting accomplished what clients wanted but without regard for the long-term consequences of those accomplishments. That singleness of purpose has been wholly incompatible with the use of these aggregations of capital for either the welfare of the investors or the good of the public.[66]

Sustainable reform necessitated changing that stance, which Douglas accepted 'cannot be created by a wish, or by a commission, or by a statute. It is a gradual and slow process-as gradual and slow as any change in the ethical standards of a group. Accordingly the intermediate legal control should condition that change and accelerate it.'[67] Rhetorically such an approach was attuned to the spirit of the times. It also reflected political naïvety in that it failed to take into consideration the power of the financial services sector.

Landis became increasingly convinced that the industry needed to be faced down, in large part by requesting powers in excess of that required in order to provide a negotiating strategy. To do so he again worked in partnership with Corcoran and Cohen, with Frankfurter providing strategic advice from his sabbatical base at Oxford, where he had gone for the academic year 1933–34. Notwithstanding the distance, Moley could see Frankfurter's hand behind the move to regulate the exchanges themselves:

> Felix [Frankfurter] was a patriarchal sorcerer to their apprentice, forever renewing their zeal for reform and their pride in fine workmanship. That their zeal and their pride would sweep them into political depths far beyond their mastery, as it did the apprentice in the medieval legend, he did not dream. [68]

The initial bill was, like the initial version of the Securities Act, exceptionally tough, although this represented a negotiating tactic designed to create the appearance of making concessions. In so doing it reflected a modus operandi honed in implementing the Securities Act. As Landis wrote to Frankfurter

---

[64] Ibid.
[65] Ibid.
[66] Ibid.
[67] Ibid, 1329.
[68] See Moley, above n 21, 285. Although referring only to the relationship between Cohen and Corcoran, Moley's assessment can equally apply to Landis.

in Oxford, 'perhaps my real effort though is to meet the opposition in such a fashion as to scare them to a point where they will deal sensibly with the whole problem.'[69] The administration was, however, to face a concerted and well-organized opposition. Frankfurter, while keen to offer support was increasingly marginalized as a consequence of his Oxford sabbatical, much to his own visible consternation, as evident in this letter from Frankfurter to Cohen and Corcoran:

> I am so glad that you are having such a good time. For while I know it's usually bad for little children, whether they are piano players or draftsmen, to get too much public attention when they are very, very young, I know that you're such hard-headed little youngsters that there isn't the slightest danger of all this public acclaim of your juvenile games and performances either spoiling you or making life as its gets duller when you grow up seem too dull when compared with your gay childhood. I only wish I were a little boy or at least young enough to share a little bit in all your games.[70]

His absence, allowed, at last, the apprentices to assume craftsman status. Asked by *Encyclopedia Britannica* to provide a cogent description of the purpose of the Securities Exchange Act, Landis highlighted its strengths and weaknesses:

> The Securities Exchange Act, perhaps more than any recent legislative measure, relies upon administration. Due primarily to the highly technical and sensitive character of the subject matter, broad powers of administrative regulation are delegated to the Commission in lieu of specific legislative statement of exchange practices and transactions. The success or failure of the measure rests thus primarily upon the vision and techniques of administrative bodies.[71]

The contours of the policy debate were nicely put in an opinion piece in *Fortune* on the challenges facing the exchanges as an agent of social change. 'What's all the shouting about? Thirteen hundred junior clerks, too many lambs and that prime hazard: too good a conscience.'[72] As *Fortune* made clear, 'the problem is overwhelmingly one of administration, not legislation.' Administration required the effective interaction of two core principles: integrity and commitment to operate the Exchange

> to the fullest extent in the interests of the public. Like all such groups which have become self-sufficient in the world, the Exchange used to feel that the world could change and not affect it. But the world has changed and, rightly or wrongly, it is up to the Exchange to convince a sensitive public that it too has changed, that it really has this public's interests at heart. Over the possibility of failure hangs the horrid shadow of regulation from without.

[69] James M Landis to Felix Frankfurter, 22 December 1933, *The Papers of James M Landis*, Special Collections Department, Harvard Law School Library, Box 16-7.

[70] W Lasser, *Benjamin V Cohen: Architect of the New Deal* (New Haven, Yale University Press, 2002) 98 (citing a 15 May 1934 letter from Frankfurter to Cohen and Corcoran in which the Harvard professor effectively dismissed the intelligence, cunning or maturity of his charges).

[71] Extract of entry to *Encyclopedia Britannica*, 18 December 1934, *The Papers of James M Landis*, Special Collections Department, Harvard Law School Library, Box 6-4.

[72] 'The New York Stock Exchange,' *Fortune*, January 1934 (on file in *The Papers of James M Landis*, Harvard Law School Special Collections Unit, Box 8-2).

The operation and control of the codes of conduct was to be a vital role in this dispute. The Investment Banking Association began a public relations offensive. On 31 January 1934 its president, Robert Christie, formally enlisted the NRA to endorse its code of conduct:

> When approved the fair practice rules will become part of the investment banking code and should go a long way towards rounding out the NRA's comprehensive plan for investment banking in the scheme of business recovery. Altogether, this broad reconstruction program for investment banking offers unparalleled opportunity for the greater usefulness and sound development of the business and the rules are being built on that basis. What we are doing in formulating rules of fair practice is a matter of such vital public interest that it is just as important for the public as for investment bankers to know and understand the character and purpose of this effort.[73]

It was very much open to question, however, whether the code departed in its fundamentals from the earlier draft. As we have seen, the FTC was far from convinced but it found itself in the midst of a media firestorm. The influential columnist Walter Lippman sought to chart a compromise through a binding code of conduct that facilitated ongoing oversight over all traded securities. Such an approach transcended a dispute, which he claimed owed more to legal semantics and ego than principle:

> For what has happened is that eminent lawyers have taken positions for and against the [Securities] Act; their passions and their prestige are now staked on proving the positions they took are right. In short the Act is somewhat naïve. It attempts to stamp out all the evils of the security business by making borrowers tell the whole truth once as of a certain date. The whole truth, even once, is better than nothing. But it is not enough.[74]

Lippman saw the solution in the development of a code:

> Let there be a code for the security business which calls for all the disclosures under the Securities Act but which goes further and calls for continuing disclosures after the securities are issued, which licenses security salesmen, which sets up rules of fair practice for the whole business in all its phases, which establishes a code authority with power to put out of business an investment banker or a dealer who violates the code, with power to forbid any banker or dealer under the code from handling the securities of a corporation which does not continually publish all the facts the investor ought to know. Having created such a code, let the investment banker or dealer make his choice. If he signs the code, he is subject to the law of the code. If he does not sign it, he is under the Securities Act as now written. A procedure of this sort would require only one simple amendment to the Securities Act—empowering the President for a period of say three years, to suspend the Act in relation to any dealer in securities who accepted a code which the President has approved. Just as under NIRA an industry can get a limited and temporary exemption from the anti-trust law if it

---

[73] 'Bankers Plan Wide Program of Code Rules,' *New York Herald Tribune*, 1 February 1934 (on file in *The Papers of James M Landis*, Harvard Law School Special Collections Unit, Box 8-2).

[74] W Lipmann, The Securities Act, *New York Herald Tribune*, 6 February 1934 (on file in *The Papers of James M Landis*, Harvard Law School Special Collections Unit, Box 9-7).

conforms to certain social standards which are higher than those under the Sherman Act, so in this proposal the security manufacturers and traders could get a limited exemption from its liability clauses if they accepted the broader obligations of the code.

The proposal irked the NRA because it did not call for additional restraints.[75] Writing to Landis, Sachs at the NRA claimed that 'our proposal imposes standards and penalties and provides the equivalent of a code association for the investor.'[76] For Sachs, the government enables investors to band together to assert their claim and to enforce standards upon the banking profession:

> Our plan thus marks an improvement upon the existing Securities Act in that it expedites vindication of the investors' rights and provides a laboratory for the development and improvement of investment standards. It differs from the existing Act in that it transcends the mere Punic features, which at present impose inequitable burdens and thus paralyze activity on the part of the very members of the banking profession who are most conscious and cognizant of their responsibilities and burdens. By removing the menace of unlimited liability unrelated to the extent of the damage incurred, or the risk involved, our proposal would liberate activity on the part of those who would be at the head of the profession. At the same time, we provide a collective strength and government backing for the investor in a legal system where he is no more on a competitive parity than the individual laborer offering himself for hire is in practice, as distinguished from outmoded legal theory, entering into competitive contract. It would indeed be but a Pyrrhic victory for those interested in the Securities Act to vindicate its letter and vanquish its spirit and promise, of a new order in investment as a social economic function. To the small group of economists who have been percipient on this depression the clue to control of the business cycle lies in the directing and equilibrium of investment and saving, however difficult the task for government planners, subject to political pressure and inertia, or venturesome private entrepreneurs, subject to greed and over-reaching.

Three days later, Sachs again wrote to Landis, advocating the 'establishment of a Code Authority as a self-governing institution and professional body to exercise control and discipline over its members with a view to enforcing those additional requirements of ethical conduct which cannot be expended by legal prohibitions without hampering the functioning of any vital system.'[77]

> As to the cynical comment on this plan and a plea for a just rather than punitive regulation of the Exchanges and of old and new securities within the referencing frame of our functioning system and in accordance with its political and economic postulates—that Wall Street and big business cannot be trusted with self-government, I can only say that the contrary course embodied in your effort to enact inflexible, all-encompassing prohibition of speculative intemperance and evil has to be purchased

---

[75] See Alexander Sachs to James M Landis, 6 February 1934, *The Papers of James M Landis*, Harvard Law School Special Collections Unit, Box 9-7.

[76] Ibid.

[77] Alexander Sachs to James M Landis, 9 February 1934, *The Papers of James M Landis*, Harvard Law School Special Collection Unit, Box 9-7.

at the cost of the obviously discernible, ensuring economic deflation and disorganiza-tion of the system.[78]

From the beginning the proposal was seen as an attempt to create a public utility, with concomitant responsibilities.[79] The proposed introduction of a punitive dimension rekindled all of the simmering disputes about an unaccountable lurch towards socialism. In its initial guise, introduced on the day that Sachs wrote to Landis (and copying in Corcoran and Cohen), it constituted the FTC as a policing agency with little discretionary power. A second and more liberal bill was introduced in March, and two more, one in the Senate and one in the House in April. A battle was waged over nearly every provision of these bills first in the Senate Banking and Currency Committee and the House Committee on Interstate Commerce and then in the conference committee of both houses. Finally a greatly liberalized measure became law on June 6 1934 by the signa-ture of the president. Under the Act as passed the most far-reaching of the mandatory restrictions were removed except those relating to market manipu-lation and to short-term speculation by corporate insiders in the securities of their own companies. In place of the rigid requirements of the original draft, the newly created SEC and the Federal Reserve Board (which were substituted for the FTC as the administrative agency) were given wide discretion to govern in such manner as they might see fit.

The goals of the SEC were limited to the control of public interstate issuance of securities. As with the Securities Act, there was no attempt to adjudicate on the quality of individual offering. 'Full publicity reinforced by far reaching respon-sibility of issuers and underwriters for their statements will enable prospective investors to judge every security on its merits,' Landis maintained. 'It is not within the compass of the Commission to protect investors from their own care-lessness, their greed or their bad judgment.'[80] Secondly the SEC had a mandate to 'police the organized exchange of the Nation with the object of ensuring fair and free dealings on the floor and of preventing insiders' manipulation of every type. Here too, the basic assumption is, that the beast once brought into the open, turns innocuous and may even become serviceable.'[81]

The Securities Exchange Act, perhaps more than any recent legisla-tive measure, relies upon administrative development and enforcement. Due primarily to the highly technical and sensitive character of the subject matter, broad powers of administrative regulation are delegated to the Commission in

---

[78] Ibid.

[79] See CR Meyer, 'Exchange Act to Result in Future Advantages,' *Journal of Commerce*, 2 January 1935 (on file in *The Papers of James M Landis*, Harvard Law School Special Collection Unit, Box 6-13).

[80] JM Landis, 'Some Remarks on the Place of the Economist within the SEC,' 1 September 1934, (on file in *The Papers of James M Landis*, Harvard Law School Special Collections Department, Box 6-3). This, in turn, reflected the longstanding belief held by Landis that the regulatory agency governing market conduct should not be drawn into providing assurance. See Chapter 1, n 58 and accompanying text.

[81] Ibid.

lieu of specific legislative prohibition of various exchange practices and transactions. The success or failure of the measure rests thus primarily upon the vision and technical efficacy of the administrative bodies. In an explanatory memorandum, Landis noted that 'it is impossible to draw a sharp line between speculation and investment.'[82] The Act was not concerned with directing the flow of investment but rather with giving investors sufficient information on which to base their choices. Speculation would be permitted subject to two caveats:

> As for speculation, I would say that in general it should be regulated with two ends in view: first 'to prevent manipulation of prices to the detriment of speculators who are not on the inside—in other words if gambling is to be permitted, the dice should not be loaded.[83]

Second, by imposing restriction it sought to reduce the liquidity of the market. These were permanent reforms as

> the evils which they seek to curb have, if anything, been more rampant in times of prosperity than in times of depression, though many of their worse consequences do not appear until hard times. Of course, 'perpetual' is a broad word but I would say that government control, as exemplified in the two acts I am discussing, should continue at least as long as there is a substantial danger of a recurrence of what we have gone through as a result of the wide spread practices of the boom era.[84]

Landis accepted that the publication of annual reports could lead to a temporary collapse in share prices but that this was both inevitable and necessary:

> The requirements for more adequate corporate reports may compel the revelation of unhealthy conditions in some corporations which will be reflected in a fall in the value of their securities. But this would be merely the realization of losses which must be faced sooner or later. The aim, therefore, was to transpose the moral logic of the Securities Act to the governance of publicly listed corporations. At its core was a belief that market listing was a privilege rather than a right, and that responsibility to the upholding of broader moral norms was an essential rather than optional component of market integrity.[85]

The passage of the act did little to stop the debate over the development of the code of conduct. In keeping with the mandate of the SEC, Landis was responsible for commissioning research into whether it should play an active role. This research found a number of general objections to the possibility of administering a code for investment bankers as well as specific problems with the code presented to it for evaluation. First, the SEC noted that as a regulatory body the Commission was still at a formative stage. The last thing it wanted was to be ensnared in the agenda put forward by industry, particularly if these were seen to be in narrow partisan terms rather than the broader public interest. This was not

---

[82] JM Landis, 'Federal Control Over Finance,' 5 June 1934 (on file in *The Papers of James M Landis*, Harvard Law School Special Collection Unit, Box 6-2).
[83] Ibid, 2.
[84] Ibid, 4.
[85] Ibid.

to say that the SEC did not see value in steering the investment banks towards the articulation of voluntary restraint. Indeed, enrolling the bankers would be advantageous to the SEC's strategy of associational governance, in particular in the regulation of over-the-counter derivatives. In the policy document, the SEC noted that

> it should, however, not attempt to dominate this cooperative effort, but merely inspire and steer it, much as it has done in the case of the stock exchanges. It is one thing to steer and inspire a cooperative body and another thing to be identified with it as administrator. The Commission, if it were to become associated with the administration of the code, would be in the position of serving the industry and, at the same time, trying to formulate rules to direct investment banking in accordance with its longer views, which at a given time might not be acceptable to the industry. Furthermore, once a given set of code rules were accepted, the efficiency of the administrator would consist of freezing a state of things as formulated by the code, while, in its very nature, the SEC is a dynamic and evolutionary policy-making body. Thus there might develop conflicts and recriminations, with neither of the two sides having the desired freedom of self-expression. It is clearly to the interest of all concerned for the IBA and the SEC to work separately and cooperatively, rather than be merged in some fashion.[86]

In addition, Landis found significant problems with the code itself that demonstrated in his mind evidence of bad faith, not least the fact that it implied that the formulation of duties and responsibilities had the imprimatur and therefore the support of the SEC, something described with remarkable understatement as potentially embarrassing. Much more problematic, it also limited the SEC's freedom to suggest further changes. It would be constrained by the terms offered and the capacity to suggest amendments precisely because the code mandated the power to change terms with the code members rather than the administrator. Equally, notwithstanding the code's apparent commitment to investor protection, the SEC saw considerable wiggle room in the specific provisions, making enforcement exceptionally problematic:

> In general the association of the Commission with the Code would mean a certain public reliance on the 'regulated state' of the investment banking business, without the commission having any regulatory powers, or the provisions of the code having, in many cases, any practical worth to protect the investor. The preceding discussion should not lead to the conclusion that the code is wholly without value. There are many provisions the enforcement of which would be extremely desirable from the Commission's point of view, particularly to the extent that they regulate fields beyond the Commission's jurisdiction (in a footnote there are some fields, however, which the code makes little or no attempt to regulate. Particularly significant is the omission of any through attempt to direct advertising and sales of promotional practices or the solicitation of proxies). The Commission is not yet ready to pass wholesale judgment on the many complex problems of the investment banking industry. It is engaged in a long-term program of study for the purpose of formulating policies. It may at present have no active opposition to some of the provisions of the code, but this does not

---

[86] Ibid.

imply any finality of judgment on its part. Any wholesale endorsement of this sort would hamper our evolutionary efforts, our flexibility and freedom of action. While friendly cooperation and liaison are acceptable and advisable, the idea of administering the code should be rejected as one which will not further the purposes of our work nor the longer interests of the capital market and the investor.[87]

The administration valued the contribution made by Landis but viewed him primarily as an effective gatekeeper of the goals of the administration. As Moley explained to Roosevelt in a briefing memorandum, Landis would be 'better as member than as Chairman because he is essentially a representative of strict control and operates best when defending that position against opposition from contrary view'.[88] Instead the briefing advocated providing the chairmanship to Joe Kennedy, an early financial supporter of Roosevelt who was demanding government office in return. It was an early indication of the privileging of narrow tactical over broader strategic goals. Before the political calculation could be tabulated it was essential that the administration cauterized any reputational risk associated with such a political move. It needed to ascertain whether there was any material evidence that past success as a financier reflected the very character traits the administration placed its reputation on eradicating. Kennedy's response to the questioning was typically profane, recalled Raymond Moley:

> Kennedy reacted precisely as I thought he would. With a burst of profanity he defied anyone to question his devotion to the public interest or to point to a single shady act in his whole life. The President did not need to worry about that, he said. What was more, he would give his critics—and here again the profanity flowed freely—an administration of the SEC that would be a credit to the country, the President, himself, and his family—clear down to the ninth child.[89]

Kennedy, however, was a shrewd operator. He recognized from the beginning the value in working closely with Landis and his fellow commissioner, Ferdinand Pecora. Along with Pecora, whose congressional investigations had created the contingency for fulfilling electoral pledges in relation to regulating securities, separating investment and commercial banking and replacing caveat emptor with a disclosure philosophy, Landis was invited to the White House:

> Roosevelt met us—well he was in bed when he interviewed us, gave us an interview. He had stacks of papers around him, I know. I recall that. Well Ferdi didn't know anything about the Boss. Great investigator the guy was, really a great investigator, but from the standpoint of a creative artist, he just didn't have that quality. Of course, we built on his work. We built completely on his work. But he just doesn't have that quality of putting together the work in the form of draft legislation. But we both went up to you him, to see the President and the President asked a few questions about the bill. I don't think we spent more than 20 or 30 minutes. We covered this,

---

[87] Ibid.
[88] Moley, above n 21, 286.
[89] Ibid, 288.

we covered that—quite intelligent questions—and he hadn't read the bill. The he said, 'All right. Go ahead.'[90]

How Landis was to proceed reshaped corporate law and corporate governance. Throughout his subsequent career Landis determined to ensure flexibility without subjecting administrative agencies to accusations of economic or ideological bias, a leitmotif that underpins *The Administrative Process*, his retrospective theoretical justification for what amounted to a new form of government. It remains the defining text of the field.[91] Before evaluating its cogency, it is essential to investigate practical manifestations of regulatory practice.

---

[90] *The Reminiscences of James M Landis*, above n 5, 199. This freedom to act is a constant refrain in the reminiscences. Recalling another meeting Landis, noted '[H]e might not have helped you at all. He might have just thrown the problem right back at you. The feeling of joviality that he gave you, the stimulation and what not—then you'd go back and solve the damn problem yourself, without too much advice from the President': 244.

[91] Landis dedicated the book to Senator Sam Rayburn, the charismatic Democrat who facilitated the passage of the securities legislation. The gesture was greatly appreciated by the lawmaker: see Sam Rayburn to James M Landis, 26 September 1938, Harvard University Archive, Deans Office 1937–39 UAV.512.20: Correspondence, Box 4 ('It will remain of course one of my very prized possessions as my admiration of the author is as much as it should be for any man and to have you dedicate this volume to me is an honor that I will appreciate to my last day').

3

The Activist: Institutionalizing the New Deal

A critical factor in the recent global financial crisis was the provision of a de facto guarantee to institutions deemed too big to fail. It remains one of the thorniest issues in capital market governance. From London, New York to Sydney industry has engaged in sustained pushback against any serious attempt to limit the structural operation of the market or place limits on globally or regionally significant actors within it. Ring-fencing is the preferred option of the United Kingdom.[1] It may enhance transparency but it is questionable whether it is possible to achieve such orderly resolution in practice.[2] Restrictions on proprietary trading or private equity holdings in the United States, as outlined in the Volcker Proposal, have been undermined by a wave of exceptions.[3] In both, the guiding imperative is to be seen to be doing something. Even in jurisdictions such as Australia, which escaped systemic collapse, policy reform has created an impression that failure will be tolerated.[4] Despite the depth of proposed reform measures, coordinated

---

[1] See *Independent Commission on Banking* (Vickers Report), London, September 2011 (advocating ring-fencing rather than forced break-up as the preferred regulatory solution).

[2] See Sir John Grieve, then Deputy Governor of the Bank of England in evidence to the Draft Financial Services Bill Joint Committee, HM Parliament, Westminster (27 October 2011) ('It is a sensible proposal. I do not think it will work in the sense it will make it possible to let Barclays or Barclays Capital go to the wall in a crisis. When there is a real crisis of confidence the main channels of contagion are not the mechanical question of who owes what to whom and uncertainties over that; it operates much more through confidence. We definitely reached the stage in 2008 when we had to save everything—there was really nothing too little to save—in order to prevent a contagious loss of confidence across the system': Q681).

[3] See P Volcker, 'Central Banking at a Crossroads' (speech delivered at the Economic Club of New York, New York City, 29 May 2013) 8–9 (according to Volcker, '[T]he regulatory landscape has been little changed. The result is that we are left with a half dozen distinct regulatory agencies involved in banking and finance, each with their own mandate, their own institutional loyalties and support networks in the Congress, along with a an ever growing cadre of lobbyists equipped with the capacity to provide for campaign financing. ... [T]he present overlaps and loopholes provide a wonderful obstacle course that plays into the hands of lobbyists resisting change. The end result is to undercut the market need for clarity and the broader interest of citizens and taxpayers'); for dissatisfaction with the SEC in particular, see D Michaels, 'Ghosts of 2008 Haunts SEC "Outsider" as She Pushes for Tighter Rules, Bloomberg, 21 July 2014, www.bloomberg.com/news/2014-07-21/ghosts-of-2008-haunt-sec-s-outsider-pushing-tough-rules.html; see also J Eisinger, 'Once Powerful, Mary Jo White's SEC Seen as Sluggish and Ineffective,' Dealbook, *New York Times*, 13 August 2014, http://dealbook.nytimes.com/2014/08/13/once-powerful-the-s-e-c-is-seen-as-sluggish-and-ineffective/?_php=true&_type=blogs&ref=business&_r=0.

[4] *Financial System Inquiry Interim Report* (Murray Inquiry), Sydney, 15 July 2014, http://fsi.gov.au/files/2014/07/FSI_Report_Final_Reduced20140715.pdf.

at global level by the Financial Stability Board, therefore, the political economy questions at domestic level remain unresolved. Mark Carney, Governor of the Bank of England and the head of the FSB, set out a progress report at the 2013 G20 Summit in St Petersburg. Much, he claimed, had been achieved but more was required in order to allow for the orderly resolution of systemically important financial institutions.[5] These remained too interconnected, too complex and subject to 'worryingly large differences' in the nature and quality of internal risk models.[6] With remarkable understatement, Carney argued that:

> [O]ur work is not yet completed. It is crucial that the G20 stay the course in implementing reforms in a consistent manner. More remains to be done to strengthen the resilience of the institutions. The G20 should also concentrate in particular on completion of three crucial areas of reform: ending too-big-to-fail; reforming shadow banking and making derivative markets safer.[7]

Decoded, three of the primary causes of the global financial crisis remain.

The policy goals articulated by the FSB are inherently connected. The failure of prior internal risk management systems at major financial institutions magnified informational asymmetries. Market participants and regulators alike remain unclear as to the size, nature and direction of risk-profile, most notably in the derivatives markets. Given the fact that 90 percent of the over-the-counter (OTC) global derivatives market is driven by 12 banks, credible reform of systemically important institutions necessitates global coordination. The dispiriting reality is that proposals to regulate the derivatives market have been in place since the 2009 G20 Summit. There is an international consensus, for example, that a centralized infrastructure will at the very least provide more granular data on how the market is operating. This performs both monitoring and accountability purposes. The reform agenda also involves commitment to develop trade repositories, centralized clearing and, where appropriate, subsequent trading on exchanges. In order to incentivize progress towards standardization, derivative contracts not centrally cleared are proposed to be subject to higher capital charges. The primary justification for such an approach is, on the face of it, justified.

The global reach of major banking entities and their counterparties provides multitudinous transmission channels for contagion. Bilateral contracts negotiated out of sight of the market have created tightly connected webs that span the globe. By the end of 2012 the notional value of outstanding contracts was estimated to be $633 trillion, nine times the size of global GDP, of which only $52 trillion were traded on exchanges.[8] While the value at risk is estimated at $25 trillion, it is notable that reserves for systemically important institutions have

[5] M Carney, 'Financial Stability Board Chairman's Letter to G20,' 5 September 2013, http://www.financialstabilityboard.org/publications/r_130905.pdf.

[6] Ibid.

[7] Ibid.

[8] Deutsche Bank, 'Reforming OTC Derivatives Markets' (Frankfurt, Deutsche Bank Research, 2013).

increased by only some $500 billion.[9] Six years since the collapse of Lehman Brothers and little progress has been made in the wholesale funding market, 'a $4.6 trillion arena operating on trust, which can disappear in an instant.'[10] Progress in financial regulation reform comes 'dripping slow.'[11] The problems associated with managing the resolution issue demonstrate all too clearly the power of organized lobbying to stymie legislative and regulatory action. As William Dudley of the Federal Reserve Bank of New York has recently pointed out, much more has to be done to change the incentives within financial institutions 'so that firm managements will act more forcefully and much earlier to put their firms on more solid ground before they encounter greater difficulties.'[12]

These problems are, however, not new. As in so many other areas of financial regulation, there is much to digest from the lessons of history. Faced with the problem of regulating 'too big to fail' in the 1930s, the United States was faced with a similar existential question. Then the problem was the interdependence between investment banking and the electricity and gas markets. The lack of coordination applied at state–federal rather than international level. Radical change then, as now, was equally bitterly opposed by industry. It was to spawn one of the most sustained and vicious lobbying campaigns in history. Crucially, however, it was a battle in which the investment industry worldview was faced down and, ultimately, if only temporarily, defeated. It is a lesson that we do well to remember, as well as the central role of James M Landis in guiding the success of the strategy. What becomes clear from this reevaluation is the importance of a strong normative underpinning, informed by adroit administrative tactics, effective litigation strategy and resolute political backing. All three, necessary for transformative change, were instrumental in securing the passage in August 1935 of the Public Utility Holding Company Act (PUHCA), the most far-reaching piece of legislation passed in the New Deal.[13]

The legislation built on the formal separation of commercial and investment banking and the introduction of a disclosure regime for the issuance of

---

[9] M Carney, 'A Plan to Finish Fixing the Global Financial System', *Financial Times*, 9 September 2013), www.ft.com/intl/cms/s/0/a0e95652-1960-11e3-83b9-00144feab7de.html#axzz2ev0cG9pe.

[10] G Morgenson, 'After a Financial Flood, Pipes are Still Broken', *New York Times*, 14 September 2013, B1.

[11] S Heaney, *The Cure at Troy* (Dublin, Field Day, 1991).

[12] W Dudley, 'Ending Too Big to Fail' (speech delivered at the Global Economic Forum, New York City, 7 November 2013). As Dudley accurately summarizes, there are three structural problems associated with the too-big-to-fail paradigm: 'The first problem is that it creates an uneven playing field between large and small financial firms, with larger financial firms gaining a funding advantage from the perception that they may be too big to fail. The second problem is that this funding advantage creates incentives for financial firms to become bigger and more complex. The third problem is that there is a positive feedback loop. As the banking system becomes more concentrated and complex, that just increases the financial stability risks, making the too big to fail problem even more acute.' See also W Dudley, 'Remarks at Workshop on the Risk of Wholesale Funding' (speech delivered at the Federal Reserve Bank of New York, New York City, 13 August 2014) noting that overreliance on short-term funding for long-term financing pervades the banking system.

[13] See J Seligman, *The Transformation of Wall Street* (New York, Wolters Kluwer, 2003) 122 (describing the PUHCA as the 'most radical reform measure of the [first] Roosevelt administration').

new securities and trading of publicly traded companies. It went much further, however, in its recognition that some industries are so important and potentially so destabilizing that disclosure was an insufficient regulatory tool. By forcing the dissolution of highly leveraged corporate structures that relied on the capital markets for their rationale and expansion, the legislation was the most ambitious attempt to steer the direction and purpose of not just the electricity and gas sectors but also the power of finance to dictate public policy.[14] Its purpose was to eliminate unfair business practices and abuses by closing down dispersed entities that evaded state oversight. They were blamed for putting corporate profits ahead of reliable electricity services. They were also seen as having privileged speculation over sustainable investment. The goal, therefore, was as much to redirect capital market practice as it was designed to keep the lights on and prices low.[15] Unprepared to countenance the implications of the changes, the financial industry used the battles over the PUHCA to undermine the operation of the entire disclosure regime.[16] With good reason the industry saw intervention in such a politically salient sector a lightening rod for even more invasive oversight.

The rise of the holding company model had been explosive. It is telling that in 1924 just under three-quarters of all electricity generated in the United States was produced by operating companies, which were component parts of holding companies. By 1930, the dynamics of the industry meant that 90 per cent of all operating entities were controlled by just 19 holding companies. This concentration of economic power had profound political implications. It was indicative of the identified political risks that between 1929 and 1936 no less than 53 utility companies with outstanding securities of $1.7 billion went into receivership or bankruptcy.[17] The manner in which the companies had operated had been a live political action throughout the 1932 election, most notably after the collapse of the Insull trading empire in Chicago. Samuel Insull's eventual personal acquittal on charges of embezzlement two years later did little to stave off an indictment

---

[14] For discussion of the advantages of the holding company model, see W Mosher and F Crawford, *Public Utility Regulation* (New York, Harper & Brothers, 1933) 322–24.

[15] See S Schwarcz 'Ring-fencing' (2013) 87 *Southern California Law Review* 69, 105 (noting that the case for ring-fencing utilities is stronger because of the need to provide continuous supply of services). This strikes one as unduly restrictive. It is indicative that Schwarcz does not reference the battles over the passage of the PUHCA, which was designed to counter speculation in the securities market as much as to keep the lights on. The rationale provided by Schwarcz of path dependency is historically inaccurate. The public utility model was taken on precisely because of its links to investment banking.

[16] See T McCraw, *Prophets of Regulation* (Cambridge, MA, Harvard University Press, 1984) 202 (noting 'a more general barrier to reform was the simple refusal of an industry to cooperate'); for justification of state intervention, see L Jaffe, 'A Pilgrimage: Reflections on a Career in Administrative Law' (1970) 45 *Indiana Law Journal* 171 ('The State had failed to curb capitalist exploitation. The State had to protect and promote collective bargaining, to provide social security, to control the credit and security markets. ... The remedy was clear–massive governmental intervention and regulation; the establishment of administrative bodies with a permanent mandate to apply state [*sic*] power to the solution of our economic problems': 172).

[17] Seligman, above n 13, 127.

of the system.[18] Indeed, it appeared to justify it. As Roosevelt had made clear in December 1934, 'the only utility securities which are all wrong are the securities of holding companies, which securities represent no cash invested in electrical development itself. They represent merely financial transactions.'[19]

The president received support from Felix Frankfurter, who on his return from a sabbatical year in Oxford, during which he missed out on the key battles over the establishment of regulatory control over finance, wrote that the holding companies 'really have no ultimate economic and social justification. That the national interest requires their elimination I have no doubt.'[20] Frankfurter was responding to and amplifying concern about how financial imperatives diverted attention from the needs of the underpinning economy.[21] As Arthur Schlesinger, the eminent historian of the New Deal, has accurately noted, the pyramid nature of the holding company, with its interlocking directorates and licensing arrangements, 'enabled an astute promoter to build a gaudy empire on a trivial investment of his own cash,' citing in evidence a report prepared by Robert Healy of the FTC that 'the holding company system is to a degree more or less of a parasite and excrescence on the actual operating companies.'[22] Standard Gas and Electric, for example, with assets of $1.2 billion was controlled by just $23,100 of common stock.[23] Similarly, the National Public Power Commission (NPPC), established by Roosevelt to develop a national policy and on which Benjamin Cohen, the primary architect of the PUHCA served as general counsel, saw unsustainable risks in inaction. The NPPC reported that 'such intensification of economic power beyond the point of proved economies not only is susceptible of grave abuse but is a form of private socialism, inimical to the functioning of democratic institutions.'[24]

The primary logic and justification of the draft legislation focused on the fact that the utilities were engaged in interstate commerce. It placed oversight with the SEC precisely because the primary problems identified were not operational but in the financial instruments that held them together. The purpose was to trade provision of a licence to operate within contiguous borders in return for formal regulated oversight, restrictions in financial chicanery and capped

---

[18] For a sympathetic account, see F McDonald, *Insull* (Chicago, University of Chicago Press, 1962) 308–33 (noting domestic political factors mandated the initial investigation by the Illinois State Attorney General in 1932, extraordinary rendition in securing arrest and deportation from Turkey, trial in New York in November 1934 on embezzlement charges and eventual acquittal).

[19] FD Roosevelt to National Executive Council, cited in A Schlesinger, *The Politics of Upheaval* (New York, Mariner Books, 2003) 302–03; see also P Funigello, *Towards a National Power Policy: The New Deal and the Electricity Utility Industry, 1933–41* (Pittsburgh, University of Pittsburgh Press, 1973).

[20] Felix Frankfurter to FD Roosevelt, 24 January 1935, cited in AC Pritchard and R Thompson, 'Securities Law and the New Deal Justices' (2009) 95 *Virginia Law Review* 841, 864.

[21] Seligman, above n 13, 127 (noting that 'the restructuring of the public utility industry historically has been the SEC's single most useful accomplishment. It was also by far the most difficult to attain').

[22] Schlesinger, above n 19, 304.

[23] Seligman, above n 13, 128.

[24] Schlesinger, above n 19, 305.

pricing.[25] The holding companies themselves were to be abolished if no economic purpose could be found to justify ongoing existence. This became known as the 'death sentence' clause. Roosevelt outlined the plan in a message to Congress on 12 March 1935:

> Regulation has small chance of ultimate success against the kind of concentrated wealth and economic power which holding companies have shown the ability to acquire. ... I am against private socialism of concentrated economic power as thoroughly as I am against governmental socialism. The one is equally as dangerous as the other; and destruction of private socialism is utterly essential to avoid governmental socialism.[26]

Tom Corcoran and Ben Cohen were given the task of both drafting and then selling the legislation in Congress.[27] In early negotiations in the Senate, Corcoran argued forcefully the rationale for change:

> The idea of the capitalistic system is that we have competitive free enterprise. What we are afraid of when we talk about socialism, is that one directing, benevolent hand will have disposition of all business. ... There is more socialism in that setup right there ... more concentrated disposition of business in one hand and more killing of competition than you could get in any system of State socialism that we could possibly set up in this country.[28]

The choice of language is instructive. Corcoran, one of the most influential aides in American history, was consciously echoing the language of his political master but remained sufficiently distant to give the administration flexibility in the event that compromise was necessary.[29]

The first major battle centered on the 'death sentence' clause. Opponents,

---

[25] See M Forer, 'A Postscript to the Administration of the Public Utility Holding Company Act: The Hydro-Electric System Case' (1959) 45 *Villanova Law Review* 1007 ('Probably the most dynamic piece of New Deal legislation, [PUHCA] was revolutionary in that it required not only the immediate eradication of specific and now all too familiar abuses, but also in that it provided for the minute supervision of actions and programs then conceived as being safely reposed in management. This statute aimed not only at the remedial, but, shooting at the escaping present, had also as its target a better economic future').

[26] Schlesinger, above n 19, 312.

[27] For contemporary assessment of their power, see 'Corcoran and Cohen Make and Break the Third New Deal,' *Life*, 9 August 1937, 18–19 ('Tom Corcoran, the voluble front man of the team, was credited with becoming a virtual alter ego of Franklin Roosevelt, bludgeoning Congressmen into line with patronage threats, editing if not totally ghostwriting the President's important speeches'); see also Janeway, above n 9, 6–7 (describing Corcoran and Cohen as 'two of the most significant White House aides in history. ... They personified the fact that the intellectual force of all of these men was of greater note than their actual job titles').

[28] Schlesinger, above n 19, 307 (Schlesinger also notes sardonically that 'the business community rushed to defend the holding company system as if it were the ark of the American covenant': 308); see also Funigiello, above n 19, 75–76.

[29] For Corcoran's influence at this stage, see D McKean, *Peddling Influence: Thomas 'Tommy the Cork' and the Birth of Modern Lobbying* (Hanover, NH, Steerforth Press, 2004); W Lasser, *Benjamin V Cohen: Architect of the New Deal* (New York, The Century Foundation, 2002); see also M Janeway, *The Fall of the House of Roosevelt: Brokers of Ideas and Power from FDR to LBJ* (New York, Columbia University Press, 2004) 5 (describing the coalition of forces behind Corcoran as 'less a faculty club meeting than a networked fraternity [that] stood for regulation of markets, aggressive antitrust measures, public investment in the economy, and its indirect guidance through fiscal policy').

including Wendell Wilkie, a future Republican presidential candidate, warned of a process of nationalism by default as a 'great bureaucracy in Washington will be regulating the internal affairs of practically all utility operating companies in the United States.'[30] The House of Representatives wanted the death sentence to be commuted if determined by the SEC to be in the national interest.[31] For the architects of the legislation as well as for senior echelons at the SEC, which was required to administer it, such an extension of discretion, while superficially attractive, would be disastrous.[32] Moreover, following the Supreme Court's decision to render the National Industrial Recovery Act unconstitutional at the height of the battle, it could also be construed as a deliberate trap.[33] In a letter to the president, Joe Kennedy expressed severe doubts about the administration of the public utilities legislation if passed with the discretion on the national interest amendment included:

> It is my strong conviction that it is poor policy to vest in any one group of men the tremendous responsibility involved in this grant of power. Certainly this is true unless such a grant is hedged with precise and defined standards set up by the Congress itself. I have an appreciation of the great need in our modern life of flexible language in statutes, so that the administration of the law may be responsive to an ever-changing existence. But in a matter of this kind where there are at stake the interests of millions of people, investors and the consuming public alike, I do not believe that any Commission should be given unfettered discretion to decide matters of such transcendent importance.[34]

It was a view endorsed by Landis, who was soon to assume the chairmanship and thus carry ultimate responsibility for its implementation. Landis saw inevitable court challenge and ongoing political controversy attach to such discretion. 'It seemed to me completely impossible for any commission to administer a statue of that nature, because the pressures on the commission would be insufferable,' Landis recalled.[35]

> Physical standards such as was proposed—that was capable of administration. But to draw a distinction between good and bad holding companies seemed an impossible

---

[30] Schlesinger, above n 19, 310.

[31] See Funigiello, above n 19, 80 (noting that the death sentence alone was sufficient to unify opposition).

[32] The invalidation by the Supreme Court on 27 May 1935 of the NIRA, which was justified by Justice Cardoza on the grounds that delegation of authority to the NIRA chairman was 'delegation running riot,' provided sound empirical evidence for such suspicion: see Funigiello, above n 19, 82. It also reflected a longstanding suspicion by Landis that attempts to force the SEC to validate the relative worth of securities would leave the agency hostile to political and judicial fortune, see Chapter 1, n 58 and accompanying text; see also Chapter 2, n 80 and accompanying text.

[33] *ALA Schechter Poultry Corp v United States*, 295 US 495, 542 (1935).

[34] Joseph Kennedy to FD Roosevelt, 1 July 1935, SEC Historical Society, www.sechistorical.org/museum/galleries/kennedy/friendly_d.php; for Landis' support for this position, see JM Landis, *The Administrative Process* (New Haven, Yale University Press, 1938) 56 (noting it 'meant nothing less than that the Commission, rather than Congress, would become the focal point for all the pressures and counter-pressures that had kept the Congress and the press at a white heat for months').

[35] *The Reminiscences of James M Landis* (Columbia University Oral History Project, 1964) 217.

thing. If the Congress couldn't draw some standard of that nature, how could they expect a commission, which is subject to more pressure in the sense that it's smaller than the Congress is, how could they expect the commission to handle it?[36]

Despite an initial rebuke by the House of Representatives, the 'death sentence' provision was retained in the final legislation, with a compromise brokered by Felix Frankfurter that diluted the national interest exemption by suggesting that size would be determined by an evaluation of the 'advantages of localized management, efficient operation, or the effectiveness of regulation.'[37] The compromise was only possible, however, because of overreach by the utility company lobbyists. In pursuit of evidence of public anger at this threat to American free enterprise they decided to fabricate it. The tactics prompted an investigation by Senator Hugo Black over the provenance of telegrams inundating individual members of Congress from constituents protesting the reform agenda as an assault on the American way of life.[38] With forensic skill Black determined many of these were fake and were coordinated by the industry in association with its professional advisors.[39] The revelations did little, however, to quell the battle over the legitimacy of the legislation, or the ire of individual members of Congress caught up in an investigation as brutal in its methods as the public relations campaign that prompted it in the first place. This fight, which was to continue unabated for decades, placed intolerable pressures on the SEC and on Landis in particular.

The SEC was bombarded with lawsuits even before the act became operational.[40] Landis and the SEC were caught in an impossible position, which could not be resolved without judicial determination. On the one hand, opposition from the utilities and the finance industry that facilitated their expansion undermined the agency's capacity to secure consent for other aspects of its attempts to recalibrate the capital markets. On the other, any aggressive move on the broader enforcement agenda risked further alienation.[41] Media commentary at the time of Landis' elevation was suspicious of what direction the agency would take.[42] Landis, in a pattern that was to be replicated throughout his tenure at

---

[36] Ibid.

[37] M Parrish, *Felix Frankfurter and His Times: The Reform Years* (New York, Free Press, 1982) 250.

[38] See Schlesinger, above n 19, 319 (quoting *Time* of the appearance before the committee by Howard Hopson, the chief executive of Associated Gas & Electric, who 'dug a pit into which the utility tycoons of the United States fell and writhed in despair'); see also *The Reminiscences of James M Landis*, above n 13, 219 ('When Hugo investigated he investigated with bare fists. That helped a great deal'); see also Funigiello, above n 19, 98.

[39] The bare-knuckle fight cemented relationships between many of the key participants on the administration's side. It also accrued political debts that Roosevelt was to repay with alacrity. Black was to be rewarded with a seat on the Supreme Court, so too were Felix Frankfurter, who was to draft the compromise section on the death sentence, and Robert Jackson, brought in to defend the constitutionality of the legislation. Landis, Corcoran and Cohen were not rewarded with material advancement but their influence in Washington increased exponentially.

[40] Pritchard and Thompson, above n 21, 843–44.

[41] Ibid, 880.

[42] See D Ritchie, *James M Landis: Dean of Regulators* (Cambridge, MA, Harvard University Press, 1980) 67.

the SEC and beyond, combined tactical and strategic tactics. Each was based on the acquisition of detailed empirical evidence. Notwithstanding the pressures and the goading, he refused to expose the agency to easy judicial challenge by precipitate action. His primary modus operandi, informed by political realities, was to exude reasonableness. This is not to say that Landis was cowed.

Surrounding himself with the top legal minds in the country, he mapped out a strategy to reduce the perception of arbitrariness within the SEC and at the same time paint the opposition in the PUHCA as, at best, duplicitous. In one of his first public addresses as SEC chairman, for example, Landis rebuked the utilities industry for attempting to stack a test case in Baltimore. From the start, it was abundantly clear that the case was a fraud. The plaintiff questioned whether it was necessary to file registration papers given the alleged unconstitutionality of the act. The alleged opposing side retained counsel who had been on the record as a vehement opponent of the legislation.[43] Excised from the litigation, the SEC, under Landis' direction and presented by John Burns, filed an amicus brief. It suggested the proceedings were nothing less than an insult to the rule of law. The strategy was to fall on deaf ears on both the industry and the judiciary. Judge William Coleman ruled the act unconstitutional on 7 November 1935. With the deadline for submitting registration weeks away, the ruling strengthened the resolve of industry simply to ignore the SEC. The stage was set for a battle of epic proportions.

It was now an imperative for the SEC to seize the initiative by developing a test case narrowly enough drawn to limit Supreme Court disproval. To do so it needed to divert attention from the more controversial aspects, such as the application of the corporate death sentence. Its test case would focus judicial determination on whether the SEC had the right to demand registration under the interstate commerce provision of the constitution. Moreover, it needed to ensure that its choice of opponent was sufficiently important to capture the attention of the industry as a whole. As Landis recalled, '[W]e came to the conclusion that, let's pick a big one, a top one, take a big one and topple that one, and then the little ones would fall into line.'[44]

The legal team found its target in Electric Bond & Share, one of the largest utility companies in the country. As part of Landis' twin-prong strategy of engagement and guile, he personally oversaw the registration negotiations with Electric Bond & Share, attending meetings with its executives in the week prior to registration deadline of 1 December 1935. Following Electric Bond & Share's inevitable failure to register, Landis pounced with alacrity. He directed his field staff to file a pre-arranged suit in the prestigious Southern District of New York, then as now the most important securities law jurisdiction in the country. Just as the industry had forum shopped its choice of jurisdiction,[45] Landis dictated

---

[43] bid, 69.

[44] *The Reminiscences of James M Landis*, above n 29, 221–22.

[45] It is indicative, for example, that the litigation on the death sentence was filed on the same day but in the District of Columbia: see *North American Co v Landis* 85 F2d 398 (DC Circuit 1936).

the jurist most likely to be sympathetic to its cause, Judge Julian Mack. 'I had been friends with Mack when I was teaching at the [Harvard] Law School. He was always very much interested in the law school and a friend of the law school. He was a liberal-minded judge, a very competent one and extremely fair.'[46] Not surprisingly Mack held the constitutionality of the Act, a decision that was upheld on appeal in January 1937.[47]

As the legal challenges and counter-challenges meandered their way through the court system, the political mood darkened. Roosevelt captured what was at stake with a particularly strident call to arms delivered in the final days of the 1936 election campaign. The fiery rhetoric retains its power to shock.

> For twelve years this Nation was afflicted with hear-nothing, see-nothing, do-nothing Government. The Nation looked to Government but the Government looked away. Nine mocking years with the golden calf and three long years of the scourge! Nine crazy years at the ticker and three long years in the breadlines! Nine mad years of mirage and three long years of despair! Powerful influences strive today to restore that kind of government with its doctrine that that Government is best which is most indifferent. For nearly four years you have had an Administration which instead of twirling its thumbs has rolled up its sleeves. We will keep our sleeves rolled up. We had to struggle with the old enemies of peace—business and financial monopoly, speculation, reckless banking, class antagonism, sectionalism, war profiteering. They had begun to consider the Government of the United States as a mere appendage to their own affairs. We know now that Government by organized money is just as dangerous as Government by organized mob. Never before in all our history have these forces been so united against one candidate as they stand today. They are unanimous in their hate for me—and I welcome their hatred. I should like to have it said of my first Administration that in it the forces of selfishness and of lust for power met their match. I should like to have it said of my second Administration that in it these forces met their master.[48]

Nowhere was this more apparent than in the legal challenges to the regulatory agencies. In ruling unconstitutional flagship programs, such as the National Recovery Authority and Agricultural Adjustment Act, the Supreme Court sharpened an existential dispute about the relative authority of the federal government and business elites that dated back to its infamous 1905 decision to strike down state-based working-hour restrictions in New York bakeries on the basis that it was 'unreasonable, unnecessary and arbitrary interference with the right and liberty of the individual to contract.'[49] Following his landslide re-election it was

---

For details, see Pritchard and Thompson, above n 21, 880–81. The Supreme Court ruled in 1936 that final determination must the decision in the SEC's New York's test case, see *Landis v North American Co*, 299 US 248, 259 (1936). The procedural victory played into the hands of the SEC.

[46] Landis, above n 44, 222.

[47] Pritchard and Thompson, above n 21, 882.

[48] FD Roosevelt, 'Campaign Address' (speech delivered at Madison Square Garden, New York City, 31 October 1936).

[49] *Lochner vs New York*, 198 US 45 (1905). Leading progressives saw such an approach as both unsustainable and unworkable: see F Frankfurter, *The Public and its Government* (New Haven, Yale University Press, 1930) 45 (noting that 'members of the Supreme Court continued to reflect the

clear that an emboldened Roosevelt had had enough of this debate and what he perceived to be the recalcitrant justices who fanned its flames.

In the 1936 presidential campaign he had hinted that something must be done to deal with Court activism and the threat he deemed it to pose to the functioning of democratic order. This despite the fact that the Supreme Court appeared to have moderated its position in relations to agency discretion, at least insofar as the SEC was concerned in terms of the application of the PUHCA.[50] In his second 'fireside chat' following re-inauguration, broadcast on 7 March 1937, he reiterated the campaign promise and announced a plan to dilute the poison by expanding the number of federal judges up to and including the Supreme Court:

> If these problems cannot be effectively solved within the Constitution, we shall seek such clarifying amendments as will assure the power to enact those laws, adequately to regulate commerce, protect public health and safety, and safeguard economic security. ... I [have come] by a process of elimination to the conclusion that, short of amendments, the only method which was clearly constitutional, and would at the same time carry out other much needed reforms, was to infuse new blood into all our courts. We must have men worthy and equipped to carry out impartial justice. But, at the same time, we must have judges who will bring to the courts a present-day sense of the Constitution—judges who will retain in the courts the judicial functions of a court, and reject the legislative powers which the courts have today assumed.[51]

To generate support for this goal it is no surprise that Roosevelt turned to Landis. As early as 1930 Landis had dismissed any restrictions on agency discretion as little more than an attempt to curtail the legitimate exercise of public power for

social and economic order in which they grew up and "sought to stereotype ephemeral facts into legal absolutes" turning "abstract conceptions concerning "liberty of contract" ... into constitutional dogmas'). See also, however, D Bernstein, *Rehabilitating Lochner: Rediscovering a Lost Constitutional Right* (Chicago, University of Chicago Press, 2011) 3 (noting that 'the bakers' maximum-hours law invalidated in *Lochner*, like much of the other legislation the Court condemned as violations of liberty of contract, favored entrenched special interests at the expense of competitors with less political power').

[50] *Landis v N Am Co*, 299 US 248, 259 (1936) (Justice Cardozo, writing on behalf of a unanimous court noted, '[W]e must be on our guard against depriving the processes of justice of their suppleness of adaptation to varying conditions. Especially in cases of extraordinary public moment, the individual may be required to submit to delay not immoderate in extent and not oppressive in its consequences if the public welfare or convenience will thereby be promoted. In these Holding Company Act cases great issues are involved, great in their complexity, great in their significance').

[51] FD Roosevelt, 'Fireside Chat on the Reorganization of the Judiciary', public radio address, 7 March 1937, www.wyzant.com/Help/History/HPOL/fdr/chat/ ('In the last four years the sound rule of giving statutes the benefit of all reasonable doubt has been cast aside. The Court has been acting not as a judicial body, but as a policymaking body. When the Congress has sought to stabilize national agriculture, to improve the conditions of labor, to safeguard business against unfair competition, to protect our national resources, and in many other ways, to serve our clearly national needs, the majority of the Court has been assuming the power to pass on the wisdom of these acts of the Congress—and to approve or disapprove the public policy written into these laws. ... We have, therefore, reached the point as a nation where we must take action to save the Constitution from the Court and the Court from itself. We must find a way to take an appeal from the Supreme Court to the Constitution itself. We want a Supreme Court which will do justice under the Constitution and not over it. In our courts we want a government of laws and not of men').

the public good.[52] Landis had stewarded the SEC through early legitimacy and accountability firefights with the financial sector, showing as much acumen in navigating the complexity of political contingency and judicial gamesmanship as in legislative drafting.[53] Landis was sanguine about the efficacy of the SEC's approach, in part because of the cautious nature of his initial stewardship. He was much less certain about the future of the New Deal itself. By the time that he had decided to retire from the SEC much broader questions of regulatory authority were at stake. This was most apparent in the debate over the fate of the PUHCA. The constitutionality of the PUHCA remained in play in the 1937 docket. A negative ruling would have severely curtailed the SEC.[54]

When Roosevelt broadcast the fireside warning to the Supreme Court, Landis was in a unique position to provide intellectual as well as practical help in justifying the threat of judicial reorganization. He was about to return to Cambridge in triumph as Dean of the Harvard Law School, taking over from Roscoe Pound, his nemesis as critic of the administrative state.[55] It was a task that Landis was more than willing to engage in. It was an opportunity to both settle old scores and present a theoretical justification for the administrative state just as conflict between the forces of capitalism, socialism and democracy was reaching an unavoidable denouement.[56]

Dispatched to Chicago in March 1937 at the height of the court-packing controversy, Landis enwrapped himself in the language of Roosevelt. He there put forward an argument for agency discretion that was to form the basis for his influential Storrs lecture series at Yale soon after his formal return to Harvard, which is discussed more fully below. Chicago was about communicating the message to the informed public. Landis argued that the 'real issue we face today is not a new one. It is the old issue of the degree to which this nation shall be a government of laws or men.'[57] Noting that the 1787 Constitutional Convention had twice rejected amendments put forward by James Wilson to give the Supreme Court power to strike down legislation, 'more than one hundred years

---

[52] JM Landis, 'A Note on Statutory Interpretation' (1930) 43 *Harvard Law Review* 886; for a critique of the Landis approach, see R Pestritto, 'The Progressive Origins of the Administrative State: Wilson, Goodnow and Landis' (2007) 24 *Social Philosophy and Policy* 16, 26–37.

[53] J Burk, *Values in the Marketplace: The American Stock Market Under Federal Securities Law* (New York, de Gruyter, 1988) 43.

[54] The constitutionality of the Act was subsequently upheld in *Electric Bond and Share v SEC* 303 US 409 (1938).

[55] Pound played a pivotal role in writing the ABA Report of the Special Committee on Administrative Law, see *Annual Report of the American Bar Association* (1938) 331–68 (referring to the rise of administrative absolutism.).

[56] Landis, above n 29, 300 ('The National Labor Relations Act, the Holding Company Act, Social Security, Minimum Wage—all these things were pending and if they went down as unconstitutional, the whole effort of the New Deal would fail. ... I was scared and I think the President was scared of the potentiality of what could happen here').

[57] JM Landis, 'The Power the Court has Appropriated' (speech delivered at Fourth Annual Woman Conference, Chicago, 10 March 1937, reprinted in *Vital Speeches of the Day* (1 April 1937) 358, http://web.ebscohost.com/ehost/pdfviewer/pdfviewer?sid=ea9e0eb3-63db-41a9-bfdd-2960ba8ffd95%40sessionmgr4&vid=2&hid=17.

later, in 1905, as though James Wilson had himself inspired it, the Supreme Court had aggregated to itself the immense super-legislative power that the Constitutional Convention had so deliberately denied it.'[58] Quoting Justice Holmes' famous dissent in *Lochner*,[59] Landis argued that the conflict

> arises out of the disregard of constitutional limitations by a majority of the members of the Supreme Court who insist upon writing their own individual economic prejudices and predilections into the fabric of constitutional law. ... It means today an attitude towards constitutional law which incites to litigation, incites to defiance of government, and too frequently leads to the paralysis of a program before it even has a chance of initiation.[60]

Landis endorsed wholeheartedly the president's proposal to inject new blood into the court, dispensing with any pretense that the move was designed to enhance the efficiency of court business. Instead, the unalloyed political reality was presented in forceful terms: '[T]he issue is not one of the Constitution but an issue of men whose interpretations of that document makes it a straitjacket upon our national life.'[61]

The plan to stack the court marked a defining moment in New Deal politics. It sparked enormous opposition and created new coalitions that challenged Roosevelt's hold on power. Crucially, the plan coincided with a remarkable volte-face in the Court's jurisprudence. There remains considerable academic controversy over the rationale and timing of the reversal. The Supreme Court decision upholding Washington State's minimum wage provision,[62] for example, was handed down on 29 March 1937 to be followed by separate decisions upholding the National Labor Relations Act[63] and the Social Security Tax.[64] The 1937 session marked the point that the court (if not coalitions of the disaffected, mainly comprised of industry participants) finally recognized the legitimacy of administrative power.[65] It was this legacy that Landis was most concerned with

---

[58] Ibid.

[59] *Lochner v New York* 198 US 45 at 75 ('This case is decided upon an economic theory which a large part of this country does not entertain. If it were a question whether I agreed with that theory, I should desire to study it further and long before I made up my mind. But I do not conceive that to be my duty, because I strongly believe that my agreement or disagreement has nothing to do with the right of the majority to embody their opinions in law').

[60] Landis, above n 57, 360

[61] Ibid, 361

[62] *West Coast Hotel Co v Parrish*, 300 US 379 (1937).

[63] *NLRB v Jones & Laughlin Steel Corp*, 301 US 1 (1937).

[64] *Steward Machine Co v Davis*, 301 US 548 (1937).

[65] Landis, above n 35, 302 ('I made a series of speeches after that, but the most important speech I made was the Chicago speech. That one, in fact. I made at the request—I don't think it was the direct request of the President but someone near him. ... It was a trial balloon. Not that the fight in the end was successful, but it was successful in getting away from the false ideas that were current, or had been made current. ... A lot of people opposed this. Frankfurter for instance. He opposed it. Q: He said so to you?

Landis: Oh yes. Yes. He had no use for it at all. Of course he is a traditionalist in many ways'); see also Peter Irons, *The New Deal Lawyers* (Princeton, Princeton University Press, 1993) 280–89.

protecting, hence his willingness to debate the issue in Chicago as a protagonist and flesh out in Yale over the fall of 1937.

There could be no doubting that as with *The Modern Corporation and Private Property* (1932), the classic Berle and Means treatise on the implications of the separation of ownership and control in major corporations, Landis' lectures were designed to inform an increasingly polarized debate over corporate purpose and responsibility.[66] Their central premise and critical thrust was to position regulatory lawmaking as an essential precondition for democracy.[67] In a critical passage Landis argued:

> [I]f the doctrine of the separation of power implies division, it also implies balance, and balance calls for equality. The creation of administrative power may be the means for that balance, so that paradoxically enough, though it may seem in theoretic viola-tion of the doctrine of the separation of power, it may in matter of fact be the means for the preservation of the content of that doctrine.[68]

Therefore, for Landis the rise of the administrative state was an exercise in modernization, legitimated by 'the inadequacy of a simply tripartite form of government to deal with modern problems.'[69]

[66] Landis wrote to Professor Paul Sayre of Iowa that '[S]ome day I hope I can get time to really explore and extend some of the ideas that were there advanced in a rather tentative manner, or better, I hope that someone else will do it.' JM Landis to Professor Paul Sayre, University of Iowa Law School, 14 February 1939, Harvard University Archive, Dean's Office UAV512.20: 1937–39, Correspondence Box 5.

[67] For his critics, foremost among them his predecessor as Dean at Harvard, Roscoe Pound, the rise of the administrative state was something to be feared: see MJ Horwitz, *The Transforma-tion of American Law 1870–1960: The Crisis of Legal Orthodoxy* (New York, Oxford University Press, 1992) 219. The political disagreements were matched by personal rivalries. Landis noted that 'faculty politics is about as dirty politics as can evolve': see *The Reminiscences of James M Landis*, above n 29, 150–51; see also JM Landis to Walter Gellhorn, Columbia Law School, 22 February 1946, Harvard University Archive, Dean's Office UAV.512.20: 1940–47, Correspondence Box 11 ('It is curious how much the New Deal has been tied in with the development of administrative law and how frequently men who damn it are really doing so because they hate to see effective instru-mentalities evolve to achieve the policies of the New Deal. Pound's attacks, for example, seem to me to have two prime sources: one of them is a Republicanism that saw no good in the rise of populism despite the scholarly mind that knew it was inevitable, and the second is an experience with the administration of prohibition. I often tell my class that they have to discount my views on administrative law because they have been formulated as a result of contact with fairly high level commissions, but for the same reason they must discount Pound's ideas because they have been fashioned out of experiences with prohibition agents, than which I suppose it would be difficult to get a lower class of administrative officials').

[68] Landis, above n 34, 46. For contemporary review, see C Rorhlich, "Business Administra-tion and the Law," *New York Times*, 16 October 1938 (noting support for Landis' admonition that 'governmental administration should be determined by needs rather than numerology'). Academic colleagues had noted that the book was in fact a manifesto. On the lectures, the Dean of Yale Law School, Charles Clark, wrote that 'they state positively, with force and reasoned argument, what to date has been so generally said only by way of defense from attacks. I think they well might prove a Bible for the Washington departments.' Charles Clark, Dean of Yale Law School, to JM Landis, 27 January 1938, Harvard University Archive, Dean's Office UAV.512.20: 1940–47, Correspondence Box 9.

[69] Landis, above n 34, 1. See also EL Glaeser and A Shleifer, 'The Rise of the Regulatory State' (2003) 41 *Journal of Economic Literature* 401–25 ('The regulation of markets was a response to the dissatisfaction with litigation as a mechanism of social control of business': 402).

Landis believed that legitimacy originated in how the initial grant of authority was framed. This grant must 'specify not only the subject matter of the regulation but also the end which the regulation seeks to attain.'[70] Once delegated, regulatory rulemaking, like law itself, was merely 'an instrument, or a social institution, if you will for the advancement of the health of society as a whole.'[71] According to the legal historian Jessica Wang, the formulation 'reflected legal pragmatism's view of law as a process and ongoing experiment, rather than a set body of rules.'[72] Landis considered it a much more complete agenda. 'The expansion of regulatory activity is, of course, the most outstanding characteristic of the nature of twentieth century governmental development,' which is founded on the 'creation rather than the restriction of liberties,' he wrote in 1939.[73] For Landis, the administrative process was designed ultimately as a place of reason, where the complicated questions of the time could be deliberated, governed by a social philosophy in which expertise is valued.[74] This state of affairs was impossible to achieve given the political circumstances of the time. Rational debate had fled in the face of ongoing contestation. He declaimed hysterical 'language hardly indicative of academic restraint' that informed criticism of the administrative agencies.[75] His ultimate aim was to secure the legitimacy of the administrative process as an essential bulwark to the rule of law. In so doing the relationship between the administrative and the judicial would reduce from a binary battle to a rivalry 'that attends the academic scene, where a passionate desire for truth makes for recognition and not resentment of achievement.'[76] For an academic who had made his name studying the value of Supreme Court precedent,[77] there was practical value in such an approach. In Landis' view, the administrative bulwark was essential precisely because of judicial bias, hence his public stance in relation to the court-packing debacle. Administrative practice had the capacity to augment and make substantive rather than reduce the rule of law. For Landis, the rule of law required those adjudicating it to be guided by moral strictures.

---

[70] Landis, above n 34, 51.

[71] J Wang, 'Imagining the Administrative State: Legal Pragmatism, Securities Regulation and New Deal Liberalism' (2005) 17 *Journal of Policy History* 257, 264 (citing a letter sent by Landis to Harvard colleague Sidney Simpson, 27 May 1936).

[72] Ibid, 265. The following two chairmen of the SEC, William O Douglas and Jerome Frank (both of whom were academic lawyers), mirrored this approach, taking a much more aggressive view of enforcement. Wang underplays the extent to which Landis was constrained by initial legitimacy battles. Without clearing the space, it is unlikely that Douglas could have adopted his more aggressive approach.

[73] JM Landis, 'Law and the New Liberties' (1939) 4 *Missouri Law Review* 105, 105–06.

[74] See T Arnold, *The Symbols of Government* (1930) 258–59 ('The question that confronts the student of government is what kind of a social philosophy is required to make men free to experiment—to give them an understanding of the world, undistorted by the thick prismatic lenses of principles and ideas, and at the same time undamaged by the disillusionment which comes from the abandonment of ideas').

[75] Landis, above n 34, 4.

[76] Ibid, 54.

[77] F Frankfurter and JM Landis, *The Business of the Supreme Court* (New York, Macmillan, 1927).

It is a recurrent theme in his writings that the judiciary had consistently failed to recognize advances in both the drafting of legislation and in the capacity of expert tribunals to determine operational outcomes, largely as a consequence of adherence to 'an outmoded age and a narrower experience.'[78] For Landis, it was imperative that in teaching, research and practice 'law must be made to look outside itself.'[79] It was only in so doing that a broad vision of statesmanship could be achieved. As he famously argued 'statesmanship is impossible without a broad vision, unattainable as long as the focus is simply the single case.'[80] This in turn shows the administrative as a unique experiment, the success of which lay precisely in its integrated nature:

> The administrative differs not only with regard to the scope of its powers; it differs most radically in regard to the responsibility it possesses for their exercise. In the grant to it of that full ambit of authority necessary for it in order to plan, to promote, and to police, it presents an assemblage of rights normally exercisable by government as a whole.[81]

Not surprisingly the exercise of this power challenged vested interests and he saw in legal disputes over implementation a strategy to privilege inaction. 'The easiest course is frequently that of inaction. A legalistic approach that reads a governing statute with the hope of finding limitations upon authority rather than grants of power with which to act decisively is thus common.'[82] Similarly, Landis saw in the administrative process a protection from congressional and executive interference in which policy application is clouded by an atmosphere informed by the proximity of self-interested lobbying to those who have the power to bend policy in pursuit of their interests rather than the public interest as a whole.'[83] This leaves open the question of how the administrative process was to be governed.

As early as 1936, empirical study in the allied field of political science had revealed the competing dynamics at play.[84] Landis concurred that this was the problem but argued that explicit and narrowly defined mandates could and should isolate the agencies from the 'turmoil of the legislative chamber or committee room'[85] and ensure 'that calmness of atmosphere in which wise

---

[78] JM Landis, 'The Study of Legislation in Law Schools' (1931) 39 *Harvard Graduates' Magazine* 433, 437
[79] Ibid.
[80] Landis, above n 78, 435.
[81] Landis, above n 34, 15.
[82] Ibid, 75
[83] Ibid, 25.
[84] EP Herring, *Federal Commissioners: A Study of their Careers and Qualifications* (Cambridge, MA, Harvard University Press, 1936) 96 ('We want good men but we are unable to define virtue. ... We do not know just what sphere is proper for these commissions. We dare not make them purely expert bodies because we distrust experts; we dare not lease them to lawyers because we recognize the limitations of the legal approach; we dare not place men of vision because we know not where their vision will take them').
[85] Landis, above n 34, 70

administration flourishes.'[86] This in turn required strategic vision, neutral administration and evidence-based policy. It was the absence of such restraint, for example, that undermined in Landis' view the National Industrial Relations Agency, where 'passion for energetic action was too fierce to permit time for the play of disinterested expertness.'[87] There was a danger that in following political imperatives, the impartiality and, therefore, legitimacy and authority of the agency in question could be threatened. At the same time, independence necessitated working with political constraints of what was possible. Following delegation of authority, in Landis' view the processes of administration must be apolitical. As long as this is taking place, the executive and Congress—as well as the judiciary—must withdraw. As Landis concludes, it is this interference that impedes or distorts progress:

> Such difficulties as have arisen have come because courts ... assume to themselves expertness in matters of industrial health, utility engineering, railroad management, even bread baking. The rise of the administrative process represented the hope that policies to shape such fields could most adequately be developed by men bred to the facts. That hope is still dominant, but its possession bears no threat to our ideal of the 'supremacy of law.' Instead, it lifts it to new heights where the great judge, like a conductor of a many-tongued symphony, from what would otherwise be discord, makes known through the voice of many instruments the vision that has been given him of man's destiny upon this earth.[88]

In this formulation, Landis is suggesting that through careful accretion of precedent and insolation from political processes the administrative agency not only acquires legitimacy but also has the capacity to advance societal preferences in a sustained coherent and cohesive manner that the other branches of government have neither the time, resources nor willingness to achieve.[89] For Landis, therefore, the courts were a necessary ally but only if they recognized the limitations of their knowledge. He based his claim on the development of the

---

[86] Ibid, 140.
[87] Ibid, 87.
[88] Ibid, 155.
[89] Ibid, 122. It was a view that was endorsed by some senior figures in Wall Street, see eg Frank Scheffey, co-director of the Investment Bankers Conference to JM Landis, 16 January 1939 ('Your explanation of the place in Government of commissions would go a long way towards eliminating some of the misunderstandings in regards to their functions. I am particularly impressed with the emphasis you develop as a basic principle underlying the Administrative Process to take care of and foster and develop the well being of the industry over which it has jurisdiction. ... Investors cannot have much confidence in going into public utilities or other securities if they have the feeling, whether or not justified, that Government agencies are giving more attention to policing and punishing than to fostering'), on file Dean's Office 1937–39 UAV512.20 Correspondence: S–Z Box 5, Harvard University Archive. This also reflects antagonism about the manner in which William O Douglas privileged enforcement over building of broad coalitions, a view that Landis also shared, see JM Landis to Frank Scheffey, 25 January 1939 ('The quarrel that I have with some of the administrative process is that many of the administrators think of their duties purely in terms of police ... to leave any permanent impress upon the industry something would have to be done to get into the inside of it as well as the outside. I only hope that the small efforts we participated in in this connection won't go completely on the rocks'), on file Dean's Office 1937–39 UAV512.20 Correspondence: S–Z Box 5, Harvard University Archives.

common law itself, with the rise of specialist courts. 'In contract, in tort, in negotiable instruments, in trusts—the body of our law is judge-made and represents the successive reactions to practical situations of a professional class that was nurtured in the same traditions and was subject to the limitations of the same discipline,' Landis admonishes his audience.[90] Indeed he acknowledges justifiable pride before warning of hubris. 'That class has had pride in its handiwork. Nor can one deny its right to pride. But the claim to pride tends, especially in the hands of lesser men, to be a boast of perfection.'[91] Working with the administrative agencies, under properly delegated discretion and accountable governance structures, provided, for Landis, the basis for liberty as it channeled decision-making to those best-equipped for the task, which in turn is dependent on both the specific circumstances and evaluation of which branch of government has the appropriate procedures, analytical methods, design and constitutional safeguards to take on the task.[92]

The exhortation to accept the administrative was not, therefore, a settled position. It could only prosper in delineated circumstances. The administrative option worked best when political contestation was reduced to a minimum. Suitably empowered the judicial model of oversight could be supplemented by administrative decision-making that had the power of precedent and which defined the public interest. It was a model that found quiet acceptance on the Supreme Court itself. Justice Harlan Stone, for example, wrote to Landis praising *The Administrative Process*:

> I think you have done an exceedingly good job and one that will be helpful to those who take the trouble to read. Your emphasis on the importance of understanding what the real function of the administrative agency is, and the effect on judicial action, of the way in which the agency does its work, should be taken to heart by the judges, by the agencies themselves, and by those who create them. The last lecture was of special interest to me. It seems to me an accurate and thoughtful analysis of the present status of court review of administrative action. I have long thought that many administrative bodies have underrated the importance of the careful preparation of findings. In a good many cases the judicial overturn of administrative action has been invited and facilitated by sloppy findings and might have been avoided by the care now exhibited by some, but unfortunately not all, of the government agencies.[93]

The model, however, required an able regulator, with the kind of intellectual brilliance that Landis himself encapsulated. Landis advanced throughout his writing an idealized image of an able regulator, a view that also informed the thinking of Tom Corcoran, who when asked how expertise could be evaluated suggested 'you have to have the power to make rules and regulations in every administra-

---

[90] Ibid, 135.
[91] Ibid.
[92] Ibid, 153.
[93] Harlan Stone to JM Landis, 17 October 1938, Dean's Office 1937–39 UAV512.20 Correspondence: S–Z Box 5, Harvard University Archives.

tive body. The answer is to pick good men on your commissions. ... It is the ultimate answer to any governmental problem.'[94]

There could be no doubt that in Cohen, Corcoran and Landis, Roosevelt had found advisors capable of traversing the political and judicial stages, most notably in the presentation of oral arguments to the Supreme Court on the Electric Bond & Share case.[95] Writing to Landis in November 1937, Cohen acknowledged Landis' role in making the SEC as small a target as possible. 'It really was a cooperative victory and no little credit belongs to you for the effective manner in which you kept the Commission from being involved in any threats of enforcement. It did require a great deal of self-restraint on the part of the Commission.'[96] The feeling was mutual. Oral arguments on the PUHCA were heard in February 1938, with Ben Cohen and Robert Jackson, soon to be elevated to the Supreme Court, representing the government. While the jurisprudential turn of the previous year gave the strategists room for confidence, they could take nothing for granted. When the Supreme Court handed down its decision in April 1938, Landis was effusive in his praise for the diffident but brilliant Cohen:

> You certainly deserve congratulations for I doubt whether the annals of the Supreme Court history would show any case better presented than you presented the Bond and Share case. And more than that, you can now feel great pride in your own draftsmanship for your technique in this respect was no less a basis for the victory than your spoken arguments. I just wanted you to know that I take my hat off to you with the deepest respect.[97]

In reply Cohen again acknowledged the tactical guile in litigating the case.

> It was a truly cooperative endeavor and that is why it succeeded so well. And not a little credit belongs to you for the admirable restraint you showed under the provocation of the enemies' fire. I thought the Chief Justice must have chuckled a bit when he wrote his opinion. He seemed almost consciously to say if you really want me to confine myself to the strictly judicial issues and not to allude to matters of legisla-

---

[94] Seligman, above n 13, 49.

[95] Even those in Wall Street acknowledged the manner in which Cohen, Corcoran and Landis provided a formidable team, that dated back to the Securities Act but which saw full expression in the PUHCA litigation, see Gilbert Montague to Benjamin Cohen, 3 February 1938 ('This is a masterly performance, and is entirely in line with the perfect legal work which you and Tom Corcoran and Jim Landis have done in each job of bill drafting and brief writing from the date when the Administration called you in to save the New Deal. Future historians are going to have a very special place for you three men, who have magnificently proved what can be accomplished by thorough scholarship united with practical good sense'), on file Dean's Office UAV.512.20: 1937–39 Correspondence I–M Box 3, Harvard University Archives; see more generally, B Cushman, 'Securities Laws and the Mechanics of Legal Change' (2009) 95 *Virginia Law Review* 927, 938 (the Court's jurisprudence concerning the power of the Commission changed not because Hughes and Roberts altered their positions, but because Roosevelt had by 1940 placed five appointees on the Court).

[96] Benjamin Cohen to JM Landis, 8 November 1937, Dean's Subject Files c. 1932–46, UAV.512.25 Benjamin Cohen [1937–40] Box 2, Harvard University Archives.

[97] JM Landis to Benjamin Cohen, 2 April 1938, Dean's Subject Files c. 1932–46 UAV.512.25 Benjamin Cohen [1937–40] Box 2, Harvard University Archives.

tive policy, I will show you how innocuous and harmless a really important judicial opinion can be made to appear.[98]

The importance of the case was that it gave the SEC the authority to begin enforcing the PUHCA in all of its dimensions, a task that was entrusted to William O Douglas. For Douglas there was early recognition that the changed dynamics of the Supreme Court as well as careful preparation had provided him with a once-in-a-lifetime opportunity. In typical fashion he seized it with gusto but he could not have achieved his goal without the patience of Landis in embedding the administrative process in American political life. Landis' belief in the supremacy of democratic will linked to the capacity of expert agencies, isolated from the travails of politics and with the resources to enforce mandate, lies at the heart of the New Deal experiment in regulating the capital markets. Tracing the rationale from initial framing to the publication of *The Administrative Process* (1938) provides an indication of the centrality of specifying regulatory purpose in legitimating this process. It provided a dual function. First, it limited the grounds for judicial challenge on constitutionality. Second, it limited the grounds for suspicion of the exercise of arbitrary power. Within this framework, disclosure, for example, was designed to inform the investing public of actual practice, thereby incrementally changing the boundaries of what could be constituted as acceptable. It is in this context that the abiding strength (and limitations) of the Landis approach to governance, which combines elite wisdom and capacity to both capture and utilize populist sentiment, becomes clear.

At the heart of the compromise lies an uneasy compact on how to evaluate expertise. In the initial framing, this was conceived as the remit of impartial career-driven bureaucrats, prepared to forgo personal material advancement in exchange for societal improvement. The critical flaw pivots on what happens when claims to expertise are evaluated according to different criteria. It could only achieve its dominance because of the extraordinary political circumstances of the time. The unresolved question was what to do with this power. Here, too, we see evidence of a coordinated approach built on gaining consensus rather than the imposition of externally generated dictates. Notwithstanding his own complex character in both government service and at the law school, Landis became a beacon.[99] Landis' commitment to that model was soon to be tested in the most profound manner.

[98] Benjamin Cohen to JM Landis, 5 April 1938, Dean's Subject Files c. 1932–46 UAV.512.25 Benjamin Cohen [1937–40] Box 2, Harvard University Archives.
[99] Charles Wyzanski to JM Landis, 28 March 1939 ('I have always cherished the highest regard not merely for your great intellectual qualities but more particularly for your capacity to bring men to the realization of their capabilities'), on file at Dean's Office UAV.512.20: 1940–47 Correspondence We–Wz Box 24, Harvard University Archives.

4

The Firefighter: The Existential Choice

As we have seen in previous chapters, at the heart of Landis' conception of regulatory purpose was the articulation and delivery of societal objectives, tailored to political choices. In no field other than finance was essentially political dispute more acutely tested than in labor relations. The stakes were raised if the target for well-financed lobby operations was an alleged communist conspiracy. If the target could be shown to be a foreigner, the political risks magnified further. The unresolved question was whether an examiner charged with running an administrative hearing on deportation had the agility and skill to ensure that the model propagated by Landis could work in practice. It was to be a test that Landis himself would conduct.

Throughout the 1930s a political battle was being fought out with intensity on the waterfront all along the west coast. Union control of the main shipping ports of Los Angeles and San Francisco provided a degree of leverage that those in other urban centers lacked. The question of how to deal with this was to ensnare Landis in a volatile political issue. Landis' appointment as a hearing examiner in the deportation proceedings brought against key union powerbroker Harry R Bridges on charges that he was an undesirable alien as a consequence of alleged communist leanings was to test both his integrity and the strength of the paradigm with which the Dean of Harvard Law School was most closely associated. The critical question was whether the administrative process could traverse the political chasm, retaining legitimacy in the adjudication of such a contested case? Revisiting the thought and practice of Landis in the carriage of the Bridges hearing demonstrates the existential choice to be made between bowing to populism and demonstrating the efficacy of independence. It is only by detailing both the way in which the hearing was conducted and the granular nature of the findings that the symbiotic relationship between law and practice that informed Landis' career can be fully understood. His conclusion was both unexpected and, in the circumstances, exceptionally brave. 'The Bridges aims are energetically radical may be admitted but the proof fails to establish that the methods he seeks to employ to realize them are other than those that the framework of democratic and constitutional government permits,' he ruled in findings that read like the political thriller it was.[1]

---

[1] JM Landis, *In the Matter of Harry R Bridges: Findings and Conclusions of the Trial Examiner* (Government Printing Office, 1939) 133; see also E Ward, *Harry Bridges on Trial* (New York, Modern Age Books, 1940).

The decision brought Landis both praise and opprobrium in equal measure. As the leading judge Charles Wzinski wrote:

> [Q]uite apart from the political and social factors which made this case so important in the history of this country, this report is certain to become famous as an example of the administrative process as a whole. There is perhaps no task more difficult for a lawyer, or judge than to make an impartial statement of facts in a case where emotion runs high, perjury abounds and economic and social forces clash. But you have done it. And every citizen has reason to be grateful not merely for your labor, but more particularly for the sacrifice of your personal interests which the job involved.[2]

Not surprisingly, Landis was also to receive plaudits from Ben Cohen and Tommy Corcoran. Cohen summed up the issues involved with his comment that:

> I thought it was a fine and courageous thing for you to take on, a job which was bound to involve stepping on a number of toes. Nonetheless you have done it with rare distinction and I think it should give you great satisfaction to know you have performed a most difficult public service with superb tact, skill and ability.[3]

Corcoran was equally ebullient, his own experience in bruising encounters on Capitol Hill apparent:

> I do want to tell you belatedly, just to relieve the monotony of the brickbats I suppose you'll get for months that I think your courage to speak the truth in the Bridges matter was worthy of you and the hopes of many of us in you and the traditions of the greatest job in the United States which you now hold [as Dean of Harvard Law School]. The more I see of these shifting sands and the endless irreconcilability of political ambition, the more I know you were a million times wise in choosing to build where you were entirely your own master.[4]

Corcoran was correct. Along with the plaudits came a substantial amount of hate mail delivered to the Dean's office in Cambridge.[5] Given the political resources expended in bringing Bridges to the hearing, this was neither surprising nor unexpected. The way in which the initial investigation was handled, however, was to bring into disrepute state and federal authorities alike. The deportation attempts were nothing less than a witch-hunt dressed up as due process. In detailing how this had corrupted core American values, Landis simultaneously upheld them and demonstrated how the administrative process could safeguard democracy rather than undermine it. It was to be one of his most significant achievements.

---

[2] Charles Wyzinski to JM Landis, 10 December 1940, Harvard University Archive, Dean's Office UAV.512.20: 1940–47, Correspondence Box 24.

[3] See Benjamin Cohen to JM Landis, 18 January 1940, Harvard University Archive, Dean's Subject Files, 1932–46 UAV.512.25 Benjamin Cohen [1937–40] Box 2.

[4] Thomas Corcoran to JM Landis, 11 January 1940, Harvard University Archives, Dean's Subject Files, c. 1932–46 UAV.512.25, 1937–40, Box 2.

[5] See eg Reginald Robbins to JM Landis, 1 January 1940 ('It seems that Reds will be Red, whether they are in Washington, San Francisco, Moscow or Cambridge,' on file in *The Papers of JM Landis*, Harvard Law School Special Collections Unit, Box 5-3).

Harry Bridges had arrived in the United States from Melbourne in 1920 with a fiery temper and commitment to workers' rights. Following a succession of jobs, he settled in San Francisco and became heavily involved in labor politics on the waterfront. Exposed to the efficacy of the general strike as a political weapon before he left Australia, he seized upon it as conditions on the waterfront deteriorated in 1934. Bridges, who had also participated in trades union activism in Melbourne, had natural leadership abilities. He rose to become the head of the International Longshoremen's and Warehousemen's Union following the breakdown of negotiations to end a general strike in which martial law was declared in San Francisco.[6] Although not accredited as the leader of the union movement, his volubility and strident rhetoric made him a symbol of dissent, not least because the federal mediator brought in to resolve the dispute blamed, without evidence, communism for preventing compromise.[7] Bridges soon attracted the attention of the authorities, but an investigation in 1936 found insufficient evidence to deport him. A subsequent extensive investigation in 1938 determined that the Australian-born Bridges, a long-term resident who had not taken naturalization papers, was secretly affiliated with the Communist Party. This was sufficient ground at the time to authorize his deportation as an undesirable alien subject to a hearing by an examiner appointed by the Department of Labor.[8]

The investigation caused intense political problems for Frances Perkins, Roosevelt's Labor Secretary, who had consistently been lobbied to deport the bombastic Bridges. As early as 1937 the House of Representatives had established a Committee on Un-American Activities under the direction of Martin Dies. It had recommended her impeachment on the grounds that Perkins had failed to deport Bridges despite cause.[9] Although the case against the Labor Secretary was dismissed, the question of how to deal with Bridges remained politically toxic for the administration and for Perkins in particular.[10] She accepted that it was 'difficult to say whether the problem of the deportation of Harry Bridges was a problem in industrial relations or a plain problem of justice.'[11] Disentangling the complexities of the case required acute legal and political judgment, as an internal memorandum prepared by the Department of Labor pointed out:

[6] For an extended profile of Bridges and his importance, see H Schwartz, 'Harry Bridges and the Scholars: Looking at History's Verdict' (1980) 59 *California History* 66; see also W Saxon, 'Harry Bridges, Docks Leader, Dies at 88,' *New York Times*, 31 March 1990, www.nytimes.com/1990/03/31/obituaries/harry-bridges-docks-leader-dies-at-88.html (noting 'like Landis' he was a 'dapper, hawk-faced with a disarming smile who mellowed with age'). On Bridges' death, the San Francisco mayor ordered flags to be flown at half-mast.

[7] CP Larrowe, 'Did the Old Left Get Due Process—The Case of Harry Bridges' (1972) 60 *California Law Review* 39, 40.

[8] See M Radin, 'The Case of Harry Bridges' (1940) 14 *Social Science Review* 1, 2–3.

[9] TJ Parnell (John Parnell), 1895–1970 and United States Congress (76th 1939–41), 'House Resolution 67: Resolution for the Impeachment of Frances Perkins, Secretary of Labor, 56,' *Columbia University Libraries Online Exhibitions*, https://exhibitions.cul.columbia.edu/items/show/444.

[10] See M Dies, *The Trojan Horse in America* (New York, Dodd, Meand, 1940) 176–95 (for specific criticism of Bridges); see also E Lyons, *The Red Decade: The Stalinist Penetration of America* (Indianapolis, Bobbs-Merrill, 1940) 219–34 (for general criticism of union activism).

[11] F Perkins, *The Roosevelt I Knew* (New York, Penguin Books, 2011) 301.

Inasmuch as the ranking officers of the Department had already been smeared as being pro-Bridges, and the West Coast officials of the Service had been smeared as anti-Bridges, and that since the evidence in the case was highly conflicting and depended primarily upon the relative credibility of the witnesses already interviewed, it was highly desirable that a lawyer of distinction and ability, having no ties with any of the West Coast factions, and whose standing was such that his judgment would be beyond suspicion of possible influence by the Secretary, the Administration, or employee groups, be appointed to sit as trial examiner.[12]

Faced with the difficulties associated with disentangling this Gordian knot, it was not surprising that the administration would turn to James M Landis. All agreed that Landis had the standing, status and impartiality to adjudicate a case of this importance.[13] In some ways, the most surprising aspect was that Landis agreed to take it on in the first place. As Dean of Harvard Law School his personal and professional reputation was at stake. He had already ruffled the powerful alumni network because of his public support of the stalled plan to stack the Supreme Court in 1937. Moreover, his lifelong association with and support for labor issues made the assignment potential professional suicide. Many expected that he would acquiesce in the political pressure to deport. Landis, ever the pragmatist, would only recommend deportation on the basis of evidence and the evidential trail took him on a dangerous and unexpected journey.

The warrant for the arrest of Bridges had been prepared on 2 March 1938 and served in Baltimore three days later. The four-charge indictment argued that after his arrival in the United States, Bridges became a member of an organization that advises, advocates and teaches the overthrow by force and violence of the Government of the United States; that he became affiliated with such an organization; that he became a member of an organization that causes to be written, circulated, and affiliated with such. On 12 June 1939 the warrant was changed to state that he was and is a member of or affiliated with such an organization but did not specially name the Communist Party. The hearing was set for San Francisco and Landis made the journey across the continent in the early summer of 1939. He had imposed two conditions: first, the report was to be public; and second that he was to have complete control over the hearing process itself.[14]

To safeguard the integrity of the hearing process, held amid tight security on Angel Island in San Francisco Bay, Landis determined that it should be conducted in the full glare of publicity. Passes were made available to all who requested them, including support groups as well as the media, who each day made the journey across the bay in a patrol launch.[15] In making the decision to open the proceedings to public scrutiny, Landis had imbibed the lessons imparted by Brandeis well.[16] As one of the journalists covering the proceed-

---

[12] See Larrowe, above n 7, 48.
[13] See Ward, above n 1, 17.
[14] *The Reminiscences of James M Landis* (Columbia University Oral History Project, 1964) 53.
[15] Ibid, 20.
[16] L Brandeis, 'What Publicity Can Do,' *Harpers Weekly*, 20 December 1913, 10–13 ('Publicity is

ings colorfully explained, 'Dean Landis, lower kip protruding, and brows drawn into a heavy scowl, seated himself behind his table, and tapped for order with a yellow pencil.'[17] Order, however, was never fully achieved in the presentation of the government's case, which weaved conspiracy onto conspiracy to depict an elemental threat to American society that was as far-fetched as it was hysterical. The media coverage was grist to the mill for radio personalities such as Father Coughlin, who from his base in Detroit fulminated across America of the dangers posed to its social fabric by the influx of agitators such as Bridges. Not surprisingly, many of the hate-mail missives that arrived in Landis' office in Harvard throughout the hearing and in its aftermath came from areas such as Brooklyn, far-removed from the heat of battle on the West Coast but within the ambit of the mercurial preacher. The hearings took over 11 weeks to complete, during which 45 days were spent taking direct evidence, the vast majority of which on Angel Island itself, with the exception of two days at San Quentin maximum security prison, where two witnesses were serving sentences for second-degree murder, symptomatic of the characters that populated the case.[18]

The evidence against Bridges was largely circumstantial. Landis saw the parsing of conflicting claims as the core task.[19] Indeed, the issue was nicely put by Carol King, Bridges' lead attorney, in her opening statement:

> [S]ince 1934 Harry Bridges has been a stormy petrel around whom has raged such a storm as only the most violent labor struggles engender. He has become such a symbol of labor strength to certain employer groups that they have spent, and continue to spend large sums of money to get rid of him.[20]

Landis, by the end of the hearing, concurred. As he put it in the final report:

> [T]he alien's response to the charges against him was a complete and unequivocal denial. Not only did he deny that he was a member of the Communist Party but he also denied that he had ever been a member of that party. Further the theory of the

---

justly commended as a remedy for social and industrial diseases. Sunlight is said to be the best of disinfectants; electric light the most efficient policeman': 10).

[17] Ward, above n 1, 23.

[18] For representative letters written to Landis from the general public both during and in the immediate aftermath of the hearing, see *The Papers of JM Landis*, above n 4, Box 5-2 to 5-6. See eg Mary Amelia Fashay to JM Landis (undated): 'Will you please use all of your offices to send this man Bridges to the country where he belongs and that at once. Why are we as a nation so dilatory? The millions that he has cost our country, the insults that he has offered our statesmen and the communist propaganda that he has spread—and surely all three should put him far from America' (Box 5-2); Byron Bishop, NYC to JM Landis, 4 August 1939: 'A strong man is on trial before you, strong because Harry Bridges has been given the opportunity to state publicly what millions of American workers believe privately. If he is guilty, then I am guilty, a native born American, as are all of my friends. From the press reports you have acted with great fairness and in the best traditions of Americanism. Vindicate our faith in you by admitting Harry Bridges to citizenship' (Box 5-2); EG Frairley to JM Landis (undated): 'If Bridges is allowed to remain in this country it will mean a free rein to the Reds. Why this expensive trial? He is an alien and just look at what he has done on the West Coast. As one American I say throw him out and the rest of his kind' (Box 5-2).

[19] *The Reminiscences of James M Landis*, above n 14, 53 (in which Landis noted that he had 'never seen a case as poorly tried, on behalf of the government, as that case was').

[20] Cited in Larrowe, above n 7, 50

defense was that the charges made against the alien were the result of a conspiracy, engaged in by persons on the Pacific Coast who were bent on getting rid of Bridges because of his admittedly militant and radical labor leadership.[21]

What made the case so politically combustible were the interactions between these forces and the official investigation. Of particular relevance was the close relationship between Harper Knowles, head of radical research at the California Department of the American Legion, Captain John Keegan, chief of detectives at Portland Police Department, and Stanley Doyle, a special agent of the State of Oregon. Doyle in particular was regarded as an unreliable witness:

> [His] conduct throughout evidence a desire not to testify and efforts were made to interpose every trivial legal technicality that could be conceived of to avoid truthfully detailing his relationship to the fact put in issue—efforts that were promoted by tactics of his counsel that at best can be designated as shabby.[22]

Laurence Milner, employed by the Military Department of the State of Oregon, was also regarded as unreliable, not least because as an undercover operative he had failed to even join the party. 'Milner throughout had very little independent recollection of the events to which he testified. He had constantly to rely upon his notes to refresh his recollection. Even this was frequently insufficient so that he was compelled on occasion to read the reports himself.' For Landis, it was simply implausible that he had gained the trust of the secretive Communist Party:

> Nothing in his testimony or these reports gives any indication that he ever reached a position of responsibility. ... Indeed as one ponders his excuse for not joining the party, the conclusion seems inevitable that normally astute leaders in the party would have hesitated on that ground alone to have thrust responsibility upon him or to have admitted him into their confidence.[23]

As a consequence,

> Milner's testimony in this proceeding is deserving of little if any credence. His reports, his oral testimony both fail to convince that he was either careful in his observations or acute in his perceptions. ... His spectrum provides no measurement for distinguishing labor-union activity from communism. ... Milner can best be dismissed as a self-confessed liar, a man who had admittedly tried twice—once successfully–to make falsehood parade as truth.[24]

More damningly, Landis also found an unhealthy relationship between the police investigation and the political aims of the Knowles committee:

> There is abundant evidence to indicate that the work of the Knowles committee came perilously close to that of those organizations whose sole effort is to combat militant unionism. ... A close differentiation was not always made between labor

---

[21] *In the Matter of Harry R Bridges*, above n 1, 7
[22] Ibid, 5.
[23] Ibid, 13.
[24] Ibid, 19.

agitators and those truly engaged in subversive activities. Indeed, the close alliances that existed between Knowles committee and the powerful employer associations lead to the conclusion that Knowles, whether wittingly or not, was frequently made the tool of their policies.[25]

The suggestion by the government that the police investigation was either routine or conducted with probity was, according to Landis, both far-fetched and dangerous. In this regard, Landis found particular fault with the chief of detectives at Portland Police Department, Captain John Keegan:

> Keegan's testimony from the beginning shows an effort to conceal his activities and the activities of his men. True, he and they were in contact with witnesses of very doubtful character. But it is not necessarily odious for the police to seek evidence from men of questionable character and with criminal records. The administration of justice frequently requires resort to such aids. A reason that could motivate such consistent concealment was that the means employed were in themselves disreputable, means that might discredit the evidence that had been adduced.[26]

As for Bridges himself, Landis was obviously captivated. Bridges was both resolute and forthright on the stand:

> There is no doubt but that Bridges had at that time and has since friends and associates who are communists. At no time was he hesitant to admit these associations nor to deny that on occasion he had sought the help of the Communist Party, as he has sought the help of the Democratic and Republican Parties as allies in the industrial and political struggles in which his unions were involved.[27]

Bridges 'seemed never hesitant in expressing his political faiths and convictions. Indeed, quite the contrary; for given an opportunity to express himself, he forcefully and volubly expatiated upon the viewpoints that he held and his methods of propagandizing for them.'[28] As Landis makes clear:

> Bridges' own statement of his political beliefs and disbeliefs is important. It was given not only without reserve but vigorously as dogma and faiths of which the man was proud and which represented in his mind the aims of his existence. It was a fighting apologia that refused to temper itself to the winds of caution. It was an avowal of sympathy with many of the objectives that the Communist Party at times has embraced, an expression of disbelief that the methods they wished to employ were as revolutionary as they generally seem, but it was unequivocal in its distrust of tactics other than those that are generally included within the concept of democratic methods. The Bridges aims are energetically radical may be admitted but the proof fails to establish that the methods he seeks to employ to realize them are other than those that the framework of democratic and constitutional government permits.[29]

[25] Ibid, 51.
[26] Ibid, 59.
[27] Ibid, 124.
[28] Ibid, 126.
[29] Ibid, 133. It was a view shared by correspondents assigned to cover the case. Arthur Eggleston of the *San Francisco Chronicle*, for example, wrote that 'For those who would like to keep Bridges a mythical monster and the labor movement something unknown and feared, the deportation hearing may turn out to be the worst thing that ever happened,' cited in Larrowe, above n 7, 65.

The manner in which Landis handled the investigation and the clarity of his final report was essential in demonstrating the efficacy of the administrative process, securing its legitimacy and upholding the rule of law.[30] Landis' forensic demolition of the government's case retains its power to shock:

> However much it may disclose lack of judgment or associations that may be regarded by others as reprehensible or unfortunate, [the evidence] falls short of the statutory definition of affiliation. Persons engaged in bitter industrial struggles tend to seek help and assistance from every available source. But the intermittent solicitation and acceptance of such help must be shown to have ripened into those bonds of mutual cooperation and alliance that entail continuing reciprocal duties and responsibilities before they can be deemed to come within the statutory requirement of affiliation. ... To expand that statutory definition to embrace within its terms ad hoc cooperation on objectives whose pursuit is allowable under our constitutional system, or friendly association that have not been shown to have resulted in the employment of illegal means is warranted neither by reason nor by law.[31]

That Landis refused to be bound by political considerations reflected considerable personal and professional bravery.[32] At the conclusion of the public hearing the *San Francisco News* editorialized of Landis that 'a man of Supreme Court caliber, he brought to the hearings a rich philosophy of what American justice means, he held both sides to the issues and he was imminently fair.'[33] Such fairness, however, was not to attach to his final report. Landis made no apology for either the length of the findings or the implications for the nature of political investigations. As he noted in the opening pages,

> [A]ny other method of approach seemed to me futile, for conclusions as to the credibility that should attach to the witnesses in this proceeding can be satisfactorily reached only after painstaking and minute analysis of their testimony. That process alone permits a fleeting doubt to be dismissed or to ripen into the conviction that what is paraded as truth bears the unmistakable marks of falsehood.[34]

For Landis the critical fact was to limit adjudication to the narrow issue at its core.[35] For those journalists who covered the proceedings there was uniform praise;[36] less so from the editorial pages. Typical was the *Los Angeles Times*, which argued:

---

[30] *The Reminiscences of James M Landis*, above n 14, 57 ('Sure, a guy might be sympathetic to certain Communist ideals, But that doesn't prove he is a Communist').

[31] *In the Matter of Harry R Bridges*, above n 1, 133–34.

[32] See K Downey, *The Woman Behind the New Deal: The Life of Frances Perkins, FDR's Secretary of Labor and his Moral Conscience* (New York, Doubleday, 2009) 283–84.

[33] Cited in Larrowe, above n 7, 78.

[34] Ibid, 1.

[35] JM Landis to Jackson Corbet, 26 January 1940, *The Papers of JM Landis*, Box 5-6 ('By pointing out that Bridges advocated certain political changes I do not understand that I was impliedly saying that it is a good thing for aliens to engage in these activities. What I did say was that when the advocacy of those changes is sought by constitutional means only, such advocacy has long been recognized by the courts as being an insufficient basis upon which to deport an alien. I say this simply to indicate the very narrow issue that was before me for disposition').

[36] James Chestnut et al to JM Landis, 10 January 1940, *The Papers of JM Landis*, Box 5-6 ('Some

Landis makes his ruling in some 75,000 words. It would take 75,000,000 words to explain its affront to common sense and it would still be unexplained. ... That Mme Perkins has been hoping for just such a report as she now has before her, however, will generally be believed. She brought the proceedings in the first place with the most obvious reluctance, and doubtless will dismiss them with a sigh of relief. There will be other administrations and other Secretaries of Labor, however.[37]

The antipathy shown by the West Coast newspapers was by no means limited. The *Chicago Tribune* was particularly hostile, editorializing in February 1940 that Landis had engaged in a frame-up to protect a violent revolutionary. Landis was incandescent but sanguine. Writing to Carl Mote, Landis gave an uncharacteristically expansive assessment of the pressures the case had placed on both him and American democracy itself:

> I was aware of the statement in the *Chicago Tribune* to which you refer. I was also aware when I took the original assignment that no matter what the evidence might be, a decision either way in the Bridges case would result in severe excoriation from certain groups and newspapers in this country. It hardly surprised me to find the *Chicago Tribune*, whose violence and utter disregard for facts is too well known to call for further comment, should indulge in statements of this nature. To combat them by a statement on my part would simply encourage further misstatements from such sources. It might, of course, be possible to seek redress at law for such action but to do so, as you are aware, involves time and energy and expenditure of emotion that I can ill-afford. I am afraid that I shall have to rest content with having my judgment vindicated in quarters where there is a real concern for the maintenance of American traditions of justice and fairness. Certainly I cannot boast that I am the only one against whom libelous attacks are being directed.[38]

There could be no doubting, however, the gratitude of the administration, and

---

of the boys who were there wish to compliment you on an eminently fair and brilliantly analytical opinion in the Bridges case'). Replying the next day, Landis remarked: 'I appreciated your telegram very much. I don't believe my appreciation stems only from the fact that I like roses better than brickbats. I have been more annoyed by some of the scattered bits of praise that have come my way than by those of a contrary hue because laudations generally derive only from the fact that I reached a result they wished me to reach regardless of what the evidence might me. But yours is otherwise and so I feel free to speak my thanks. One reflection refreshes me these days and points to the hardiness of our democratic ways. Surely, if so many of our people can indulge in invective and feel free to do so, the dangers of dictatorial control are pretty far away. Then too I am learning something more about invective as a fine art. Will you give my sincere regards to your associates[?] I liked not only the uniform courtesy that you people gave me last summer but more the opportunity to be received as a friend'.

[37] Editorial, 'An Affront to Intelligence,' *Los Angeles Times*, 31 December 1939; see also Editorial, 'Bridges Cleared Will Stay,' *Stockton Recorder*, 1 January 1940 ('It must be admitted that some of the Government's witnesses did not make an impressive appearance at last summer's hearing. Some seemed unreliable and their testimony unconvincing. Nevertheless it is difficult to see why Professor Landis should have been so diligent in lumping them in a liar's club while accepting as gospel the word of Harry Bridges. Californians will be bound to ask why the waterfront leader whose word has meant less than nothing and who considers agreements as scraps of paper should impress Landis with his veracity').

[38] JM Landis to Carl Mote, 7 February 1940, *The Papers of JM Landis*, above n 4, Box 5-6.

in particular Frances Perkins. Writing to Landis on 16 January 1940 she was unstinting in her praise:

> Although I thanked you for the report on the day when you handed it to me I had not then read it. Therefore I was not in a position to tell you how admirable it is. I have read it very carefully, checking it with the testimony and the evidence offered. It is really a splendid piece of work, painstaking and punctilious, but at the same time lucid and convincing. The conscientious manner in which you have analyzed all of the evidence and exposed your own mental processes in weighing and analyzing it seemed to me to place this report at an unusual level of fairness and thoroughness. Needless to say, it was important in this particular case that such fairness and such conscience should be exercised. Permit me to express my appreciation and hearty thanks for the time, effort and intelligence which went into it.[39]

In a statement Harry Bridges himself was to acknowledge the wider power of the Landis critique:

> Dean Landis has supported through his analysis of the evidence our consistent declaration that red-baiting is the method of reaction, used either economically or politically to attack the fundamentals of American democracy. Realistically speaking we cannot expect reactionary employers and politicians to discard this method. ... Their methods are not the exposure of a radical or the deportation of a man. Their motives are to depress wages, lengthen hours of work and place their tools in public office so that, on every front, they may obtain greater profit and privilege. They wish to return the worker to slavery, to rob him of education, wife, children, home, security. This program of theirs even includes robbing the worker of peace, by driving him into wars for which losses and death are his only rewards. They have done it before, and they will do it again—if they can. They wish, in short, to steal Americanism from the many and make it an instrument of private power. The opinion of Dean Landis gives us a guide by which we may, in the future, avoid such dangers.[40]

Effort and intelligence was, however, in short supply. In 1940 Congress passed the Alien Registration Act, making past membership of the Communist Party grounds for deportation. The legislation was widely regarded as specifically targeted to deport Bridges.[41] A second hearing was held under the auspices of the Department of Justice under the command of retired Judge Charles Sears, who advocated deportation, a ruling endorsed by the Attorney General, Francis Biddle.[42] The decision was appealed to the Supreme Court, which ruled that past communist affiliation had not been proven, in large measure by returning to the evidential core offered by Landis.[43] This did not stop further investigation and

---

[39] Frances Perkins to JM Landis, 16 January 1940, *The Papers of JM Landis*, above n 5, Box 5-6.
[40] Cited in Ward, above n 1, 239.
[41] See Schwartz, above n 6, 68.
[42] *The Reminiscences of James M Landis*, above n 14, 59–60 (According to Landis, recounting a conversation with the Attorney General, Biddle made the decision because 'he thought it was politically wise to do so. ... He was scared on the political consequences of the thing').
[43] *Bridges v Wixen*, 326 US 135 (1945); for discussion, see D Dickson (ed), *The Supreme Court in Conference (1940–1985): The Private Discussions Behind Nearly 300 Supreme Court Decisions* (New York, Oxford University Press, 2001) 199–204 (revealing the political calculation behind the decision, most notably the rationale for Felix Frankfurter's notorious dissent on the grounds that reversing the

the case against Bridges was eventually dropped in 1953.[44] As Milton Konvitz has noted, '[I]t was our administration of justice that was on trial; and the verdict of history will probably be that, taking the case as a whole, as it extended over a period of nineteen years, it was America ... that lost the case.'[45]

The great innovation of the initial Landis presentation of the hearing examination was in its melding of administrative and judicial methods. Not bound by the rules of evidence, he was able to employ a range of extrajudicial tactics to explore the broader political forces at work. As Max Rodin put it with prescience in a contemporary review:

> [T]he net result has been a demonstration that something very like a trial could be conducted in an intelligible fashion and that a trial need not be, as actual court trials are often permitted to be, mere contests of skills between opposing counsel in which the judge is little better than a secluded umpire. This difference is, as a matter of fact, the striking difference between administrative and judicial trials in general and must seem to modern observers as marked a difference as that which in the early days of the common law distinguished the procedure of the royal courts from that of the old local courts.[46]

In so doing, Landis revealed in practice the triumph of the administrative process. As he explained to an irate correspondent:

> I do not think that our Administrative agencies are best manned by men who do not believe in the content of the rights which it is their sworn duty to maintain. I make no claim—and I think that is clear from my writings—that officials of the Labor board, to take a specific example, should be partial to employees as against employers; I do claim that officials of the Labor Board could be zealous in their sworn duty to maintain the right to collective bargaining against unfair, labor practices. Yet it is the former you accuse me of, not the latter.[47]

Attorney General's decision limited government discretion. In a concurring opinion, Justice Frank Murphy argued that '[T]he record in this case will stand forever as a monument to man's intolerance of man. Seldom if ever in the history of this nation has there been such a concentrated and relentless crusade to deport an individual because he dared to exercise the freedom that belongs to him as a human being and that is guaranteed to him by the Constitution': see *Bridges v Wixen*, 326 US 135, 157).

[44] *Bridges v United States*, 346 US 209 (1953). The decision was widely reported in Australia, see 'Harry Bridges Freed in US by Supreme Court on Appeal,' *Canberra Times*, 17 June 1953 (highlighting the dismissal of perjury claims on grounds that the case was taken after the statute of limitations had already run out).

[45] M Konvitz, *Civil Rights in Immigration* (Ithaca, NY, Cornell University Press, 1953) 120–21; see also V Hallinan, *A Lion In Court* (New York, Putnam, 1963) 242 (the author, who represented Bridges in the second hearing, complained, with cause that: '[I]n dealing with many agents of the US Government, you must assume, until the contrary is completely established, that these representatives might commit felonies, suborn perjury, conceal evidence, bribe witnesses, intimidate jurors, convey information to judges, and otherwise engage in practices which would be the cause for disbarment or imprisonment for a private attorney,' cited in Larrowe, above n 7, 81. Hallinan himself was prosecuted for tax evasion and disbarred. For sympathetic review of the Hallinan book, see J Carpenter, 'Books for Lawyers: A Lion in Court' (1963) 49 *ABA Journal* 1114.

[46] Radin, above n 8, 5–6.

[47] JM Landis to Julius Smith, February 8, 1940, Harvard University Archives, Dean's Office UAV.512.20: 1940–, Correspondence Box 21.

Fulfilling that duty was to destroy a career but not a legacy. The hearing had demonstrated that the administrative process could indeed handle the complexities of modern life. To do so on a sustained manner, however, required men and women of integrity and demonstrable commitment to the social purposes of the institutions in which they served. It was this task that Landis committed to securing through his stewardship of Harvard Law School. For Landis, education was not simply a condition of entry and then to be discarded. It was an essential component of continuous professional development.

5

The Transformational Dean:
Law, Lawyers and Society

In May 2013 the major New York investment bank Goldman Sachs published the results of its *Business Standards Committee Impact Report*.[1] Goldman Sachs' intention was to present to the markets a reframed conception of business ethics and accountability. The apparent gravity of the task was set by the prodigious workload. The report, it was claimed, derived from 'tens of thousands of hours of discussion, analysis, planning and execution, and importantly training and development, which alone totaled approximately 100,000 hours.'[2] Drawing upon the scarifying experience of the global financial crisis, the report begins with a stated recalibration of the firm's strategy. It emphasizes the need to put the interests of clients first. Two additional drivers are also referenced, namely 'reputational sensitivity and awareness and the individual and collective accountability of our people.'[3] Curiously, there is no mention that the stated commitment to reform derives from a settlement agreement with the SEC over allegations that existing standards and practices at the bank violated each of these noble objectives.[4]

Goldman Sachs was far from being the only offender. The global financial crisis demonstrated in startling detail the externalities caused by emasculated or compartmentalized conceptions of responsibility and accountability. Corporate executives and their professional advisors conspired to push through deals and strategies informed by legal technicalities and accounting conventions as well as market norms. If not, arguably, in direct violation of the letter of the law, these strategies led to suboptimal results for both the sustainability of specific corporate models and the professional standing of their advisors.[5] This was as

---

[1] Goldman Sachs, *Business Standards Committee Impact Report* (New York, May 2013) www.goldmansachs.com/a/pgs/bsc/files/GS-BSC-Impact-Report-May-2013.pdf.

[2] Ibid, 3.

[3] Ibid, 3.

[4] *Securities and Exchange Commission v Goldman Sachs & Co and Fabrice Tourre* 10 Civ 3329 (SDNY, 15 April 2010); Securities and Exchange Commission, 'Goldman Sachs to Pay Record $550 million to Settle SEC Charges Related to Subprime Mortgage CDO' (Litigation Release 21592, Washington DC, 15 July 2010); for discussion of the case and the rationale for settlement, see J O'Brien, 'The Façade of Enforcement: Goldman Sachs, Negotiated Prosecutions and the Politics of Blame,' in S Handelman, S Will and D Brotherton (eds), *How They Got Away With It: White Collar Criminals and the Financial Meltdown* (New York, Columbia University Press, 2013) 178–204.

[5] See *Final Report of the National Commission on the Causes of the Financial and Economic Crisis in the United States* (New York, Public Affairs, 2011) xxii–xxiii (noting 'a systemic breakdown of accountability and ethics … to pin this crisis on mortal flaws like greed and hubris would

evident in the United Kingdom as in the United States.[6] The fines, although escalating in severity, have not necessarily led to a change in practice, leading to the suspicion that they represent just one further cost to doing business. Such is the level of judicial disquiet that one prominent jurist, Judge Jed Rakoff of the Southern District of New York, described Citigroup, for example, as a 'recidivist' offender.[7] The judge's concern related to a settlement between Citigroup Capital Markets and the SEC. The settlement focused on claims that the financial services conglomerate had deliberately created a billion-dollar fund to dump dubious assets on misinformed investors.[8]

> If the allegations in the Complaint are true, this is a very good deal for Citigroup; and even if they are untrue, it is a mild and modest cost of doing business. It is harder to discern from the limited information before the Court what the SEC is getting from this settlement other than a quick headline.[9]

Although Rakoff's refusal to endorse the settlement was overturned in an appeal brought by both the SEC and Citigroup, the case highlights a much broader issue. In its exercise of discretion, do the SEC's enforcement strategies, and indeed the more aggressive deployment of potential criminal sanction by the Department of Justice, privilege illusion over substance?[10]

---

be simplistic. It was the failure to account for human weakness that is relevant to this crisis. ... Collectively, but certainly not unanimously, we acquiesced to or embraced a system, a set of policies and actions, that gave rise to our present predicament'); D Kershaw and R Moorhead, 'Consequential Responsibility for Client Wrongs: Lehman Brothers and the Regulation of the Legal Profession' (2013) 76 *Modern Law Review* 26, 27 (noting that 'the idea that the lawyer's primary function is to zealously advance their clients' interests has acted as an ideological justification for the alignment of the profession's commercial interests with their clients' interests and as a barrier to close investigation of the role and responsibilities of transactional lawyers').

[6] See eg Parliamentary Commission on Banking Standards, *HBOS: An Accident Waiting to Happen* (London, HM Stationary Office, 4 April 2013) 52 ('In the view of this Commission, it is right and proper that the primary responsibility for the downfall of HBOS should rest with Sir James Crosby, architect of the strategy that set the course for disaster, with Andy Hornby [his successor as Chief Executive Officer], who proved unable or unwilling to change course, and Lord Stevenson [the Chairman], who presided over the bank's board from its birth to its death. Lord Stevenson, in particular, has shown himself incapable of facing the realities of what placed the bank in jeopardy from that time until now'); see also Financial Services Authority, *The Failure of RBS* (London, Financial Services Authority, 2011) 7 (noting that many will be 'startled' to read the RBS board voted to proceed with the acquisition of ABN-Amro, which is described as an 'extremely risky deal', based on information provided by the target within 'two-lever arch files and a CD', but also noting that incomplete due diligence could not form the basis of a credible prosecution. This is attributed to the fact that 'there are no codes or standards against which to judge whether due diligence is adequate, and given that the limited due diligence, which RBS conducted, was typical of contested takeovers': 8).

[7] *Securities and Exchange Commission v Citigroup Capital Markets* 11 Civ 7387 (SDNY, 28 November 2011) 11.

[8] Ibid, 1.

[9] Ibid, 11. Rakoff's refusal to sign off on the settlement, which he described as nothing more than 'pocket change to an entity as large as Citigroup', was successfully appealed by both the SEC and Citigroup, see *Securities and Exchange Commission v Citigroup Capital Markets*, 2014 WL 2486793 (2nd Cir 4 June 2014). The Second Circuit upheld the discretion of the SEC to determine how to prosecute and whether to pursue settlement rather than litigate to a judicial conclusion.

[10] A later settlement also involved Citigroup: see M Corkery, 'Citigroup and US Reach $7bn Mortgage Settlement,' *New York Times*, 14 July 2014, http://dealbook.nytimes.com/2014/07/14/citigroup-and-

It is this context that the revitalized Goldman Sachs business standards initiative is potentially so interesting. The bank's 'voluntary' strengthening of its code of conduct signals the strength and limitations of market ordering. Its approach is based on a determination that self-assessed surveillance and stated commitment to changed practice are sufficient to manage client relationships, conflicts of interest, structured products, transparency and disclosure, broader governance, and training and development. The stated commitment is laudable but does or will it work? Can or should trust be so readily given to an institution subject to SEC enforcement proceedings? On this front, the evidence is decidedly mixed. In sharp contrast to earlier reliance on caveat emptor, the bank now claims that its suitability framework has been enhanced. This, it is claimed, will 'help us [ie Goldman Sachs] better assess whether our clients have the background, experience and capacity to understand the range of outcomes from transactions they execute with us, particularly those transactions that are strategic or complex.'[11] Secondly, the firm has introduced what it claimed to be a 'systematic, integrated and comprehensive firm-wide framework for reputational risk monitoring and management.'[12] Thirdly, Goldman Sachs makes explicit reference to the importance of culture. 'We know that while formal processes and rules are important, they cannot alone substitute for sound judgment and experience and an environment in which every person in the firm feels equally accountable for the firm's reputation,' the report concludes.[13] So far so good, one might say. Reputation, however, is determined by risk. In this regard the report reads much more defensively.

The defensive tone rings or should ring alarm bells. It suggests the commitment to enhanced disclosure and transparency reflects the need to respond to external dynamics rather than internalized reflection. Indeed, the report is explicit on this point. Goldman Sachs notes 'the uncertain impact of regulatory reform on both our clients and the firm currently is a consistent theme across our businesses.'[14] Simultaneously, it seeks refuge in its storied past. It notes that 'suitability will always be an important focus for us as will conflicts and business selection.'[15] The failure to provide effective mechanisms to deal with these foundational problems within a functioning ethical framework, however, is what got Goldman Sachs into such trouble in the first place. Moreover, presenting

u-s-reach-7-billion-mortgage-settlement/?_php=true&_type=blogs&action=click&pgtype=Homepage&version=HpSum&module=first-column-region&region=top-news&WT.nav=top-news&hp&_r=0. Since 2009 more than $100 billion has been 'extracted from balance sheets' in the US alone: see Editorial, 'Shining a Light on Bank Misconduct,' *Financial Times*, 19 June 2014, www.ft.com/intl/cms/s/0/911c759e-f7c0-11e3-b2cf-00144feabdc0.html?siteedition=intl#axzz37RbnrLpj. It is indicative of the limited effect of such sanctions that on the day Citigroup released information to the market in relation to the fine, its share price increased 3 percent, see M Paul, 'Citigroup Earnings Drive Global Values,' *Irish Times*, 15 July 2014, B7.

[11] Goldman Sachs, above n 1, 3.
[12] Ibid, 13. Moreover this is deemed to be 'one of the main achievements of the BSC.'
[13] Ibid, 5.
[14] Ibid, 7.
[15] Ibid, 7.

enhanced levels of disclosure and transparency as voluntary initiatives when in fact they are mandated through legislative change is dissembling of the first order. It takes much away from the authenticity of the report. Paradoxically, the report itself goes on to spell out the forced nature of change. 'Our Investment Management Division has been concentrating on new regulations and require-ments related to suitability, many of which impact a broader range of clients than in the past and call for enhancements to disclosure, documentation and controls,' it notes rather plaintively.[16]

Goldman Sachs remains sanguine that 'professional investors generally have the background, experience and risk profile to make their own invest-ment decisions.'[17] It has, nonetheless, established vetting procedures related to the design and purpose of specific instruments offered by the firm to ensure 'the instrument is appropriate for the markets and that the relevant risk factors associated with the instrument are adequately addressed and disclosed.'[18] The unmistakable message is that Goldman will design, market and sell the product if it thinks it can get away with it, not on whether it is appropriate or socially useful. *Plus ça change, plus c'est la même chose.*

This extended vignette tells us much about the limitations of the corpo-rate and regulatory response to the global financial crisis and the failure of the professionalization agenda as a credible strategy. Seen in this context, the oper-ation of leading corporate and law and professional advisory firms and their conception of what constitutes obligation are part of the problem rather than the solution. It is not credible that the Goldman Sachs report was released without extensive legal consultation, not least to ensure it was compliant with the SEC-enforceable undertaking. The result is a minimal approach to social obligation. Without an acceptance of the social obligations that attend to those who hold or aspire to hold professional status, however, there is a real danger that we risk a repetition of the same hubris that was so instrumental in generating the crisis. This existential question animates current policy development in, for example, the United Kingdom and Australia.[19] At its core, enhancing ethical standards requires sustained evaluation of how to embed restraint. Just because something

---

[16] Ibid, 7.

[17] Ibid, 14.

[18] Ibid, 15.

[19] See British Parliamentary Commission on Banking Standards, *Changing Banking for Good* (London, HM Stationary Office, 2013) vol II, paras 567–611 (noting 'in the absence of true profes-sional requirements in banking, it is questionable to what extent existing bodies focus on behav-iour as opposed to the technical skills likely to be more prized by employers': 581). The move to push towards professionalization is also evident in Australia, see Parliamentary Joint Committee on Corporations and Financial Services, 'Inquiry to Lift the Professional, Ethical and Educational Stand-ards in the Financial Services Industry' (Canberra, Press Release, 14 July 2014). The inquiry covers 'the adequacy of current qualifications required by financial advisers; the implications, including implications for competition and the cost of regulation for industry participants of the financial advice sector being required to adopt: (a) professional standards or rules of professional conduct which would govern the professional and ethical behaviour of financial advisers; and (b) professional regulation of such standards or rules; and the recognition of professional bodies by ASIC [Australian Securities and Investments Commission].'

is technically permissible does not make it ethical. Moreover, this investigation necessitates parsing whether serving the interests of the client necessitates acquiescence or challenging courses of action that could harm the public good. These are not new questions. Finding mechanisms to manage this dilemma was one of the most vital issues in the development of legal education in the 1930s.

None was to play a more pivotal role in that development than James M Landis, who was to return to Cambridge at the beginning of the 1937 academic year as Dean of Harvard Law School. At the age of 37, Landis was the youngest leader in the school's illustrious history but was already a household name given his role at the SEC. As we have seen, Landis was an outstanding practitioner and theoretician of regulatory design. His pragmatism further complicated perceptions. From the beginning he had stressed purpose over regulatory form, cooperation over coercion and, critically, the need to guide industry to understand and provide socially beneficial outcomes. Whether that made him a slave of Marxism or market forces remained exceptionally contested.[20] All, however, recognized that in returning to Cambridge, Landis was making a deliberate if misunderstood choice. From the beginning it was apparent that the primary attraction of the position was its stewardship role. Control of the Harvard Law School allowed him to enlist the profession of law as a critical gatekeeper for wider system integrity, particularly in the operation of the capital markets. The primary mechanism to achieve this was through a recalibration of the curriculum, comprehensively revived within a year of arrival.[21] At its core was the placing of the profession of law at the service of the public interest. In doing so, Landis forsook the immediate gains from cashing in on government experience by going into private practice. He sought an altogether more lucrative prize: the capacity to shape the direction of legal education. There were, of course, partisan reasons for doing so. Such an approach justified Landis' own role in stewarding regulatory agencies as a new form of experimentalism in democratic governance. A further and by no means secondary objective was how Harvard provided a unique and exceptionally well-regarded venue to institutionalize the gains of the New Deal. No other university in the United States had the same cachet or influence. The attractiveness of the opportunity was set out in a major speech in Washington soon after the announcement that he would be returning to the

---

[20] See 'Public Service,' *Princeton Alumni Bulletin*, 22 January 1937, 334 (citing approvingly the *New York Times'* opinion that the choice was a 'noble' one. The Princeton journal noted that Landis remained a polarizing enigma. '*The Weekly*'s charter does not merit speculation upon the merits of the SEC or Mr Landis's chairmanship thereof. We are allowed no opinion on whether the conservatives were right three years ago in fearing Mr Landis as an agent of the Kremlin or whether the radicals have been right more recently in fearing him as an agent of Wall Street. We are allowed to observe, however, that, with the possibility of continuing to play a leading role in government, or of earning a respectable fortune in private law practice, one of the country's most prominent public figures has elected to "retire" to a university').

[21] See JM Landis, 'The New Curriculum of the Harvard Law School' (1938) 51 *Harvard Law Review* 965.

banks of the Charles River, not as a retirement sinecure, as slyly suggested by his own alma mater at Princeton,[22] but as a beachhead for radical change.

From the beginning Landis saw the need for legal education to integrate technical expertise with a sound understanding of the changing postulates of society. He proposed, therefore, a tripartite solution. Technical expertise needed to be leavened by a sound appreciation of political economy and willingness to engage with wider society through applied academic exploration and rigorous research:

> The emphasis on technical competence protects us against newness for the sake of newness, instilling as it does the discipline that one must know the present progress of an art before one essays its further advance. The emphasis on centrifugal forces means absence of moulds of opinion, the freedom of choosing ones own way of living, and the joy of finding that the law can be its avenue. The tradition to pioneer means more than the glory of exploration. It means the insistence of refreshing the law through continual reference to the needs of the nation.[23]

There can be no doubting the scale of the ambition. It was also inevitable that such an approach preordained conflict with not only the powerful alumni network but also the even more powerful American Bar Association (ABA). Landis, however, was blessed in his enemies. He returned to a faculty so riven by division over the form and function of the law that the President of the University was forced to mediate weekly meetings.[24] Landis' status as a former chair of the SEC and his close relationship with Roosevelt more than offset the barbs from white-shoe firms. Tactical calculation combined with strategic prowess in navigating the complexities of academic politics. Shrewd financial management helped address glaring gaps in the school budget, augmenting the level of support at the highest echelons of the university administration. As in so many other areas, Landis was adroit in reading the wider political mood. He was prescient in recognizing that calibrating academic learning to ensure obligation was embedded throughout the curriculum fed into wider political dynamics. In exploiting this opportunity, recognized by both his faculty and the wider university, Harvard cemented its dominance at the intersection of legal theory and administrative practice. In a media statement accompanying the launch of the new curriculum, which was covered extensively, Landis argued that:

> [W]hatever form our internal politics for the next two decades will take, it seems certain that government as such will remain important in affecting the rights of the individual against individual, and the rights of the individual against the State. Adequate instruction and adequate emphasis on those public aspects of law therefore becomes essential if we are thinking in terms of a bar that deserves the name of leadership.[25]

[22] *Princeton Alumni Bulletin*, above n 20.

[23] JM Landis, 'Address to the Third Annual Eastern Students Conference' (speech delivered at the Catholic University of America, 20 March 1937) 3.

[24] D Ritchie, *James M Landis: Dean of Regulators* (Cambridge, MA, Harvard University Press, 1980) 80–81.

[25] 'Harvard to Alter Law Curriculum,' *Lewiston Daily Sun*, 4 November 1938, 11; see more gener-

Change, for Landis, began at entry level. For Landis, the University performed a core educative function that transcended initial attendance in Cambridge. He argued that the strategy of transcending the limitations of technical instruction was more likely to be effective if entry-level students had a broader understanding of the natural and social world. It was as important if not more so for the student to be able to think. Writing in 1939 to the president of Liberty National Life, for example, Landis noted the importance of a general liberal arts and science education prior to entry to law:

> A young man should have acquired by that time a capacity to handle the English language well, he should be able to express himself both orally and in writing and he should have a broad acquaintance with the field of English literature. I cannot stress this point too much because I find so many of our young men are deficient in this respect. The second matter to stress is acquaintance in a broad way with the history of our civilization. This means knowledge not only of its political evolution, but of its intellectual evolution as well. For that reason I think that philosophy as well as history should be part of such a program of study. The third suggestion is that a man should be acquainted with the nature and methods of both the social and natural sciences.[26]

His approach was encapsulated in a characteristically blunt letter to the chair of the Committee on Legal Education of the New Jersey Bar Association. 'More and more,' Landis complained, 'I am convinced that the great majority of the men who fail in the Law School do so because they have never learned to express themselves, not only to others but also to themselves.'[27]

There were further reasons for privileging such an approach. First, basing entry on prior academic ability would reduce the high level of attrition, which had previously informed the operation of the Law School. According to Landis, an experiment to limit access to those who had demonstrated ability, 'reduced the "flunking ratio" from thirty percent to twenty percent.'[28] Second, it would enhance the capacity of the students and indeed scholars from other institutions to engage in meaningful research, which in turn reflected on Harvard's academic standing. Landis noted with satisfaction that:

> We have some thirty to forty men annually doing work for advanced degrees or doing advanced work without regard to degrees. That group consists of some of our best

ally R Gordon, 'The Geologic Strata of the Law School Curriculum' (2007) 60 *Vanderbilt Law Review* 339; see also R Gordon, 'The Case For (and Against) Harvard' (1995) 93 *Michigan Law Review* 1231. Gordon argues that the emphasis on change flatters to deceive. The underpinning method of instruction or core did not change. This he traces primarily to the fact that 'teaching law explicitly as what it inescapably is, a body of principles and procedures for ordering social life, is bound to land the teacher in the thick of greatly controverted issues. When one is running a school whose success must be underwritten by a powerful and often very conservative profession, that thicket is not necessarily where one wants one's teachers to be': 1259.

[26] JM Landis to Frank Sanford (President of Liberty National Life), 26 June 1939, Dean's Office 1937–39 UAV512.20 Correspondence: S–Z Box 5, Harvard University Archives.

[27] JM Landis to Josiah Stryker, 3 November 1939, Deans Office 1937–39 UAV512.20 Correspondence: S–Z Box 5, Harvard University Archives.

[28] JM Landis to Charles Rugg, 9 June 1939, Dean's Office 1937–39 UAV.512.20: Correspondence N–R Box 4, Harvard University Archive.

men, the best men from many other law schools, teachers from other law schools and some practitioners. They frequently go from that work into teaching and thereby carry on the ideas they have gotten here in the law school all over the country.[29]

Third, it would carve out a distinct niche for Harvard in the debates over the form and function of law. 'The great thing to be achieved, of course, is to excite the student's interest in things that are outside the range of the mere technique of the law.'[30] Nowhere was this integrated strategy more pronounced than in the field of administrative law itself, which informed the changing dynamic between government and business. The drive and strategic positioning impressed Erwin Griswold, who succeeded him as Dean in 1946. Griswold would later concede merit in Landis' strategic calculation that 'it is not going to make any difference who controls the government in Washington. They can be Democrats, Republicans, Socialists or whatnot—the pervasive character of government would continue.'[31]

Landis saw in the intervention of the state nothing sinister, rather the institutionalization of changed consciousness, itself the result of democratic choices. Adaptation was the only rationale response to increased complexity. As he pointed out in a draft article for *American Scholar*:

[B]usiness, because of its ramifying effects upon the public, must take upon itself the responsibilities of so conducting its activities as to meet not merely the simple ethical standards of the nineteenth century but also to produce positive gains for the public as a whole. Coincident with this movement has been the enormous rise of administrative law.[32]

Not only did an aspiring lawyer seeking to engage with the administrative state require new educational training, so too did the profession itself. This reinforced Harvard's centrality in both practical and theoretical terms. While the curriculum review maintained faith in the case study method, the increased use of electives, along with secondment of professors to New Deal agencies, created an elite within an elite. More than anyone else, therefore, Landis was to provide the intellectual foundations of the administrative state:

The new obligations that have been created, the new human claims that have been recognized, have been entrusted in the main to administrative tribunals for their protection rather than to courts. In part, this movement represents a need for expert advice that the common law failed to develop. In part, it demonstrates a belief that better results can be achieved by these tribunals, free to develop procedures and techniques differing from those that traditionally have held sway. The effects of this movement upon our systems of administering justice are likely to be as permeating

[29] Ibid.
[30] JM Landis to Justice Harlan Stone, 29 November 1939, Dean's Office 1937–39 UAV512.20 Correspondence: S–Z Box 5, Harvard University Archive.
[31] Ritchie, above n 24, 88.
[32] JM Landis, 'Draft Article for American Scholar,' Dean's Office 1940–47 UAV.512.20, Correspondence A–Az Box 6, Harvard University Archive.

and as profound as those that attended the rise of equity more than four hundred years ago.[33]

For Landis the gains in such an approach had theoretical as well as practical manifestations. At a more theoretical level, the rise of the administrative process fundamentally challenged the prior assumption that law is to be found not made:

> An earlier generation held to the faith that judges do not make law but only find it. Today the issues turns upon the materials that they may justifiably use in the process of making law and the nature of the law they have made. That the judge occupies the role of statesman in law is recognized; but his occupation of that role in private adjudication is equally apparent. An appreciation of these facts tends to make law a human, dynamic institution for the achievement of justice between man and man, observable and subject to criticism for its shortcomings and not the majestic brooding in the sky of an earlier age.[34]

This appreciation of the dynamic interplay between political economy, policy development, legislative framing and judicial precedent by its very nature complicated both the nature and quantity of teaching materials. It was also, Landis reasoned, necessary. As he wrote to Walter Gelhorn at Columbia:

> The big trouble with administrative law, certainly in the field of separation and delegation of powers, is the enormous amount of reading one must do in order to turn anything up. But that process seems almost essential to a study of this subject, and in a way you have to put your class through that process.[35]

The aim, however, was not simply to train one side of the debate. From the beginning Landis recognized the importance of a revolving door between Wall Street and Washington, DC (and indeed the role of Harvard Law School itself as a critical knowledge broker):

> Personally I do not encourage public service as a career in the sense of suggesting to men that they devote their entire lives to public service. I believe that considering the nature of American public service the best way to deal with the problem is to encourage men to serve for a number of years with their Federal or State Governments and then return to practice. Then when the opportunity comes again to serve for a period of time they can go back to it. These men are usually the most efficient in handling their responsibilities in public service and in turn they carry a better sense of idealism into their work at the bar as a consequence of that service.[36]

For Landis, the implications of this approach transcended the narrow area of administrative law. What he sought to institutionalize was the view that law is

---

[33] Ibid.
[34] Ibid.
[35] JM Landis to Walter Gelhorn, 18 February 1946, Dean's Office UAV.512.20: 1940–47 Correspondence Encyclopedia–Ge Box 11, Harvard University Archive.
[36] JM Landis to Ella Graubart (Patterson, Crawford, Arensberg & Dunn, New York), 10 May 1946, Dean's Office UAV.512.20: 1940–47 Correspondence Encyclopedia–Ge Box 11, Harvard University Archive.

and always has been a mechanism of social control.[37] What was required, there-fore, was both practical expertise and political judgment.[38]

The thinking behind the transformation, initially sketched out while still in Washington, was revealed in a major lecture in a high-profile series convened in New York in 1938–39. Profoundly aware of the unease with which experimen-tation was viewed by powerful alumni networks, and opposed by large sections of the ABA, which saw it as a threat to established power-relations, Landis' aim was targeted. He sought in his address to ensure that those who had gradu-ated continued to imbibe what was taught in law school. In so doing, he hoped to reduce the commitment of the ABA to market ordering and legitimate the administrative process. Under the provisional title 'Democracy in Crisis: The Conservation of Industrial Capitalism,' the lecture series was convened by the Bureau of Personnel Administration.[39] It was designed to examine the changing structure of the American economy, with particular reference to the impact of increased financial concentration and the interdependence between economic, social and political spheres.

Landis' starting point in New York was the articulation of what had become a familiar refrain. Societal complexity generated the need for specialization. The emergence of new professions, including economics and sociology in the academy and industrial engineering in the real world, reflected that dynamic. Law could not and should not, he argued, insulate itself from this reality. Instead, across all its dimensions, from student to professor, practitioner to Supreme Court justice, law as a profession needed to respond to it by privileging fealty to the integrity of truth. For Landis that truth was the need to accept changing societal preferences. Expressed at the ballot box and tempered in operation by respect for the rule of law, these preferences had to be respected.[40] The role of

---

[37] JM Landis to Milton Hanler, CLS, 28 March 1946, Dean's Office UAV.512.20: 1940–47 Corre-spondence Ha–Hon Box 13, Harvard University Archive.

[38] See eg JM Landis to Julius Smith, 8 February 1940, Dean's Office UAV.512.20: 1940–47 Corre-spondence Sh–Statistics Box 21, Harvard University Archive, ('It is true that I have urged expedi-tion but I cannot recall ever having urged expedition at the expense of fair play in regard to the opportunities for the presentation of evidence, argument and the like. … I do not think that our Administrative agencies are best manned by men who do not believe in the content of the rights which it is their sworn duty to maintain. I make no claim—and I think that this is clear from my writings–that officials of the Labor board, to take a specific example, should be partial to employees as against employers; I do claim that officials of the Labor Board should be zealous in their sworn duty to maintain the right to collective bargaining against unfair, labor practices')

[39] *The Papers of JM Landis*, Harvard Law School Special Collection Unit, Box 5-8. Landis' lecture was delivered on 30 March 1939, and the text is included in the Harvard papers: see JM Landis, 'The New Responsibilities of the Professions (Law, Engineering, Banking) in Their Interrelationships with Business Management' (speech delivered at the Conservation of Industrial Capitalism Lecture Series, New York, 30 March 1939). The lecture series was subtly amended to 'The Conservation of Industrial Capitalism: A Challenge to our Collective Intelligence.' It is indicative of the standing of the conference that a further participant was Professor Berle, who spoke on the subject of 'The Modern Corporation as a Democratic Instrument' (speech delivered at The Conservation of Indus-trial Capitalism Lecture Series, New York, 23 March, 1939).

[40] Landis, above n 23, 2 (in which he argued that 'the bond of a Faculty can never be loyalty to particular truths but the deeper one of loyalty to the idea of truth').

the profession was to facilitate this process of change rather than block it because of predetermined bias. According to Landis:

> The rise of the [new] professions corresponds with the shift in our economy from laissez-faire to a type of collectivism. This synchronization makes it necessary for us, in order to fit our professions into our economy, to phrase the far-reaching postulates upon which our society now depends.[41]

In this Landis maintained he was not advancing a partisan point of view. Rather, he suggested that the complexity of modern life challenged previous limitations on the role and scope for governmental intervention at either state or (increasingly) federal level. This need for adaptation, he argued, was 'truly revolutionary', noting that 'today it is the right of organized society to impose obligations upon enterprises, which at one time were considered individual property.'[42] Landis was in no doubt of the impact of this on existing power relations. Law's primary responsibility for upholding social control was challenged by the emergence of new forms of knowledge and expertise. This in itself was ground for a changed focus. According to Landis, the assault on law's primacy in setting the parameters of policy development was necessary and required a response above the level of petulance:

> Law was the only profession that had any professional concern with social problems. The other professions that today deal with social problems were then non-existent. Law, after all, is little more than a method of brokering appropriate solutions between competing claims made by individuals and this process thus devolved almost exclusively upon lawyers. In this way a substantial monopoly over statecraft came into the hands of the lawyers. This situation was particularly acute in this country, largely because our system of judicial review over governmental action. Lawyers thus had the power to determine what the postulates of our society should be. How effectively this worked is another matter.[43]

For Landis,

> it was sheer egotism on the part of one profession to say that they and they alone could articulate such fundamental postulates of our society. When one considers the way in which the judicial process reaches results in its field, one must be worried and concerned about the enunciation of doctrine of this character.[44]

The main impediment to progress, as Landis viewed it, was therefore the legal profession's rejection of evidence and the elevation of dogma. Landis proclaimed the value of the introduction of a more scientific method in the presentation of cases, in particular to the Supreme Court. He noted the enormous influence of Louis Brandeis' argument to the Supreme Court in 1908 that 'the question them

---

[41] Landis, above n 39. 1.

[42] Ibid, 2.

[43] Ibid, 4. In a reflection of his disdain for the innate conservatism of the courts, in the original speaking notes Landis went on to say 'The Courts believed that they were the guardians of our destiny.'

[44] Ibid.

before them—the validity of maximum hour legislation for women—was not to be determined by abstract speculation but upon the basis of examination the available scientific data as to the physical and moral effects of fatigue.'[45] Moreover, for Landis, the growing sophistication in the presentation of evidence in advance of the passage of legislative instruments to establish administrative tribunals was a further indication of both the utility and the democratic foundations of modern political decision-making. For Landis, building on the jurisprudence of Brandeis and Holmes, the courts and the legal profession were beholden to accept this reinforced legitimacy and put aside ideological bias.[46] The emergence of specialist administrative tribunals, led by neutral experts, provided, in his estimation, much better ways to resolve complex ongoing disputes, he argued, reprising the arguments made in his Storrs lectures at Yale in 1937, which were

---

[45] Ibid, referencing Brandeis brief to the court in *Muller v State of Oregon*, 208 US 412, 419 (1908). The Supreme Court held: 'It may not be amiss, in the present case, before examining the constitutional question, to notice the course of legislation, as well as expressions of opinion from other than judicial sources. In the brief filed by Mr Louis D Brandeis for the defendant in error is a very copious collection of all these matters, an epitome of which is found in the margin. ... While there have been but few decisions bearing directly upon the question, the following sustain the constitutionality of such legislation. ... The legislation and opinions referred to in the margin may not be, technically speaking, authorities, and in them is little or no discussion of the constitutional question presented to us for determination, yet they are significant of a widespread belief that woman's physical structure, and the functions she performs in consequence thereof, justify special legislation restricting or qualifying the conditions under which she should be permitted to toil. Constitutional questions, it is true, are not settled by even a consensus of present public opinion, for it is the peculiar value of a written constitution that it places in unchanging form limitations upon legislative action, and thus gives a permanence and stability to popular government which otherwise would be lacking. At the same time, when a question of fact is debated and debatable, and the extent to which a special constitutional limitation goes is affected by the truth in respect to that fact, a widespread and long continued belief concerning it is worthy of consideration. We take judicial cognizance of all matters of general knowledge. It is undoubtedly true, as more than once declared by this court, that the general right to contract in relation to one's business is part of the liberty of the individual, protected by the 14th Amendment to the Federal Constitution; yet it is equally well settled that this liberty is not absolute and extending to all contracts, and that a state may, without conflicting with the provisions of the 14th Amendment, restrict in many respects the individual's power of contract.' For discussion of the importance of this approach, see A Mason, 'Mr Justice Brandeis: A Student of Social and Economic Science' (1931) 79 *University of Pennsylvania Law Review* 665.

[46] Landis, above n 29, 5; for support for Landis' position, see also P Freund, *Standards of American Legislation* (Chicago, University of Chicago Press, 1917), the central argument of which is that judicial opposing of legislative discretion through judicial discretion cannot command sustainable societal support. It was indicative of Landis' strategic repositioning of the Harvard Law School that as Dean he recruited Freund to the faculty, in part because of his role as both an advocate of legislative action and experience preparing briefs to the Supreme Court while serving secondments to New Deal Agencies, and in part because they had both clerked for Brandeis and been schooled by Frankfurter; see also P Freund, *On Understanding the Supreme Court* (Boston, Little, Brown & Co, 1949) 50 (noting the importance of a 'morality of mind' informed by 'an insistence on knowledge as indispensable to judging; a rejection of opportunism; and insistence of jurisdiction and procedural observances and a rejection of sentimentality', features that animated Brandeis as a jurist). For Brandeis, as with Holmes, striking down state legislation on grounds of bias was unacceptable. For forthright expression of this point of view, see Holmes' dissent in *Baldwin v Missouri* 281 US 586, 595–96 (1930) 'As the decisions now stand, I see hardly any limit but the sky to the invalidating of those rights if they happen to strike a majority of this Court as for any reason undesirable. I cannot believe that the Amendment was intended to give us *carte blanche* to embody our economic or moral beliefs in its prohibitions.'

published in book form to wide acclaim the following year.[47] He acknowledged, however, that in order to reduce contestation, these disputes must be resolved in an accountable manner. For Landis, expedited solution did not necessarily equate to efficacy.[48] Instead, it must demonstrate effectiveness:

> In the field of labor, for example, it has always seemed to me that it is wise to delegate the efforts to solve these problems to agencies other than courts. The courts are already busy with all sorts of routine legal business—wills, divorce cases, contracts and similar matters. To hope that the courts alone can take the time to work out the difficult perplexing problem of collective bargaining seems rather hopeless. Members of some other professions, having some knowledge of the labor situation, some additional expertness are also needed.[49]

Landis was acutely aware of the extent of judicial resistance to such forays into areas of past competence, and noted that he was, in this context,

> distressed ... by several of the decisions of the Supreme Court which seem to have disregarded this truth. They disturbed me because the Court instead of reversing the actions of the administrative body on the grounds of law, reversed in on the grounds of policy. Whether or not breach of a collective agreement on the part of employees should be grounds to disbar them from their rights as set forth under the National Labor Act is a problem of labor engineering not law. I do not see why lawyers should be particularly qualified to judge this. I think it should be decided by persons who have dealt with these problems over a long period of time and I am disturbed that the Court should seek to superimpose its judgment upon the administrative in a matter such as this.[50]

This distrust of the expert reflected, in Landis' view, an out-of-date conception of the contemporary state that extended well beyond the courthouse. It reflected the social mores of large swathes of the profession, in particular graduates of the Harvard Law School itself.[51] Just as the courts had to curb the risk of confusing political sentiment with legal justification, so too had the legal profession to inform their clients of changing and legitimate expectations of what was considered acceptable conduct. This, in turn, required a change to the very basis of

---

[47] JM Landis, *The Administrative Process* (New Haven, Yale University Press, 1938) 123–55. For discussion of the theoretical importance of the book, see Chapter 3; for application in practice, see Chapter 4; for opposition of the ABA to its message, see Chapter 6.

[48] See JM Landis to Julius Smith, above n 38 ('It is true that I have urged expedition but I cannot recall ever having urged expedition at the expense of fair play in regard to the opportunities for the presentation of evidence, argument and the like. ... I do not think that our Administrative agencies are best manned by men who do not believe in the content of the rights which it is their sworn duty to maintain. I make no claim—and I think that is clear from my writings—that officials of the Labor board, to take a specific example, should be partial to employees as against employers; I do claim that officials of the Labor Board should be zealous in their sworn duty to maintain the right to collective bargaining against unfair, labor practices').

[49] Landis, above, 5.

[50] Ibid, 6 (referring to *National Labor Relations Board v Fansteel Metallurgical Corporation*, 306 US 240 (1939).

[51] See Ritchie, above n 24, 84 (noting that as early as April 1937 the President of Harvard had to mollify alumni at a Harvard Club event about the danger associated with elevating such a talismanic figure of the New Deal to the Deanship of Harvard Law School).

legal instruction, which had been the primary focus of academic management the previous two academic years:

> We are all aware of the tendency on the part of men with professional training to be somewhat narrow in their approach to problems, and that fact disturbs us. But that seems to me to follow from the educational methods that heretofore have character-ized professional training. We have not sufficiently emphasized the significance of a broad general education as preliminary to professional training. ... The responsibili-ties of the professions are greater than they ever were, for whether it be business or government, there is the duty to define and to articulate for us the postulates that govern for today and will govern for tomorrow the society in which we each must find our place.[52]

For Landis, this provided an opportunity for the professions to advance social progress, which he argued was central to their privileged position in society. The professions, therefore, were better regarded as guardians than hired guns; the aim of legal education was to impregnate the major law firms with enhanced social consciousness. This was, he argued, a laudable ambition that ultimately justified the continued leadership of law and lawyers in modern society. According to Landis, the privilege of professional status necessitated responsibility to guide those who by virtue of their other priorities had not time to reflect on changing expectations:

> The complexity of modern political life meant that business leaders did not have the time to reflect on the kind of obligations it was reasonable and fair for industry to assume because of changing conditions and this was the primary function of the professional disciplines.

This guidance would not necessarily in Landis' view lead to formal regulation. Indeed, he explicitly told his New York audience that the aim of the New Deal architecture was to reduce contestation by getting industry to accept its respon-sibilities. He cited the administration of the Securities and Exchange Act as an example of how cooperation could reduce contestation:

> The Commission was given enormous power to regulate almost every activity on the Exchange. However, the members of the Commission never resorted to that power unless they had to, hoping that management itself would adequately carry out these obligations. If they did, that was all that was necessary. If these postulates are observed, the particular solution lies in the hands of industry. But if industrial management will not recognize the obligation which society as a whole insists upon, then we will be in for an unfortunate time.[53]

This legacy was first reduced and then glossed over entirely. For example, one of

---

[52] Landis, above n 39, 8–9.

[53] Landis, above n 39 (transcript of Q&A following Landis' speech). For Landis it was also unfor-tunate that he was not paid. In an apologetic note the convener informed Landis that 'I regret terribly that I cannot say that the honorarium is enclosed. But this recession has hit us badly and put us behind in some of our obligations': see Henry Metcraft to JM Landis, *The Papers of JM Landis*, Harvard Law School Special Collections Unit, 29 May 1939, Box 5-8.

the first things that his successor, Erwin Griswold, did was to assume intellectual ownership of the Landis model. When asked for an update of Landis' statement of pre-law requirements, Griswold passed it off as his own:

> I have always thought that Landis' statement was excellent, and if it is agreeable with you, I would be glad to have you use it with my name under it. As a matter of fact, although Landis did the basic work of preparing the statement, as I recall it, he discussed it with a large number of us and revised it somewhat in the light of what we had to say. Therefore, it really has the status, to some extent, of a Law School statement, and I should think it was entirely appropriate to put it out under my name on behalf of the Law School.[54]

Griswold's conceit also involved taking ownership of an even larger part of Landis' legacy: the review of the entire curriculum in the aftermath of the war.

Landis had long been convinced that the end of hostilities would further transform American discourse about the nature of society, not least because of the provision of free education to former combatants. Writing to Frankfurter, he was also aware that it could strain relations with the school's extensive alumni network:

> Of course the GI Bill is affecting the situation enormously. It means that men who never had the financial resources to come here before are now able to do so. I think the infusion of that type is all to the good even though it does mean that we have to deny our facilities even to sons of our graduates who would before have been admitted under the pre-war standards. It does however bring us a volume of protests that have to be dealt with carefully.[55]

One way of so doing was to reposition Harvard as a necessary bulwark of democratic choices. To advance this agenda he convened a special committee, placing Lon Fuller as its allegedly independent chair. In a letter to Fuller, Landis outlined the audacity of the plan:

> The content of law alters and so the immediate objectives of teaching must be adapted to that fact. The second factor is that the position of the lawyer with reference to the members of other professions changes. The rise of experts in fields like economics, sociology, criminology, and the like, means that a portion of the burden that may originally have been the lawyer's is now placed on other shoulders. In some cases this may have resulted from the inability of the lawyer to assume responsibilities that he should have assumed. In other cases that shifting of responsibility is a natural evolution. In these latter cases it is not the lawyer's function, as I see it, to attempt to duplicate this expertness but to employ it in behalf of his causes. But how to do this, and indeed, how to recognize expertness are problems now before us. It is my belief that the time is now particularly appropriate to examine in the interests of legal education the role of lawyers in our society. During the past fifteen years this country has seen many great changes both in legal conceptions of the rights and duties of

---

[54] Erwin Griswold to Dean Delmar Leighton, 23 October 1946, Dean's Office 1940-47 UAV.512.20, Correspondence Jo–Li Box 15, Harvard University Archives.

[55] JM Landis to Felix Frankfurter, 10 January 1946, Correspondence of JM Landis, December 1945–April 1946 UAV.512.22, Harvard University Archives.

individuals and in methods of dealing with controversies. That experience, in which all of us have shared in part, is not now so close as to distort our vision. Its meaning deserves better and more accurate articulation in terms of what the lawyer is called upon to do and what responsibilities he may rightfully be required to assume. Also we have just won a war. That struggle, I trust, embedded in men's minds more firmly the age-old search for justice. The spiritual challenge arising out of the sacrifices that have been made should endure particularly for men who as lawyers should have a special devotion to the idea of justice. The training of lawyers cannot and must not neglect to carry on from the point where as soldiers they spent themselves in a cause they believed to be the highest good. Because I believe so firmly that the prosecution of an inquiry of this nature is worthwhile. I am asking you to act as the chairman of a small committee for that purpose. I have chosen the committee method of inquiry because in this field a pooling of knowledge and experience is particularly important. ... The results of such an inquiry are of prime importance to legal education, for out of it I hope will evolve a design for living for the Law School for perhaps the next decade that will enable it more wisely than ever to train young men for the profession of law.[56]

Fuller, assisted by Paul Freund, developed that model, which emerged in final form soon after Griswold took over the leadership of the school. Although there was no doubting Griswold's academic status, changing political priorities and a gradual dilution of direct political influence accompanied Landis' decision to leave. His conception of the lawyer has atrophied over the years, in particular in the operation of the capital markets and the result, understandably enough, has been a steady erosion of trust, the most recent manifestation of which has been the global financial crisis itself. As John Kay has astutely noted:

> [T]he most powerful mechanism for establishing a culture of trust and respect is for intermediaries and market participants to impose it on each other. Conversely, the contagious effect of failure to observe these standards at any point in the investment chain undermines them at every point in the market chain.[57]

It is in this context that the professions play a pivotal role, a point Landis made with such erudition in his address to the Bureau of Personnel Administration in New York in 1938. What is also apparent, however, is that those rules and procedures cannot be vouchsafed by allowing the communities of practice themselves to set what constitutes best practice and monitor effectiveness—a point critical in Adam Smith's (lost) essential reasoning.[58]

The failure of professional obligation in established professions should, in this context, provide a warning that zealously protecting the interests of the client can turn into ideational zealotry. Much more holistic assessment of the efficacy of existing trust boundaries is required, as is evaluation of how codes

---

[56] JM Landis to Lon Fuller, 11 December 1945, Correspondence of JM Landis, December 1945–April 1946 UAV.512.22, Harvard University Archives.

[57] J Kay, *The Kay Review of Equity Markets* (London, HM Stationary Office, July 2012) 47.

[58] A Smith, *The Theory of Moral Sentiments* [1759] (London, Penguin, 2009) 133 (arguing that 'we can never survey our own motives, we can never form any judgment concerning them, unless we remove ourselves, as it were, from our own natural station, and endeavor to view them as at a certain distance from us').

of practice police deviance from agreed institutional commitments and reinforce stated adherence to integrity. In the aftermath of the global financial crisis public trust in technical expertise is understandably unforthcoming. What is also abundantly clear is that not only has the banking industry proved incapable of rising to the level of a profession, within the financial services arena professional obligation has weakened, in large part through identification with those who are paying for services. The result is a mutual draining of legitimacy and authority, which has now reached crisis proportions for both.

All professions base their authority on the acquisition of expertise or competence. Standing within the community for each individual professional group is predicated on a latent trust that this expertise will be applied responsibly through the exercise of professional judgment. The profession itself acts as the gatekeeper for the competence and judgment of its members. There is, however, a symbiotic relationship between the individual practitioner, the individual firm or partnership in which she operates, and the professional association. At both individual level and for the profession as a whole, professional obligation is predicated on the capacity and the necessity to uphold the stated values of the profession. This, after all, is where the utility of the profession derives and its reputation rests. The specific duties that bind a professional are, therefore, defined by the expectations that the profession has itself created in the public mind. These expectations become exceptionally problematic to manage in environments such as capital markets, which are governed by specific cultural norms and mores and separated from society through (potentially) unbridgeable income disparities. Although lucrative for those providing professional advice, it is, nonetheless, questionable whether it is fair or reasonable that the externalities caused by the sector's misjudgments should be borne by those excluded from its governance.[59] Equally, in the event of failure, is it sustainable for the professions to retain status in the event that actual practice consciously (or through negligence of professional obligation) undermines the integrity of either the market or the wider justice system? It is axiomatic that credible ongoing reform necessitates that the ethos of responsibility percolates much deeper than bankers and their regulators and through to those who already hold the privilege of professional status. It must also inform the self-regard and self-referential framing of discourse by the professions.

Through ideological privileging, neglect or willful blindness, professional lawyers failed to either identify or safeguard market integrity and societal welfare.[60] In so doing they have brought into doubt both the utility and legitimacy of their function. The policy question now is how to render an alternative framework operational in a systematic, dynamic and responsive way. To

---

[59] See S Schwarcz, 'Systemic Risk' (2008) 97 *Georgetown Law Journal* 193.

[60] See Kershaw and Moorhead, above n 5, 45–46 (noting the conflation of libertarian and pluralist rationales); see also W Simon, 'After Confidentiality: Rethinking the Professional Responsibilities of the Business Lawyer' (2006) 75 *Fordham Law Review* 1543 (noting that reliance on formalism privileges technicalities and eviscerates obligation to uphold the spirit of the law).

be successful, this framework needs to balance specific economic efficiency (ie benefits to business) and professional rights to self-governance with explicit requirements that society should not be held responsible (or liable) for the failures of the former.[61] At corporate, professional and regulatory levels the framework needs to be mutually reinforcing. It needs to be capable of evaluating the calculative, social and normative reasons for behaving in a more (or less) ethically responsible manner.[62] It also requires reciprocal obligation from each institutional actor to maintain (and certainly not contribute through omission or commission to the erosion of) the integrity of the governance arrangements. These must articulate common understandings of what constitutes the ethical problem. Moreover, it must generate a framework in which disputes over interpretation can and should be resolved in a manner that is proportionate, targeted and, ultimately, conducive to the building of warranted trust in the operation of the financial sector. All of this places significant responsibility on the tertiary sector. It is the university, after all, that guarantees entry into the profession in the first place through qualifying degrees.[63]

As the Goldman Sachs *Business Standards Committee Impact Report* with which this chapter opened has revealed, these norms remain exceptionally powerful. To address them necessitates challenging the discourse and its underpinning assumptions. In short it necessitates fashioning a different narrative in an agonistic dialog and partnership and holding institutional actors as well as the professions accountable to it.[64] As we have seen, however, a command and control approach to regulation without internalization of its rationale and purpose has profound limitations. Rules are too easily transacted around. Likewise, the articulation of principles without ongoing external validation and oversight is difficult to enforce. Tackling ethical deficiencies requires we pay much more attention to the moral dimension of market conduct, which I have argued is core rather

---

[61] For application to business as an intangible asset, see J Petrick and J Quinn, 'The Challenge of Leadership Accountability for Integrity Capacity as a Strategic Asset' (2001) 34 *Journal of Business Ethics* 331; for original formulation of the model, see J Petrick and J Quinn, 'The Integrity Capacity Construct and Moral Progress in Business' (2000) 23 *Journal of Business Ethics* 3.

[62] S Winter and P May, 'Motivation for Compliance with Environmental Regulations' (2001) 20 *Journal of Policy Analysis and Management* 675; see more generally I Ayres and J Braithwaite, *Responsive Regulation* (Oxford, Oxford University Press, 1992); for study suggesting the power of outsiders to frame the emphasis on effective internal controls only if there is a perception within the company that performance is being monitored, see C Parker and V Nielsen, 'To What Extent Do Third Parties Influence Business Behaviour' (2008) 35 *Journal of Law and Society* 309 (reporting survey evidence from 999 large Australian companies); for broader theoretical issues, see M Dubnick and J O'Brien, 'Retrieving the Meaning of Accountability in Capital Market Regulation', in M Dubnick and G Fredrickson (eds), *Accountable Governance: Problems and Promises* (Amonk, NY, ME Sharpe, 2011) 282–301.

[63] For enlightening discussion of the trajectory of the role of the legal profession, see T Rostain, 'Self-Regulatory Authority, Markets and the Ideology of Professionalism', in R Baldwin, M Cave and M Lodge (eds), *The Oxford Handbook on Regulation* (Oxford, Oxford University Press, 2010) 168–200.

[64] See J Braithwaite, 'Cultures of Redemptive Finance', in J O'Brien and G Gilligan (eds), *Integrity, Risk and Accountability in Capital Markets: Regulating Culture* (Oxford, Hart Publishing, 2013) 269–97.

than incidental to the disclosure paradigm. It is essential once again to stress the ethical component of corporate and professional obligation. In so doing we can rejuvenate the paradigm and provide a meaningful basis for trust. Without it we are destined to repeat past mistakes at precisely the point that society literally cannot afford to pay for them. As Roosevelt warned in 1933, it is not enough to rely on exhortation. It is time for action. For Landis, 'the art of regulating an industry requires knowledge of the details of its operations [and the] ability to shift requirements as the condition of the industry may dictate.'[65] In 1937 Landis told the *New York Times*, somewhat optimistically, that brokers

> are beginning to realize more clearly that their interest is tied up with the public interest. They are beginning more often to subordinate their own interest to the larger interest. People are beginning also to look upon the exchanges not so much as private institutions as public utilities.[66]

The real tragedy here is not the misplaced optimism of Landis but the misplaced trust in financial services sector statements that through their disclosures they had recognized their obligations. This explicit normative foundation, which Landis did so much to inculcate in Harvard, has been lost in a debate over technicalities. Until it is regained, we will be incapable of either changing practice or shifting the calcified norms that have proved so corrosive to the body politic.

---

[65] Quoted in J Seligman, *The Transformation of Wall Street*, 3rd edn (New York, Wolters Kluwer, 2003) 62.

[66] 'Landis Retiring, Reviews SEC Acts', *New York Times*, 10 September 1937, 1.

6

The Advisor: Revitalizing and Losing Regulatory Authority

As the United States entered the 1950s the place of the administrative process in American governance appeared, on the surface, secure. A series of interlocking judicial and political compromises had settled the relationship between the traditional three arms of government. It did so by embedding the administrative process. These compromises were foundational to the rise of the regulatory state. Judicial change, both in personnel and outlook, combined with legislative setting of administrative procedure, which included the grounds of and limitations to right of judicial review. A third foundation stone was provided through ongoing presidential authority to set or change the strategic priorities and governance of the agencies themselves, provided such reorganization plans had the authority of Congress. The unresolved question was what either the executive or the agencies would do with such latent power. Of equal importance was whether the design was capable of creating sustainable governance or preordained dysfunctional outcomes.

From the beginning, there was evidence that the move back from the Supreme Court to Capitol Hill resulted in strategies that jettisoned reason based on evidence in exchange for the advancement of narrow sectional interests. Temporary alliances linked to the complexities of managing class and racial relations along with the ideological conflict spilling over from Europe played out in a debate in which opponents of the administrative process presented it as both distinctly un-American and a threat to the social order. Critically, the American Bar Association (ABA) was to emerge as a critical knowledge broker. The campaign, waged incessantly since the onset of the New Deal but intensified in 1937, placed the administrative process in immediate peril. If not managed or diffused it was a campaign that threatened to destroy it completely. As Landis put it in a pivotal article written in 1940, proposals to place legislative restrictions on agency discretion threatened 'to cut off here a foot and there a head, leaving broken and bleeding the processes of administrative law.'[1] A mere two years after the publication of *The Administrative Process* the integrity of the entire framework had eroded. How and why that occurred remains of critical importance in explaining the trajectory of postwar politics and, indeed, the ongoing nature of financial regulation in the United States.

---

[1] JM Landis, 'Critical Issues in Administrative Law' (1940) 53 *Harvard Law Review* 1077, 1102.

As we have seen, the most visible manifestation of the legitimation process was found on the Supreme Court itself. By 1946 none of those who had most criticized agency discretion remained on the bench. Presidential nominations throughout the federal judiciary allowed for a percolation that had incremental but nonetheless vital importance.[2] The decision to uphold the constitutionality of the PUHCA in 1946, after years in which the prior involvement of individual justices in securities law cases prevented the Supreme Court from reaching a quorum, marked the point at which the battle over the legitimacy of federal or state intervention was fought to a judicial if not political conclusion. 'The fact that an evil may involve a corporation's financial practices, its business structure or its security portfolio does not detract from the power of Congress under the commerce clause to promulgate rules in order to destroy that evil,' wrote Justice Murphy in a unanimous opinion.[3]

The executive had eventually triumphed not because of external pressures placed on the Supreme Court, most notably the botched threat in 1937 to 'stack the court.' More prosaically, the passage of time and personnel change was to be the key driver for change. Incremental changes to the jurisprudential outlook of the Supreme Court increased in direct proportion to the number of those associated with unease at expansionary government opting to retire.[4] Roosevelt's chosen replacements had a vested interest in protecting the administrative process from further challenge, given their partisan role in battling with the judiciary at every level throughout the early years of the New Deal. In making those choices, the president demarcated, if indirectly, the parameters of what constituted or should constitute the appropriate relationship between the executive, the legislature and the judiciary. The choices also reflected both the continued bitterness and the fundamental nature of the conflict. It was notable that his first nominee was a United States Senator, Hugo Black. The message was clear. Democratic will would triumph over judicial precedent.

Black had been an early and enthusiastic supporter of the plan to pack the court.[5] If there was any doubt about President Roosevelt's intention it was spelt out in a speech in which he argued for the necessity to take on an elite 'deeply interested in the security of property.'[6] The fact that Black had very little experience, was a populist in the mold of Huey Long and had prior links with the Klu Klux Klan, also demonstrated that no allowance would be made to the possibility that Roosevelt may be offending the sensibilities of the Court. Indeed, his landslide re-election in 1936 had evidenced a leftward turn in the administration, as Roosevelt sought to minimize any challenge from an increas-

---

[2] AC Pritchard and R Thompson, 'Securities Law and the New Deal Justices' (2009) 95 *Virginia Law Review* 841.

[3] *North American Co v SEC*, 327 US 686, 706 (1946). For full discussion of the Public Utility Holding Company Act (PUHCA) and its implications, see Chapter 3.

[4] B Cushman, 'The Securities Laws and the Mechanics of Legal Change' (2009) 95 *Virginia Law Review* 927.

[5] J Simon, *FDR and Chief Justice Hughes: The President, the Supreme Court and the Epic Battle over the New Deal* (New York, Simon & Schuster, 2012) 8, 347.

[6] Ibid, 347.

ingly discontented labor movement acutely aware that the rise of both fascism and communism fundamentally challenged the status quo in domestic as well as global politics. One way of demonstrating that resolve was to elevate to the Supreme Court a populist senator who, like Long, was seen as a champion of the working class and an ardent critic of corporate power.[7] Justice Black's very first opinion, a dissent in a utility rate-setting case, in which eight of the justices held in an unsigned opinion that the determination required reassessment, deliberately breached Supreme Court protocol.[8] Weeks later, he made clear his view that corporations could not use the protections offered by the 14th Amendment to evade state oversight. To do so, he reasoned in an opinion rooted in political philosophy if not jurisprudence, amounted to an abuse of power.[9] In a sense, it was a mirror image of the innate conservatism of Justice Sutherland, who had reasoned in 1936 that the rise of the administrative process risked institutionalizing arbitrary power.[10]

Such was the level of professional if not personal animosity that Chief Justice Charles Evans Hughes could tell the American Law Institute that 'the prime necessity in making the judicial machinery work to the best advantage is the able and industrious judge, qualified by training, experience and temperament for his office', views widely seen at the time as an indirect but explicit attack on Black's competence. [11] It was a view that both Roosevelt and Black studiously ignored. Indeed, the determination to meld political commitment to judicial thinking was also apparent in the nomination of Frank Murphy in 1940 to the highest court in the land.[12] A former liberal mayor of Detroit, Governor of the Philippines and on his return Governor of Michigan, Murphy was primarily a

---

[7] Black had played a critical role in the Senate exposing the lobbying operation of the utility companies against the PUHCA, see A Schlesinger, *The Politics of Upheaval* (New York, Mariner Books, 2003) 320–23.

[8] See N Feldman, *Scorpions: The Battles and Triumphs of FDR's Great Supreme Court Justices* (New York, Twelve Book, 2010).

[9] *Connecticut General Life Insurance Co v Johnson*, 303 US 77 (1938); for background and effect on the court, see Simon, above n 5 (noting how Justice Stone enlisted the support of a journalist to make public internal division about how Black was using the court to voice political opinions: 358); see also W Leuchtenburg, *The Supreme Court Reborn: The Constitutional Revolution in the Age of Roosevelt* (New York, Oxford University Press, 1995) 202–04 (quoting the *Christian Science Monitor* Washington Correspondent, Erwin Canham, that 'Mr Justice Black has "climbed out of the pit into which the circumstances of his appointment had hurled him, and is on the way to being regarded as another Brandeis"').

[10] *Jones v Securities and Exchange Commission*, 298 US 1, 24–25 (1936). Correspondence between Felix Frankfurter and Supreme Court Justice Harlan Stone revealed profound skepticism with Sutherland's reasoning. According to Frankfurter, 'Sutherland writes as though he were still a United States senator, making [a] partisan speech.' Stone was even more caustic in reply; the judgment, he maintained, 'was written for morons, and such will no doubt take comfort from it': cited in M Tushnet, 'Administrative Law in the 1930s: The Supreme Court's Accommodation of Progressive Legal Theory' (2011) 60 *Duke Law Journal* 60 1565–637, 1608 (quoting an exchange of letters dated 7 April 1936, on file with the Special Collections Department, Harvard Law School Library); see also *Conversations with Justice Frankfurter* (Columbia University Oral History Project, 1956) 188 (describing Sutherland as 'a very nice, extremely limited person—extremely limited. He just took those generalities and clichés as though God gave them to Moses on Sinai').

[11] Leuchtenburg, above n 9, 201.

[12] Simon, above n 5, 375.

political rather than legal operator. Loyalty was his primary qualification for the post of Attorney General, to which he was appointed in 1939.

As a critical powerbroker in Michigan he was a useful bulwark against the growing influence of Father Charles Coughlin on the Irish-American community and on conservative Catholics in general.[13] Coughlin, an early supporter of the New Deal, had become an increasingly vocal critic of Roosevelt. A weekly radio program nationally broadcast from his Michigan church made him one of the most influential commentators on social and financial matters. The devout Murphy brokered a series of meetings between the turbulent priest and Roosevelt in advance of the 1932 election and was often used an intermediary when the religiously inspired rhetoric emanating from Coughlin's radio station, broadcast from his Detroit church, became too strident or politically volatile. The convenient fact that the next vacancy on the Supreme Court arose due to the retirement of the only sitting Catholic judge was to pave the way for Murphy's elevation in 1940. Dismissed by Felix Frankfurter as someone who confused his function as a judge with that of a priest, Murphy was to retain throughout his judicial career a belief that the law cannot be isolated from politics.[14]

Along with these overt political appointments, designed in part to show scorn, came a ruthless strategic calculation to advance the administration's priorities. This was achieved through the nomination of the lawyers most publicly associated with presenting the judicial case between 1933 and 1937 that changed times necessitated changes in both the size and function of government. Stanley Reed, Roosevelt's second nominee, for example, was a much more traditional choice than Black. Here too, however, was the elevation of a partisan. As Solicitor General, Reed had played a critical role in arguing New Deal cases before the court. The elevation of William O Douglas was a further signal that Roosevelt wanted judicial deference to the agencies created by virtue of legislative decision-making.

Douglas came to the court direct from the SEC, an agency the Supreme Court had just two years previously denounced as a functional equivalent to the 'Star

---

[13] A Brinkley, *Voice of Protest: Huey Long, Father Coughlin and the Great Depression* (New York, Vintage Books, 1983) 107, 127; see Schlesinger, above n 7, 224, 250; see also *The Reminiscences of Arthur Krock* (Columbia University Oral History Project, April 1950) 18–20 ('Huey was a great demagogue and Roosevelt was afraid of him. Huey always said "I can take him. He's a phony. I can take this Roosevelt. He's scared of me," which he was. "I can out-promise him, and he knows it. People will believe me and they won't believe him. ... He was a remarkable man and Roosevelt was frightened to death of him ... politically, he was the most interesting character that I saw in the 1930s').

[14] JW Howard, 'Justice Murphy: The Freshman Years' (1965), 18 *Vanderbilt Law Review* 473 (suggesting that dramatic changes in judicial reasoning can be traced to the problems of adaptation); JW Howard, 'On the Fluidity of Judicial Choice' (1968) 62 *American Political Science Review* 43 (noting that Black was by no means the only judge to oscillate in the period 1940–49 as 'hardly any major decision in this decade was free from significant alteration of vote and language before announcement to the public. Neither was the phenomenon confined to Justices whose overt allegiances were to professional ideologies of law as reason or to philosophies of self-restraint'); on the specific conflict between Frankfurter and Black, see JW Howard, *Mr Justice Murphy: A Political Biography* (New Haven, Princeton University Press, 1968) 269.

Chamber'.[15] Most notably, Douglas developed a reputation at the SEC for aggressive enforcement. The failed attempts to build legitimacy through consensus alone, along with ongoing contestation and the emergence of scandal, both necessitated and facilitated a muscular approach to enforcement.[16] Douglas had the drive and ambition to use that enforcement to build a reputation for the SEC as well as himself. Following his elevation to the Supreme Court, however, Douglas was to recuse himself from all cases involving the SEC, making his role somewhat weaker in relation to securities law and regulation. Finally, in (belatedly) nominating Felix Frankfurter, the president endorsed the legal academic and policy entrepreneur most associated with the regulatory blueprint itself, which was designed to embed judicial restraint.[17]

The critical hybrid appointment, however, was that of Robert Jackson in 1941. As with Reed, Jackson had served as Solicitor General. More significantly, he was directly associated with the court-packing plan, justifying it in evidence before Congress that had the explicit approval of Roosevelt.[18] While serving as Solicitor General Jackson wrote a detailed account justifying the need to take action against what was seen to be an intransigent court. He argued that it had lost sight of what should be its core function, that of mediating or composing conflicts rather than imposing its own view on them.[19] On the day that Jackson was sworn in Roosevelt is reported to have told a private gathering that 'it may

---

[15] *Jones v Securities and Exchange Commission*, 298 US 1, 24–25 (1936).

[16] W Bealing, M Dirsworth and T Fogarty, 'Early Regulatory Actions by the SEC: An Institutional Theory Perspective on the Dramaturgy of Political Exchanges' (1996) 21 *Accounting, Organizations and Society* 317, 327 ('An uneasy ambivalence on the part of the regulatees was apparently tipped in favor of hostility towards the SEC by the ... appointment of the adversarial Douglas, whose appointment was perceived as a victory by the liberals'); see also T McGraw, *Prophets of Regulation* (Cambridge, MA, Harvard University Press, 1984) 195.

[17] It is somewhat ironic that Felix Frankfurter, who was instrumental in creating the design, would throughout his tenure on the court be the one most insistent on holding the agencies to direct account. His, however, was to become an increasingly shrill dissenting voice, in part because of his combative and patronizing temperament: see Pritchard and Thompson, above n 2, 891–912; Leuchtenburg, above n 9, 221; Simon, above n 5, 392–93.

[18] Feldman, above n 8, 113.

[19] R Jackson, *The Struggle for Judicial Supremacy: A Study of a Crisis in American Power Politics* (New York, Alfred Knopf, 1941) 10. Arthur Krock of the *New York Times* thought the original miscalculation was in the administration not being honest about its intentions: see *The Reminiscences of Arthur Krock* (Columbia University Oral History Project, April 1950) 54 ('I think he was thoroughly right in his objective. I thought the Court was so obsolete that it should have worn knee britches and wigs and taken snuff'). For a review of the importance of Krock, see D Ritchie, *Reporting from Washington: The History of the Washington Press Corps* (New York, Oxford University Press, 2005) 19–20 (citing Roosevelt as describing Krock as 'a social parasite whose surface support can be won by entertainment or flattery, but who in his heart is a cynic who has never felt warm affection for anybody—man or woman'). Similarly he was loathed by Felix Frankfurter, see *Conversations with Justice Frankfurter* (Columbia University Oral History Project, 1956) 8 ('There is a good deal of justification for a witty remark by Joseph Alsop [a prominent gossip columnist] apropos of my great interest in the doings of the press and the frequent forays of Mr Arthur Krock of the NY Times, into jurisprudence. There's nothing that he likes to write more about than matters legal, nor is there anything about which he is more frequently inadequate and inaccurate. Joe Alsop said "Arthur Krock is a frustrated jurist and Justice Frankfurter is a frustrated journalist." I don't know about Krock but I do know that's a fair crack about me').

not be proper to announce it, but today the Supreme Court is full.'[20] The extent to which the jurisprudence had changed was manifest in a 1955 decision in which Justice Douglas, writing on behalf of a unanimous court, could hold 'the day is gone when this Court uses the Due Process of the Fourteenth Amendment to strike down state laws, regulatory of business and industrial conditions, because they may be unwise, improvident, or out of harmony with a particular school of thought.'[21] While the legitimacy of intervention was secured, unresolved was the question of how to make the agencies themselves more accountable.

The fear of arbitrary power animated the intertwined political and judicial debates throughout the 1930s. They became ever more vitriolic as the decade progressed. These were, only in part, linked to the vexed question of what constituted expertise and on what basis should it be evaluated. A much more fundamental politics issue was at stake. As the world moved inexorably towards conflict, it was by no means evident what form of government would prevail. Significant labor unrest, particularly on the west coast, prompted suspicion that the enemy within had the capacity to destroy the very fabric of American life through a process of infiltration, most notably the National Labor Relations Board (NLRB).[22] Business leaders suggested that communists had infiltrated the NLRB and indeed ostensibly independent congressional investigations, including the long-running probe chaired by Senator La Follette into accusations that business had illegally attempted to block union membership drives.[23] As the hearings progressed, the atmosphere became even more strained in Washington and beyond. At stake were not only vested political and corporate interests but also vested professional interests, most notably those of the legal profession itself.

The roots of the conflict can be traced back to an argument first promulgated in the United Kingdom that the rise of administrative agencies contributed to the emergence of the new despotism, the eponymous title of a book written by the Chief Justice, Lord Hewart.[24] Two years later his counterpart in the United States, Chief Justice Charles Evans Hughes, accepted that that the growing complexity of contemporary society necessitated more systematic administration. As Hughes told a meeting of the Federal Bar Association:

> Experience, expertness and continuity of supervision, which could only be had by administrative agencies in a particular field, have come to be imperatively needed. But these new methods put us to new tests, and the serious question of the future is

[20] Feldman, above n 8, 203.

[21] *Williamson v Lee Optical Co*, 348 US 483, 488 (1955).

[22] See E Latham, *The Communist Controversy in Washington, From the New Deal to McCarthy* (Cambridge, MA, Harvard University Press, 1966) 124–50; for recent archival research using documents from the Soviet Union, see H Klehr and J Haynes, *The Secret World of American Communism* (New Haven, Yale University Press, 1995) 96–100 (suggesting the existence of a network within the NLRB).

[23] US Congress, Senate, Subcommittee of the Committee on Education and Labor, *Hearings Pursuant to S Res 266, Violations of Free Speech and Rights of Labor*, 74th–76th Congress, 1936–40.

[24] G Hewart, *The New Despotism* (London, Ernest Benn, 1929).

whether we have enough of the old spirit which gave us our institutions to save them from being overwhelmed.[25]

With that power came responsibility. 'The power of administrative bodies to make findings of fact which may be treated as conclusive, if there is evidence both ways, is a power of enormous consequence,' he warned.[26] It was precisely this reasoning that animated Justice Sutherland's criticism of the procedures followed by the SEC in 1936 in refusing to allow the withdrawal of a securities offering amounted to 'the assumption of arbitrary power by an administrative body.'[27] It was a reasoning that Landis had deemed simultaneously preposterous and purposeful in his famous Yale lectures:

> Such an outburst indicates that one is in a field where calm judicial temper has fled. Deep feelings underlie this unguarded language of Mr Justice Sutherland. They underlie too, the suggestion by the Chief Justice that the administrative is prone to abuse the powers entrusted it. Rhetoric of this nature has a purpose. If it is fair to apply the legal rule that one intends the natural and probable consequences of his acts, certainly the effect if not the purpose was to breed distrust of the administrative.[28]

The change in Supreme Court doctrine from 1937 did not mean that the conflict ended. Instead the key battleground moved to Capitol Hill. There was a growing recognition among both lobbyists and politicans alike that as the balance of power shifted in the highest court of the land, and throughout the federal judiciary through adroit placements, there could be no guarantee of judicial defenestration of agency authority. The question inexorably turned to how the agencies could be restrained. As the newspaper magnate Frank Gannett pointed out with remarkable candor, 'since the President now controls the Supreme Court, our only hope lies in influencing members of Congress. This we are trying to do.'[29] The mechanism to do so was through the imposition of legislative controls. This strategy was self-consciously designed to protect the positions of vested corporate, political and professional interests. The inevitable consequence of the creation of temporary alliances to limit labor and capital markets, devoid of overarching principle, was also to fracture any semblance of a national agenda for significant social change. Each interest had its own rationale for opposing Roosevelt's agenda. Wall Street wanted to reduce regulatory oversight; corporate America wanted to reduce the impact of the newly established NLRB on collective bargaining; the ABA wanted to retain its privileged intermediating position across both sectors. Southern Democrats were increasingly concerned that labor rights would lead inevitably to civil rights and social change, while conservative counterparts were concerned about the rise of presidential power and its

---

[25] *New York Times*, 13 February 1931, 18.

[26] Ibid.

[27] *Jones v Securities and Exchange Commission*, 298 US 1, 19 (1936).

[28] JM Landis, 'Administrative Policies and the Courts' (1937) 47 *Yale Law Journal* 519, 528; this essay is reprinted in JM Landis, *The Administrative Process* (New Haven, Yale University Press, 1938).

[29] Cited in J Patterson, *Congressional Conservatism and the New Deal* (Lexington, University of Kentucky Press, 1967) 212.

impact on the checks and balances. Each could advance its agenda by dressing opposition in the language of freedom. It was a charade and everyone knew it.

From his position at Harvard Law School Landis viewed the calculations in Congress with open derision. Writing to James Hanes, who had just been appointed to the SEC, Landis wished him 'all of the luck possible in your new task. And I am afraid you are going to need it. There are quite a few eddies whirling in the political current that tend to engulf people who have as much selflessness as you.'[30] The five years at the coalface negotiating with industry had taken a heavy price. 'I sometimes regret not being still on the scene, but the regrets come less frequently and less poignantly,' he wrote in September 1938 to Charles Gay, former president of the New York Stock Exchange.'[31] By the following year, however, the sanguinity had turned to despair. He was convinced that the turn to the legislature opened the administrative process to profound and pressing danger. As he complained to a prominent member of the New York Investment Bankers Conference:

> To leave any permanent impress upon the industry something would have to be done to get into the inside of it as well as the outside. I only hope that the small efforts we participated in in this connection won't go completely on the rocks.[32]

The quiescence he had detected on his retirement from the SEC had all but evaporated.[33] The increasingly aggressive use of enforcement coupled with the rising geopolitical instability placed intolerable strains on the administrative process. It was no surprise that the SEC and the NLRB were the most important targets. Landis had led one and throughout his entire career had evidenced support for improvements to working conditions, the animating purpose of the second. He could see clearly the way in which the legal profession had played a significant role in facilitating the looming conflict. For Landis the problem was both structural and ideational. In the pursuit of expeditious outcomes administrative agencies ran the risk of not following procedure or of following it to the detriment of fair play. Accountability, for Landis mattered and mattered enormously:

> It is true that I have urged expedition but I cannot recall ever having urged expedition at the expense of fair play in regard to the opportunities for the presentation of evidence, argument and the like. ... I do not think that our Administrative agencies are best manned by men who do not believe in the content of the rights which it is their sworn duty to maintain. I make no claim—and I think that is clear from my writings—that officials of the Labor board, to take a specific example, should be partial to employees as against employers; I do claim that officials of the Labor Board should

[30] JM Landis to John Hanes, 24 June 1938, Dean's Office UAV.512.20 1937–39, Correspondence D–H Box 2, Harvard University Archives.
[31] JM Landis to Charles Guy, 26 September 1938, Dean's Office UAV.512.20 1937–39, Correspondence D–H Box 2, Harvard University Archives.
[32] JM Landis to Frank Scheffey, 25 January 1939, Dean's Office 1937–39 UAV512.20 Correspondence: S–Z Box 5, Harvard University Archives.
[33] 'Landis Retiring, Reviews SEC Acts,' *New York Times*, 10 September 1937, 1.

be zealous in their sworn duty to maintain the right to collective bargaining against unfair, labor practices.[34]

In advancing this position Landis was thrown back into the political limelight, in the process deepening a schism within the academic community and threatening the ABA's relationship with the most influential law school in the country, now under his embattled direction. The conflict was also personal. His predecessor as Dean of Harvard Law School, Roscoe Pound, had been appointed chairman of the ABA Special Committee on Administrative Law in 1938. Under his direction the Committee took on a much more strident tone. No longer did the ABA suggest that in proposing technical measures to improve administrative efficiency it was engaging in public service. Instead the conflict was placed in stark ideational terms. The country was sliding it was claimed, towards 'administrative absolutism':[35]

> The ideal of administrative absolutism is a highly centralized administration set up under complete control of the executive for the time being, relieved of judicial review and making its own rules. This sort of regime is urged today by those who deny that there is such a thing as law (in the sense in which lawyers understand the term) and maintain that this lawyer's illusion will disappear in the society of the future.[36]

There could be no doubting where the barb was aimed. Pound was depicting advocates of the administrative process and legal realism more generally as fools, knaves and communists. He positioned this as an intellectual threat to the integrity of academic discourse and a pressing threat to the profession itself as well as the country.[37] As the serving Dean of Harvard Law School, Landis was in an exceptionally strong position to institutionalize administrative law and was in the process of doing so, much to Pound's evident consternation. While their personal relations remained cordial, Landis noted that the conservative turn had weakened Pound's capacity to function as a scholar and as an administrator.[38]

---

[34] JM Landis to Julius Smith, 8 February 1940, Dean's Office UAV.512.20 1940–47 Correspondence Sh–Statistics Box 21, Harvard University Archives.

[35] *Report of the Special Committee on Administrative Law*, American Bar Association Annual Report (Washington, DC, Congress, 1938) 342.

[36] Ibid, 343.

[37] Ibid, 339–40 ('Much of the case for administrative absolutism, a doctrine which has made great headway especially in American institutions of learning, with which, therefore, the legal profession must sooner or later contend, rests upon a use of "administrative law" in a sense quite repugnant to what "law" had been supposed to mean. It is urged that "law is whatever is done officially." Hence administrative law would be the actual course of the administrative process, whatever it is. But the usual and longest continued meaning of law in jurisprudence is the body of authoritative grounds of and guides to decision. Those who would turn the administration of justice over to administrative absolutism regard this meaning as illusory. They expect law in this sense to disappear. This is a Marxian idea much in vogue just now among a type of American writers': 339–40). For discussion of the implication of this dispute on legal scholarship, see M Horwitz, *The Transformation of American Law, 1870–1960* (New York, Oxford University Press, 1992) 213–46.

[38] JM Landis, *The Reminiscences of James M Landis* (New York, Oral History Collection, Columbia University, 1964), 151 (noting how Pound had become 'strangely conservative'). Pound was not alone; Raymond Moley, a critical figure in the first New Deal, became increasingly estranged frmo the president because of what he saw as 'an alliance with Labor and radical groups' and became

The dispute, already evident before Landis returned to Harvard,[39] had now taken on a vituperative tone in public.[40] The ad hominem nature of the ABA report was reflected in public disputation into the 1950s with Pound never relinquishing the central argument that administrative absolutism denigrated and threatened the rule of law.[41]

In the context of the ABA's campaign against the administrative process, Pound was to be a critical resource. His prestige, which even Landis was to acknowledge,[42] provided the proponents of reform with a cloak of intellectual legitimacy. His status allowed the ABA to defenestrate the administration as a threat to the American way of life, which the legal profession and conservative-leaning members of the judiciary were in a position to defend. It also had the effect of undermining the professional standing and intellectual authority of Landis, then the youngest Dean in the history of the Harvard Law School.[43] Armed with the reports, the ABA lent its considerable authority to a bill before Congress designed 'to provide for the more expeditious settlement of disputes with the United States and for other purposes.'[44] It did so on the basis of what was presented as a scientific investigation of the need for reform.[45] In an attempt to stave off the potential conflict, Roosevelt directed his then Attorney General, Frank Murphy, to set up an alternative research group, which could provide the evidential basis on which to guide controls, thus reprising the strategy used to justify presidential power for reorganization of federal agencies.[46] This was

anti-business, see *The Reminiscences of Raymond Moley* (Columbia University Oral History Project, 2 February 1965) 8.

[39] R Pound, 'The Future of Law' (1937) 47 *Yale Law Journal* 1.

[40] *Report of the Special Committee on Administrative Law*, above n 35, 343 (denouncing any suggestion that administrative adjudication can take place within the calm of scientific inquiry and arguing that 'the postulate of a scientific body of experts pursuing objective scientific inquiries is as far as possible from what the fact are or are likely to be'). The report at this stage deliberately references JM Landis, 'Business Policy and the Courts' (1938) 28 *Yale Law Review* 235, 237.

[41] R Pound, *Justice According to Law* (New Haven, Yale University Press, 1951).

[42] Landis, above n 38, 152–53 ('Pound's position in connection with administrative law was an extremely conservative one. Pound was the great radical in 1912. Of course the kind of work that he did through 1908, and I would say almost to 1928 was perhaps the most significant work done in law in this country in any period of time. ... Pound with his insistence upon the development of what he called sociological jurisprudence, which was a revolt against the idea that the law should live on its own entrails and that it should utilize other sciences in order to build itself up—that was a tremendous contribution. Of course he was an extraordinary scholar').

[43] See D Wigdor, *Roscoe Pound: Philosopher of Law* (Westport, CT, Greenwood Press, 1974) 270.

[44] For a definitive account, see G Sheperd, 'Fierce Compromise: The Administrative Procedure Act Emerges from New Deal Politics' (1996) 90 *Northwestern University Law Review* 1557; see also D Rosenbloom, '1946: Framing a Lasting Congressional Response to the Administrative State' (1998) 50 *Administrative Law Review* 173, 173–74 (noting that the APA was 'at the core of a broader congressional effort in 1946 to reposition itself in order to exercise greater discretion and control over the burgeoning post-New Deal federal administrative state').

[45] J Lashly, 'Administrative Law and the Bar' (1939) 25 *Virginia Law Review* 641, 658.

[46] Shepherd, above n 44, 1594. For discussion of the President's Committee on Administrative Management, see R Polenberg, *Reorganizing Roosevelt's Government: The Controversy over Executive Reorganization 1936–39* (Cambridge, MA, Harvard University Press, 1966) 28. For specific discussion of the battle over regulatory authority, see P Arnold, 'The Brownlow Committee, Regulation and the President: Seventy Years Later' (2007) 67 *Public Administration Review* 1030.

never, however, a conflict to be played out in university seminar rooms.[47] The research was always designed to further partisan agendas. The research director of Murphy's group was designated to be Walter Gelhorn, then a young academic based at Columbia. From the beginning Gelhorn, an acolyte of the Landis perspective on administrative law, was exceptionally skeptical of the evidential basis put forward by the ABA Special Committee.[48] Moreover, Gelhorn had made his name as an keenly critical opponent of judicial interference in administrative decision-making. He had given an address in Chicago in 1939, for example, noting the danger of the arrogant assumption of power by the judiciary, language that invoked Landis' critique in 1937 in the same city at the height of the court-packing controversy:[49]

> The judiciary has by myriad ways sought to foster the illusions that it alone is capable of governing justly and dispassionately, that the entrusting of responsibilities to the administrative agencies is fraught with danger unless their exercise is ultimately subject to judicial supervision, and that the supremacy of law is synonymous with the supremacy of the judges. ... Sporadic, inexpert, and superficial dictation by the courts will never produce methods of administration which are both workable and fair. On the contrary, such dictation serves chiefly to obstruct the development of sound administrative processes.[50]

By this stage, however, the battle with the courts had largely been won. It was now a question of to what extent an evidential basis could be provided to ensure coherence and consistency in the application of administrative power. Notwithstanding the provision of detailed evidence of the nature of specific administrative problems, the debate quickly degenerated into 'a bruising political brawl.'[51] As George Shepherd has astutely observed, the 'battle over administrative reform was a fight for the life of the New Deal, not a scientific debate about the most efficient administrative procedures.'[52] It was one in which the agenda was directed primarily by those to whom the evidence was supplied. The age of lobbying had begun. It has never ceased.[53]

---

[47] L Jaffe, 'Invective and Investigation in Administrative Law' (1939) 52 *Harvard Law Review* 1201; see also Lashly, above n 45.

[48] KC Davis and W Gellhom, 'Present at the Creation: Regulatory Reform before 1946' (1986) 38 *Administrative Law Review* 511, 516 ('[T]he ABA Committee continued to pick ideas out of the air without any research that one could determine. The committee members had no staff. I don't say this censoriously, but it was a fact that they had to come up with results and the results were ill-considered. I well recall having conversed with some of the people in Congress who were involved. Their level of penetration into the mysteries of administrative processes was maybe that far below the surface [indicating with his fingers a one inch span] but barely that far below the surface).'

[49] JM Landis, 'The Power the Court has Appropriated' (speech delivered at Fourth Annual Woman Conference, Chicago, 10 March 1937, reprinted in *Vital Speeches of the Day* (1 April 1937) 358.

[50] Cited in Shepherd, above n 44, 1597.

[51] Ibid, 1596.

[52] Shepherd, above n 44, 1595.

[53] A Mann, *Administrative Law in a Global Era* (Ithaca, NY, Cornell University Press, 1992) 2 (noting that deregulatory change post-Reagan de-emphasizes expertise and favors abrupt change, often with presidential power to direct providing at least superficially a veneer of accountability).

Landis, watching from Harvard, could no longer stay silent. He entered the fray with a devastating critique, much of it carried out in detailed footnotes:[54]

> It is not possible, for example, to view the recently proposed amendments to the National Labor Relations Act as simply intended to deal with procedural defects and not recognize that the outcry against the procedure is made partly by those whose desire is radically to alter substance.[55]

For Landis, the establishment of the right of collective bargaining or the regulation of investment banking and securities markets reflected fundamental changes in political principle. These were then translated into social outcomes through the administrative process. It was, therefore, both unfair and unreasonable to blame the administrative for implementing a constitutional mandate. 'Because we hesitate to take issue upon the basic questions of principle that they raise ... the focal points of attack and defense become the administrative measures employed for translating these principles into reality,' he argued.[56] Deploying his considerable experience as a draftsman and legislative scholar, Landis proceeded with cutting sarcasm to expose the political calculations behind the amendments. More particularly he targeted the partisan role played by the ABA in facilitating what was presented as technical change but which in reality affected the substance of political and regulatory action:

> Ordinarily a detailed examination of a bill is only a matter of limited concern. But this, a bill purporting to be the fruit of years of work by a learned and non-political organization, and avowedly covering a vast area of administrative action, deserves from that cursory or casual treatment.[57]

In so doing he was taking on Pound directly. It was both audacious and dangerous.

Landis' intervention in the court-packing incident in 1937 had already alienated powerful interests within the ABA, which had lobbied the Harvard President to block his appointment.[58] Now he was taking on in the most direct fashion the very organization that provided the route to employment for Harvard law graduates seeking to work for Wall Street firms. Critical to his analysis was an explication of the rationale behind exempting pre-New Deal Agencies from the operation of the bill. Was this, he surmised, a consequence of more effective procedures, or the lack of knowledge in how they operate? Perhaps, he suggested, a more ominous 'third [explanation]—a rather ugly one—is that

---

[54] Landis, above n 1, 1081–83 (Landis traces in this passage the history of the ABA investigation, the opposition it had generated within the legal community itself, and the manner in which this opposition had been glossed over by Representative Logan).

[55] Ibid, 1058.

[56] Ibid, 1078.

[57] Ibid, 1083.

[58] Landis, above n 38, 50 ('I had a lot of letters myself and I know that President Conant told me that he got a hell of a lot of letters, but he stood firm on it. I always admired him for standing firm on that, because obviously that was not a popular measure with the conservative law, and the Harvard Law School still represents much of the conservative law').

political considerations of the type from which the scholarly approach should be immune may have dictated these exemptions.'[59] Landis systematically debunked the grounds for exemption. He used examples drawn from both independent agencies and those under the control of executive departments to test whether the existing grounds for judicial review could be said to be appropriate. The Office of the Comptroller of the Currency, for example, established in 1863, had—and continues to have—enormous power to force banks to comply with suggested courses of action on the basis that it has the right to make public reports into the condition and operation of a given bank:

> When one turns to the statutes to discover what judicial restraint, if any, there exists upon the exercise of this truly significant power, the statutes, as they stand, are silent. Neither court, manner, nor scope of review is mentioned. Yet here the bill is also silent, thus hardly leaving a basis for inferring that the principle of its exemption rests upon the adequacy and clarity of the existing procedures for review.'[60]

Having dispensed with the flawed rationale behind exemption, he then turned his attention to the list of agencies that fell within the operation of the bill. Inclusion would

> in substance make for independent judicial determination of the facts. That is an end sought by many members of the bar, particularly those whose distrust of the administrative process in its new fields is deep and intense. If that is the result of this proposal, it is, perhaps, the most important innovation in the bill. ... [The implications] strike at the very heart of the administrative process itself. For the creation of the administrative [bodies] has been responsive to the desire for expertness both in the development of policy and the sifting of the underlying facts upon which the shaping of policy must rest. To subject this fact-finding again to independent judicial determination is to make pointless the process itself. Arbitrariness no one can defend; but against arbitrariness of judge, jury or administrator, the substantial evidence rule is ample bulwark.[61]

Landis proposed instead the rigorous analysis of practice across all regulatory agencies, taking into account significant differences in underpinning mandate, with the analysis of the relationship between the administrative and judiciary taking into account three specific issues:

> (1) the problem of the category of administrative acts that should be subject to judicial review; (2) the manner of invoking that review, and (3) the scope of that review.[62] Historical and traditional concepts of judicial power help to answer the first, considerations of expediency tend to dictate the manner of review and considerations that

---

[59] Landis, above n 1, 1084.
[60] Ibid, 1088.
[61] Ibid, 1093–94.
[62] This call for evidence has been a constant refrain of those proponents most in favor of the administrative process. It fails to take into account the fact that the evidence is largely a cover for what is in essence a failure to resolve an inherently political problem.

have reference to the relative expertness of administrator and judge should govern the scope of review.[63]

Critically, he argued that the Supreme Court had only the previous year already ruled on the competence of the administrative (insofar as the procedures it was following were appropriate):

> The determination of utility rates—what may fairly be exacted from the public and what is adequate to enlist enterprise—does not present questions of an essentially legal nature in the sense that legal education and lawyers' learning afford peculiar competence for their adjustment. These are matters for the application of whatever knowledge economics and finance may bring to the practicalities of business enterprise. The only relevant function of law in dealing with this intersection of government and enterprise is to secure observance of these procedural safeguards on the exercise of legislative powers which are the historic foundations of due process. [64]

For Landis, a review that encompassed the entire regulatory waterfront and ascertained whether and if so general principles had been departed from

> would have merit, arbitrarily excluding older agencies because of vested interests in the procedures they have evolved and turning the blunderbuss upon the new, as the existing proposal does, has none. In such a fashion and only in such a fashion will the problem of adequately molding this relationship ever come about.[65]

It was to be a forlorn aspiration.

All of this leaves unanswered the question of what should constitute adequate procedures. As Landis points out, the form and extent of an investigation into whether a public company holding company should be broken up differs enormously from an investigation into the mislabeling of cosmetics. The difficulty is that 'there is no solution but the painful device of overhauling critically each phase of the administrative process, made more painful because the very canons that should govern must still in the main be discovered.'[66] Landis closed, somewhat mischievously, with a lesson from recent history. Aiming his criticism directly at the proponents of reform, he suggested that they should look not at Roosevelt's or the New Deal's triumphs but rather at their talismanic failure. He noted that that the National Recovery Administration Act, signature legislation from the first term, had failed because

> no intensive survey had antedated [it]; no working papers had been consulted so as to delimit the scope of its operation. It, too, was superimposed upon an existing administrative scheme with only fleeting concern given to the problem of its joints.

---

[63] Ibid, 1099. Such an approach animated the early methodological impulses behind Pound's work on sociological jurisprudence: see R Pound, 'The Causes of Popular Dissatisfaction with the Administration of Justice' (1906) 40 *American Law Review* 729 (noting that the adversarial model resulted in 'a sporting theory of justice.'); see also R Pound, 'Mechanical Justice' (1908) 8 *Columbia Law Review* 605 (noting that discretion provided flexibility).

[64] *Driscoll v Edison Light & Power Co*, 307 US 104, 122 (1939).

[65] Landis, above n 1, 1100.

[66] Ibid, 1101.

It, too, was shot with exceptions dictated by the happy thought of the moment or the desire not to come to grips with vested interests that it necessarily affected.[67]

The Act, he concluded was bound to fail

> because behind it has none of that understanding essential to the effectiveness of reform. It is this need of understanding which must be uppermost. Its want posits the truly crucial problems not only of administrative law but of all measures of law reform. It and it alone offers the royal road to attainment.[68]

The article had an immediate impact. Writing from Washington, Ben Cohen told Landis that the article was 'a devastating answer to the American Bar Association and their cohorts. The whole work is splendid but your discussion of the exceptions is indeed a classic.'[69] Eleven days later, Cohen reported progress but also danger:

> It was a great help to have your article on the Walter–Logan Bill. We have made quite extensive use of it. We are working to stop defeat of the bill if we can, but I am afraid the politics back of the bill are so strong that it may have to go to Presidential veto.[70]

So it was prove to be.[71] It was, however, both the power and logic of Landis and Cohen that animated the president's response.

Opposition to the legal profession was one of the prime reasons Roosevelt vetoed the bill. Disdainfully the president argued that:

> [M]any of them prefer the stately ritual of the courts, in which lawyers play all of the speaking parts. ... Many of the lawyers prefer that decision be influenced by a shrewd play upon technical rules of evidence in which the lawyers are the only experts, although they always disagree. Many of the lawyers still prefer to distinguish precedent and to juggle leading cases rather than to get down to the merits of the efforts in which their clients are engaged. For years, such lawyers have led a persistent fight against the administrative tribunal.[72]

For Roosevelt this reflected interest group politics at its worst:

> There are powerful interests which are opposed to reforms that can only be made effective through the use of the administrative tribunal. Whenever a continuing series of controversies exist between a powerful and concentrated interest on the one hand

---

[67] Ibid, 1102.

[68] Ibid, 1102.

[69] Ben Cohen to James Landis, 2 May 1940, Dean's Subject Files c. 1932–46 UAV.512.25 Benjamin Cohen [1937–40] Box 2, Harvard University Archives.

[70] Ben Cohen to James Landis, 13 May 1940, Dean's Subject Files c. 1932–46 UAV.512.25 Benjamin Cohen [1937–40] Box 2, Harvard University Archives.

[71] Landis retained the utmost respect for the capacity of Ben Cohen and Thomas Corcoran and their work as technicians and lobbyists: see Landis above n 38, 263 ('They both appreciated each other and they both worked together. Ben, for example, wouldn't be good at selling, but Corcoran was good at that. Ben is an inventor and a creator, rather than Corcoran, but Corcoran peddled his goods, and very ably'). This was a case in which even their famed skills would be insufficient to sway Congress.

[72] The veto message was subsequently published in full by the ABA 'in order to complete the record': see 'Logan–Walter Bill Fails' (1941) 27 *American Bar Association Journal* 52.

and a diversified series of individuals, each of whose separate interests may be small, the only means of obtaining equality before the law has been to place the controversy in an administrative tribunal.[73]

Roosevelt made it clear that reform without the commissions and their deployment of expert judgment would be 'sterile and useless. Great interests, therefore, which desire to escape from regulation rightly see that if they can strike at the heart of modern reform by sterilizing the administrative tribunal which administers them they will have effectively destroyed the reform itself.'[74]

The president concluded:

[A]part from a general disagreement with the general philosophy of legal rigidity manifest in some provisions of the bill, I am convinced that it would produce the utmost chaos and paralysis in the administration of the government at this critical time. ... Today, in sustaining American ideals of justice, an ounce of action is worth more than a pound of argument. For these reasons I return the bill without my approval.[75]

This, however, was just the victory in an opening legislative war that was to continue for a further five years. Roosevelt attempted to play for time by suggesting that participants should await the imminent publication of the final report of the Attorney General's Special Committee on Administrative Procedure. It would, he claimed, provide an evidential basis to reflect what accountability mechanisms could or should be implemented. The impossibility of such an outcome was made manifest in the publication of that report three weeks later. Drawing on the resources of no less 27 monographs, released the previous summer, the committee would not reach a consensus. The liberal majority (unsurprisingly given Attorney General Murphy's critical role in overseeing the appointment process) proposed placing little restraint on the agencies. A separate bill from the minority suggested the imposition of a unified framework that failed to take into consideration the multiplicity of regulatory mandates. Critically, the majority view rejected the innovative imposition of mandatory notice and comment procedures for regulatory rulemaking advanced by the minority because of 'expense and a measure of delay-not always warranted in connection with regulations of minor, noncontroversial character or regulations which announce interpretations, or regulations whose rapid creation is necessary to avert dangers or prevent unscrupulous conduct.'[76] Both approaches were presented to the Senate and a series of hearings held. The vitriolic debate that

---

[73] Ibid.

[74] Ibid.

[75] Ibid. The strength of the Roosevelt denunciation was sufficient to fracture the uneasy coalition, with many of the northern conservatives and southern Democrats defecting: see Shepherd, above n 44, 1630.

[76] *Final Report*, Attorney General Committee on Administrative Procedure (Washington, DC, Congress, 1941) 108; see also Shepherd, above n 44, 1635 (noting that this is the first time that such a provision entered into regulatory discourse and formed a centerpiece of the eventual compromise that led to the passage of the APA).

accompanied Walter–Logan was essentially replayed, with only passing reference to the now-discarded evidence.[77] The hope of supporters of the administrative state that expert decision-making could occur in a neutral manner was once again dashed on the rocks of political expediency. It was to be short-lived, however. The decision by Roosevelt to declare a national emergency in relation to the attack on Pearl Harbor meant that administrative reform was off the agenda until the end of the war.

A combination of factors, however, changed regulatory dynamics in the aftermath of the war. First, the regulatory agencies, given enhanced power, proved incapable of exercising it, highlighting the need for reform, a point that the ABA lost no time in highlighting.[78] The gradual erosion of Roosevelt's commanding electoral position also contributed to a recognition within the administration that some sort of compromise must be sought, a position that was further underscored by Harry Truman's elevation to the presidency on Roosevelt's death. Eventually, in 1946, Congress reached a compromise that differentiated between rulemaking and adjudication that bore more than a passing resemblance to the minority report of the Attorney General's Special Committee on Administrative Procedure published in 1941.[79] The critical control section mandated that no rule could be imposed without first going through a substantive comment process. It furthermore noted the grounds for judicial review:

The reviewing court shall–
(1) Compel agency action unlawfully withheld or unreasonably delayed; and
(2) Hold unlawful and set aside agency action, findings, and conclusions found to be
    (A) Arbitrary, capricious, an abuse of discretion, or otherwise not in accordance
    with law;
    (B) Contrary to constitutional right, power, privilege, or immunity;
    (C) In excess of statutory jurisdiction, authority, or limitations, or short of statutory right; [or]
    (D) Without observance of procedure required by law.[80]

George Shepherd, the author of a definitive study of the debate that led to the eventual passage of the Administrative Procedure Act (APA) in 1946, surmised that 'brilliantly reasonable minds readily differed, with conviction, on whether

---

[77] See Horwitz, above n 37, 232 ('At a still deeper ideological level the divisions within the Attorney General's Committee were basically a repeat performance of the original split between Landis and Pound').

[78] *Report of the American Bar Association Special Committee on Administrative Law* (1943) 249–50 ('War has complicated and aggravated the problems of administrative law, particularly federal administrative law. The impact of administrative regulation has vastly increased both in degree and in scope. …The war has illustrated and emphasized the admitted defects of administrative justice. … [T]he citizen is more keenly aware, in a war fought for freedom and the dignity of the individual, that his freedom and rights lie under the pall of a war emergency reflected in operations of the federal administrative establishment,' cited in Shepherd, above n 39, 1642.

[79] JL Entikin Goering, 'Tailoring Deference to Variety with a Wink and a Nod to Chevron' (2010) 36 *Journal of Legislation* 18, 32 It also highlighted the ultimate triumph of 'the legalist mentality that Pound had effectively revived': see Horwitz, above n 37, 233.

[80] Administrative Procedure Act (1946) s 706.

New Deal programs' impositions on individual rights and twisting of constitutional separations were acceptable or worthwhile.[81] A darker reading has been provided by Ira Katznelson, who traces the compromises in Congress to a partnership between the Republicans and southern Democrats, who were deeply suspicious of the increasingly liberal turn of the administration in the aftermath of the 1936 landslide re-election.[82] This was most apparent in the battles over the passage of the National Labor Relations Act but for which enjoining the SEC provided effective cover. For Katznelson, the façade of national unity gradually disintegrated as southern members

> aware of the dangers that threatened the South's racial order … closed ranks in Congress to reshape the framework within which unions and the labor market could operate. For their Republican partners, labor remained an issue of party and ideology. For southern legislators, labor had become race.[83]

It was no coincidence, for example, that the primary sponsor of the Walter–Logan Bill in the Senate was Mills Logan, the junior senator from Kentucky. In introducing the Senate report, Logan claimed that:

> [U]nless this country is to become first a parliamentary and then a totalitarian government, with the States reduced to mere police provinces, and with both the legislative and judicial branches of our Government dominated by the administrative agencies of Government, these administrative agencies must be required to both observe the terms of the statutes and to exercise good faith in their administration of such statutes.[84]

Debate in the House of Representatives was even more bad-tempered, with the SEC compared to operating in a manner akin to the Gestapo in Germany.[85] In part this was designed to reduce the president's power but it led to difficulties in finding a durable compromise. Notwithstanding the passion for innovation that informed the early New Dealers, this was to be increasingly restrained as the Roosevelt administration sought to navigate its way through ever more treacherous waters. Experimentalism was increasingly constrained, as Katznelson puts, it by

> fiscal and labor policy [that] set the course for country's political system. They fashioned, in effect, a new national state that was dramatically different from its crusading face. … US politics increasingly came to be a politics of competitive bargaining among organized interests for the public purse. Under this system of pressure-group pluralism, lobbying grew. Groups pressing particular claims mobilized constituents, influenced public opinion, spent funds to elect favored candidates, penetrated regulatory agencies,

---

[81] Shepherd, above n 44, 1560. As Shepherd convincingly argues, the 'bill passed both houses unanimously not because everyone was thrilled with the bill, but because private negotiations had permitted the parties to cobble together an agreement that all could at least tolerate': 1675.

[82] I Katznelson, *Fear Itself: The New Deal and the Origins of Our Time* (New York, WW Norton & Co, 2012) 398–402.

[83] Ibid, 398.

[84] Cited in Shepherd, above n 44, 1602.

[85] Ibid, 1610.

swayed the legislative process, and built webs of influence to orient public policies in ways that would help them achieve their private ends.[86]

The APA was a classic example of this process in action. It is true to say that the APA facilitated the emergence of the regulatory state but it facilitated its emergence in a particularly dysfunctional form.[87] Under the terms of the act, agencies were provided with the discretion to advance goals within boundaries set only by quite weak procedural restraints, thus limiting the grounds for judicial review unless there was evidence of capricious disregard of due process. Writing to Gelhorn at Columbia, Landis was sanguine:

> It is curious how much the New Deal has been tied in with the development of administrative law and how frequently men who damn it are really doing so because they hate to see effective instrumentalities evolve to achieve the policies of the New Deal. Pound's attacks, for example, seem to me to have two prime sources: one of them is a Republicanism that saw no good in the rise of populism despite the scholarly mind that knew it was inevitable, and the second is an experience with the administration of prohibition. I often tell my class that they have to discount my views on administrative law because they have been formulated as a result of contact with fairly high level commissions, but for the same reason they must discount Pound's ideas because they have been fashioned out of experiences with prohibition agents, than which I suppose it would be difficult to get a lower class of administrative officials.[88]

This was to be a naïve reading of the political realities that were to result in the ABA's victory. The successful challenge opened the door for a more sustained questioning of the role of experts in the administration more generally, and set the administrative agencies on a collision course with Congress.[89] Landis had at this stage lost. The conflict, however, was not to end there. It merely went dormant, with each side bruised and battered by the experience and seeking a way of reducing the political contestation.[90] After the intense conflict of the 1930s the regulatory agencies were provided both the opportunity and freedom to advance goals, curtailed mainly by budgetary restraints and degree of executive commitment and direction.

This was to provide the third interlocking foundation stone in the building of the regulatory state. It was in this critical dimension that the real strength

---

[86] Katznelson above n 82, 401.

[87] Shepherd, above n 44, 1558 (describing the APA as a 'bill of rights for the regulatory state'); see also Rosenbloom, above n 44, 197 ('Congress responded to [the] quest for executive dominance by reengineering its constitutional position to supervise federal administration. ... It is far too late to treat congressional involvement in federal administration as haphazard or wayward. It follows the deliberate blueprint of 1946—a design that remains vibrant and shows no signs of obsolescence').

[88] James Landis to Walter Gelhorn, 22 February 1946, Dean's Office UAV.512.20 1940–47 Correspondence Encyclopedia–Ge Box 11, Harvard University Archive.

[89] See Horwitz, above n 37, 233 ('A declining faith in the ability of experts to produce neutral, and apolitical solutions to social and legal questions led in turn to a re-emergence of proceduralism').

[90] The federal courts, particularly the DC circuit, have increasingly challenged the limitations of the grounds for judicial review, in a manner that leading commentators suggest reflects political preferences: see J Fisch, 'The Long Road Back: Business Roundtable and the Future of SEC Rulemaking' (2013) 36 *Seattle University Law Review* 695.

or weakness of the regulatory paradigm could be determined. Of equal significance it would demonstrate the extent to which the agencies were independent
of or interdependent on executive power, control and oversight. The power to
direct came through presidential authority to reorganize priorities through the
tabling of plans to Congress. Introduced as an emergency measure in 1933 and
again in 1945, Congress had placed time limits on the exercise of executive
power. Moreover the 1945 legislation exempted major agencies, including the
SEC, ostensibly to safeguard their independence but also as a consequence of
effective lobbying by the commissions. The effect was to constrain decision-
making.[91] The executive was increasingly determined to show its power and
purpose. First, however, following a predictable if effectively useless fashion, it
sought evidence. Once again the academy and leading practitioners were brought
together under a presidentially appointed commission.

In an adroit move designed to show bipartisan support, Roosevelt's successor,
Harry Truman, reached back across the New Deal to Herbert Hoover, to establish a more accountable framework. The former president retained the reputation
of a skilled technocrat notwithstanding the failure of 'progressive individualism'
to deliver effective governance or business responsibility during the height of
the roaring twenties.[92] He did, however, have the capacity to institutionalize the
administrative process. Hoover was predisposed to bring the regulatory agencies
directly under the control of executive departments. He was convinced that
identified abuses and failures could be achieved by less drastic measures in large
measure by the intervention of James Landis. Landis was to play a pivotal role in
formulating the precise recommendations of the Hoover Commission not in his
own right but as an employee of Kennedy Enterprises, his home since effective
dismissal from the Civil Aeronautics Board by President Truman. Forced to take
a back seat, his work carried the imprimatur of Joe Kennedy, who sat on the key
sub-committee on regulatory agencies. Kennedy assumed patriarchal responsibility over the troubled Landis but allowed him to exercise voice if *sotto voce*.[93]

The Hoover Commission gathered evidence from 1947 to 1949, eventually
recommending the executive's right to redesign the regulatory agenda 'should
not be restricted by either limitations of exemptions.'[94] The Commission argued
forcefully that 'once the limiting and exempting process is begun it will end the
possibility of achieving really substantial results, instead adequate protection
against ill-thought out plans were to be found in both 'sound exercise of the President's discretion and in the reserved power in the Congress by concurrent resolution to disapprove any reorganization plan.'[95] Armed with this support, President Truman told Congress that temporal and structural limitations failed to take

[91] F Heady, 'The Reorganization Act of 1949' (1949) 9 *Public Administration Review* 165.
[92] See A Schlesinger, *The Crisis of the Old Order 1919–1933* (New York, Mariner Books, 2002) 83.
[93] D Ritchie, *James M Landis: Dean of the Regulators* (Cambridge, MA, Harvard University Press, 1980) 175.
[94] *Commission on Organization of the Executive Branch of the Government 1949* (Hoover Commission) 8–9.
[95] Ibid.

into account the fact that 'the improvement of the organization of Government is a continuing and never-ending process.'[96]

Truman signaled the unintended consequences that could flow from allowing exemptions. There was, he explained, a risk that

> such exemptions prevent the President and the Congress from deriving the full benefit of the reorganization-plan procedure, primarily by precluding action on major organizational problems. A seemingly limited exemption may be fact render an entire needed reorganization affecting numerous agencies wholly impractical.[97]

The political compromise was to retain the time limits but end the process of exemption, thus freeing the president to recalibrate the whole gamut of agencies subject to the approval of Congress.[98] It was to be the application of those powers that was to animate Landis' final battle to free the administrative agencies from the straitjacket imposed by a declining faith in professionalism.[99]

---

[96] Message of President Truman to Congress, H Doc 42, 17 January 1949.
[97] Ibid.
[98] Heady, above n 91, 172 ('[N]o one need be deceived that the favorite agencies of Congress have been thrown to the wolves by their congressional friends').
[99] See Horwitz, above n 37, 235.

7

The Fall: Hubris and the Making of a Greek Tragedy

The election of John F Kennedy to the presidency of the United States in November 1960 brought James M Landis back to the epicenter of political life. It was to be a tempestuous assignment. As chief architect of the regulatory project, Landis was to oscillate between outstanding success and catastrophic failure in both political and personal terms. In the space of less than four years he was to provide one of the most devastating critiques of regulatory practice, propose comprehensive mechanisms to deal with those failures and see those plans bring political defeat to the presidency, largely as a consequence of self-inflicted political blunders. His influence progressively weakened, without any discernible reason until the revelation in August 1963 that he was to plead guilty on tax avoidance charges. The final ignominy for the former Dean of Harvard Law School was the temporary loss in 1964 of his license to practice law. The conviction on the tax charges prompted an ethics investigation that no amount of special pleading could forestall. A week later, he was dead. So too with the assassination of JFK was the support necessary to arrest a terminal decline in the regulatory authority model Landis had pioneered. The law, which Landis had done so much to further, became the instrument of his final destruction. The final arc of his public life, cut short by personal hubris, political expediency and the machinations of the Kennedy White House, a contemporary House of Camelot, had all of the hallmarks of a Greek tragedy.[1]

The connections between the Kennedy family and Landis dated back to the creation of the SEC, on which the president's father had served as inaugural chairman. The political patriarch and regulatory theorist remained in contact over the years. Joe Kennedy's loyalty to a fellow New Deal loyalist periodically reignited the relationship. Kennedy had watched Landis' progression from the SEC to Harvard Law School and on to the position of chairman of the Civil Aeronautics Board (CAB) in 1946, following service overseas as a senior official with responsibility for economic development in the Middle East, with pride and admiration. While avowedly anti-communist, Kennedy saw in Landis a model of academic and practitioner integrity, not least in the handling of the controversial Bridges case in 1939. At the same time, given his own predilections, Kennedy was forgiving of foibles in Landis' personal life, including the breakdown of his

---

[1] Interview with Robert Morgenthau, New York City, 24 January 2013.

marriage. What Kennedy most admired about Landis was his pragmatism and his sense of the possibilities of public service.

In the aftermath of the war, the primary source of conflict in industrial relations had moved from the shop floor to the floor of Congress. With the passage of the Administrative Procedure Act, the primary question for industry was not how to stop governmental intervention but how to limit or direct its influence. It was a recipe for stasis. Absent the overarching support provided by a political benefactor, no regulatory agency could on a sustainable basis withstand the entreaties of regulated entities willing and able to use fragmented congressional support to challenge operational decision-making. Landis was successful in advancing international aviation agreements, largely through the executive decision to personally handle the negotiations. Although a representative of the United States, the aim was to advance the interests of American aviation. As Landis put it:

> [T]here is a tendency on the part of the State Department to be less resilient to diplomatic pressures unrelated to aviation than there is, say, on the part of somebody whose sole concern is aviation, and who naturally should have a certain flexibility and realize that there are other things in connection with aviation, but he's less willing to sacrifice aviation on the altar of other considerations.[2]

Landis was to find that it was one thing to provide support for the industry, it was quite another if he was to seek to impose any restrictions on it. Opposition from the airlines over the introduction of additional safety requirements and competition within routes to reduce passenger and freight costs, along with changes to the dynamics of regulatory governance throughout the Truman administration, conspired to make Landis surplus to requirements at the CAB.[3]

By the end of 1947 speculation started appearing in the aviation trade press that Landis would not be reappointed to a full term as chair of the Civil Aeronautics Board, speculation that the administration failed to counter. The slight had profound and pressing professional and personal implications for Landis. He was totally reliant on the income provided by the CAB. He had no savings and no fallback position. Despite repeated attempts, Landis failed to secure a meeting with the president until 27 December, days before his tenure was due to expire.[4] For an intellectual long used to public admiration, the distancing was a source of consternation, embarrassment and panic. The eventual meeting with Truman left no doubt that his star waned. As Landis later recounted:

> After some pleasantries [the president] came to the point and he said he had decided not to re-appoint me. I said, of course, that's his privilege, 'But I would like to know, Mr President, whether I have offended you in any particular.; He said 'Oh no, not at all, not at all … but shortly after I took over this job as president Ed Flynn [a leading

---

[2] *The Reminiscences of James M Landis* (New York, Columbia University Oral History Project, 1964) 535.
[3] Ibid, 497–98.
[4] Ibid, 549.

Democratic powerbroker] [said] "you'll have to be a son of a bitch half the time'"—and I am quoting him exactly. He said, 'This is one of those times.'[5]

Landis believed, but could not prove, that the airlines were behind the decision, telling an interviewer in 1963 that '[Y]ou have to recognize that in many cases, these airlines have tried to dominate the thinking of the board. ... They were quite successful with some of my associates on the Board.'[6] The dismissal and reasons for it highlighted the critical importance of political support at the highest echelons. Without political support no administrative official could survive, never mind thrive. Truman's decision marked the first time in Landis's adult life that he had been a failure. It was to destabilize him in a profound manner.

The news spread quickly throughout Washington. It inevitably reached Tommy Corcoran, the key political fixer of the Roosevelt administration and by then a leading lobbyist. Corcoran, in turn, informed Kennedy. The network, forged in the maelstrom of the New Deal, had remained surprisingly intact.[7] Joe Kennedy immediately sent word to Landis that he had a face-saving alternative to offer: Landis would resign from the CAB to manage the finances of the Kennedy family.[8] As Landis put it:

> That in a sense saved me from a great deal of embarrassment, because here was not only a prominent Democrat [Joe Kennedy extending support at a time of need] but an outstanding lay Catholic and man whose integrity is unquestionable. Of course he had no use for Mr Truman at that time, but I don't think that was the motivating fact. He and I had been friends for many years and he has that kind of generous streak in him. If somebody's in trouble, he will try to help them out. He can be means as well on occasion but on the other hand he can be gracious and extremely generous on other occasions.[9]

Landis moved down to Palm Beach and on to New York, where he established a private practice. His role at Kennedy Enterprises, the holding company that delivered the profits for the trusts designed to ensure that the children could devote their lives to public service, was never defined.[10] He did play a critical role preparing the Kennedy scion for public service. He managed the campaign of the future president for the House of Representatives in 1952 and subsequent election to the Senate in 1958. He helped prepare for publication *Profiles in Courage*, a book that John F Kennedy used to associate himself with the claimed

---

[5] Ibid, 551 (Landis continued: '[T]he interview was quite pleasant as far as that goes. There was nothing except ordinary language but after he told me that this was one of those times that he had to be a son of a bitch and that I was a victim of the thing, I wouldn't have worked for him in any job': 552).

[6] Ibid, 555.

[7] Ibid, 256 (describing his links to the Roosevelt administration, Landis noted that 'Tommy would float around through things. He was sort of a handyman for the president').

[8] Ibid, 552–53.

[9] Ibid, 553.

[10] For detail of Landis' work with the Kennedy family, see D Ritchie, *James M Landis: Dean of Regulators* (Cambridge, MA, Harvard University Press, 1981) 156–73.

American virtue of self-sacrifice. At the same time, he continued his investigation into the failure of the regulatory process he was so instrumental in creating. The forced reflection provided the opportunity to extract revenge on what he saw as his betrayal by Truman and the corruption of the administrative process itself through inappropriate lobbying.[11] Landis remained convinced that the regulatory experiment could be rejuvenated with political direction.

It was indicative of Landis' standing with the family and centrality of the proposed use by John F Kennedy of the regulatory agencies to refashion American politics that in his first public statement the president-elect announced three appointments. J Edgar Hoover would continue as head of the Federal Bureau of Investigation; Allen Dulles would remain at the Central Intelligence Agency and James Landis would be appointed as a special advisor on regulatory matters.[12] Months later the president's brother, Robert F Kennedy, soon to become Attorney General, sounded Landis out on his willingness to be nominated to the first available position on the Supreme Court. To the neophyte politician's surprise, Landis demurred. Recounting the conversation to his close colleague and confident Justin Feldman, Landis exclaimed that under no circumstances would he 'submit myself to Senate confirmation.'[13] The proposed appointment of Landis to the bench made perfect sense, however. Just as when as a neophyte academic he had provided important rhetorical and intellectual support for the creation and legitimation of the regulatory agencies in the New Deal, so to Landis' status as a former Dean of Harvard Law School and combative chair of the CAB provided the cachet to reinvigorate regulatory governance. Grandiosely termed the New Frontier, the call to action consciously harked back to the New Deal, critical elements of which bore Landis' imprint as academic, practitioner and retrospective theorist. Kennedy, of course, was not the first to recognize the political possibilities of nominating Landis to the Supreme Court. His nomination had been suggested to Roosevelt for precisely the same reason. From the world of the academy, Roosevelt instead chose the rival and rivaling Felix Frankfurter and William Douglas. According to Landis' law partner, Justin Feldman, the intended strategy was to entice Douglas to take up the ambassadorial position to India. Frankfurter, having been made aware of the maneuvering, offered to vacate his own place in favor of Landis on grounds of ill health.[14] Landis' refusal left the

---

[11] Landis, above n 2, 554 (recounting his sacking from the CAB, Landis noted that 'the whole incident left me with a little sense of distaste that I didn't get over for several years').

[12] D Nasaw, *The Patriarch: The Remarkable Life and Turbulent Times of Joseph P Kennedy* (New York, Penguin Press, 2012) 769 (noting the appointment of Landis as special advisor to president-elect John F Kennedy in 1960 and articulating that, next to family, Joseph Kennedy 'trusted no one to watch out for his son as he did Jim Landis'); see also *The Reminiscences of Justin Feldman* (Columbia University Oral History Project, 1973) 223 (noting that Landis was 'a trustee of the [Kennedy] family trusts which the children derived their income from and more or less managed [John F] Kennedy's first campaign for the Senate in 1952 and had written most of the speeches in 1958').

[13] Interview with Justin Feldman, 22 June 2004, *Securities Exchange Commission Historical Society*, 64, http://3197d6d14b5f19f2f440-5e13d29c4c016cf96cbbfd197c579b45.r81.cf1.rackcdn.com/collection/oral-histories/feldman062204Transcript.pdf.

[14] Ritchie, above n 10, 186.

plan stillborn, but as with Frankfurter in the first Roosevelt administration, there was much to be gained for having Landis remain as an external adviser.

Landis had proved his worth with a remarkable dissection of the problems facing regulatory agencies and evaluation of how through careful husbandry they could once again become essential custodians of societal growth.[15] Delivered less than eight weeks after the election, the Landis report was breathtaking in its critique. The academic and practitioner community were stunned by both its verve and far-reaching implications. Crucial, in this regard was Landis' earlier work for the influential Hoover Commission, established by Truman in a prior failed attempt to revitalize the regulatory agencies.[16] The sections on the future of regulatory agencies (for which Joe Kennedy claimed credit) provided Landis with the core material that informed his new report. Notwithstanding ongoing American rhetoric, the age of big government had become firmly embedded, the result of societal complexity and social preferences.[17] The only question was in whose interests it would be run.

Even those who questioned the logic of Landis' conclusions had no doubt that his 1960 report had shone a bright light on one of the defining questions of the time.[18] As Landis recalled in 1963:

> I knew what I wanted to say, even before I got into writing the report, because I had been watching the agencies for a long time, and I knew a great many people in the various agencies that I called on for help ... because a great deal of material came to me from the administrative agencies themselves, I think that they had confidence in how I would handle the material and well—I put that together, and [took] only about two months to complete the report.[19]

For Landis, the critical value of the report lay in the brevity and clarity of the message. 'It did go to the heart of the entire administrative process, when we enlarged the field in the thirties and the extent to which it hadn't lived up to its expectations,' he noted with satisfaction.[20] The report highlighted the ambition and the intrinsic flaws associated with the delegation of discretion.

---

[15] JM Landis, *Report on Regulatory Agencies to the President-Elect* (21 December 1960), http://c0403731.cdn.cloudfiles.rackspacecloud.com/collection/papers/1960/1960_1221_Landis_report.pdf.

[16] 'Summary of Reports of the Hoover Commission' (1949) 9 *Public Administrative Review* 49; see also J Lederle, 'The Hoover Commission Reports on Federal Reorganization' (1949) 33 *Marquette Law Review* 89 (noting, presciently, as with Landis, that '[W]hile it is conceivable that cutbacks in some services might be made, economizers in our national legislatures are never able to marshal more than generalized support. When the economizers point to specific spots where cuts should be made, their brothers jump ship. Big government is with us and likely to stay': 90).

[17] See Chapter 3.

[18] See A Keeffe, 'Practicing Lawyers Guide to the Current Law Magazines' (1961) 47 *American Bar Association Journal* 931 (noting 'his attack upon the way in which our federal agencies now conduct their business is well-nigh unanswerable. It is a joy to read as there is a chuckle a page, if you are a miserable character like me who loves to laugh at the misery of other bureaucrats'); see also, however, C McFadden, 'Landis Report: The Voice of One Crying Out in the Wilderness' (1961) 47 *Virginia Law Review* 1; for review of the underlying debates on the status of administrative law itself, see L Jaffe, 'Basic Issues: An Analysis' (1955) 30 *New York University Law Review* 1273.

[19] Landis, above n 2, 637.

[20] Ibid, 637–38.

The delegation, he maintained, remained necessary. The increased complexity of modern society, the incapacity of Congress to devote the time or the resources to deal with them and a conviction that 'the issues involved were different from [and even further removed from] those that theretofore had been traditionally handled by courts and thus were not suited for judicial determination, combined to necessitate an additional bulwark provided by the administrative process.'[21]

The problem, as Landis postulated, was that in operational terms the regulatory commission model had failed. 'Spectacular instances of executive, legislative and [industry] interference with the disposition of matters before the agencies have been uncovered,' he wrote in the introduction.[22] 'Expansion of the role, power and duties of the agencies has continued and despite the absence of effective solution of and increasing concern with their problems they now embrace within their regulatory powers almost every significant aspect of our national being.'[23] For Landis, there could be no turning back. 'Their continued existence is obviously essential for effective government,' he noted, reprising arguments first made in his Storrs Lecture at Yale in 1937.[24] 'The advent of atomic energy, of telecommunications, of natural gas, of jet aircraft, to cite only a few examples, all call for greater surveillance by government of the appropriate use of these resources to further the admittedly dim but recognizable aims of our society.'[25] The policy problem was that this created competing dynamics. First, more and more areas of government were brought within formal regulatory ambit. Second, congressional mandates were 'increasingly loosened so that not infrequently the guide in the determination of problems that faces the agencies is not much more than their conception of the public interest.'[26] This created dysfunctional path-dependency patterns and brought the administrative process into disrepute.[27]

---

[21] Landis, above n 15, 3.

[22] Ibid, 2.

[23] Ibid, 4.

[24] Ibid, 4.

[25] Ibid, 4.

[26] Ibid, 4. In part the process was even more problematic because of the lack of contrarian thinking in the agencies themselves. This, Landis argued, could be effectively dealt with through the introduction of a public interest counsel, whose job it would be to evaluate the rationale behind agency discretion: see Landis, above n 2, 575 ('The lack of public counsel [is] terrible. Its lack in the Interstate Commerce Commission is, I think, a terrible thing. Take these larger merger cases that are going on now. There is no public counsel. The Commission takes the view that it is the public interest, it represents the public interest and that they don't need anything of this nature. But that is wrong, because they allow the record to be developed by the parties in interest, and if you don't have somebody developing the record, not with to the parties in interest, but with regard to the public, the Commission will be ignorant of many things that ought to be in that record, which aren't there').

[27] It was also to result in a chasm between Frankfurter and Landis, with Frankfurter on the court siding on behalf of substantive external review: see M Horwitz, *The Transformation of American Law* (New York, Oxford University Press, 1992) 236, citing Felix Frankfurter, 'The Task of Administrative Law' (1927) 75 *University of Pennsylvania Law Review* 614, 621, 628 (advocating that one of the tasks of legal scholarship is to impart to students 'a sympathetic understanding of the major causes which have let to the emergence of modern administrative law, and must be able to move freely in the world of social and economic facts with which administrative law is largely concerned,' which could only be achieved through the development of a 'professionalized civil service' given 'flexible, appropriate and economic procedure'); see also M Parrish, *Felix Frankfurter and His Times*

Their persistence is too serious to be longer ignored, for their prevalence is threatening to thwart hope so bravely held some two decades ago by those who believed that the administrative agency, particularly the 'independent' agency, held within it the seeds for the wise and efficient solution of the many new problems posed by a growingly complex society and a growingly benevolent government. It is to these problems that this report addresses itself.[28]

The report itself highlighted ten structural problems: delays in the disposition of adjudicatory proceedings; increased costs; the lack of effective personnel; unethical conduct; flawed administrative procedures and organization; the lack of adequate policy formulation within individual agencies and the complete absence of inter-agency formulation; problems associated with the relationship of the agencies to the executive and to the legislature. On one level, the picture painted is an exceptionally bleak one. Landis made explicit the basic political reality. The administrative process could only succeed on the basis of settled political leadership and commitment by given industry sectors to shared values and acceptance of regulatory purpose. Absent that, the administrative process would fail, an analysis that reflected Landis' own experience. Roosevelt's support was essential in safeguarding the operational independence of the SEC, for example. Truman's ambivalence, however, was a key contributing factor to Landis' forced removal from the CAB. Throughout the report, however, one also detects muted optimism that calibration of purpose could breathe fresh life into the regulatory model.[29] This optimism reflected an abiding faith in rule by experts. Landis, ever the realist, also recognized that the agencies also had to adapt. In short, the agencies had also a responsibility to help themselves. This was best achieved by addressing operational deficiencies. The delays in disposing of adjudicating proceedings, for example, are described as 'inordinate' and attributed to 'inadequate budgets. A period of economic rigor if not parsimony seems to have

---

(New York, Free Press, 1982) 200; for dawning of appreciation of this view, see L Joffe, 'The Judicial Universe of Mr Justice Frankfurter' (1949) 62 *Harvard Law Review* 357, 358 ('One remembers Mr Justice Frankfurter's respect for "expertise," his reluctance even to review the agencies, and his assertion that they as well as the courts must be trusted to observe the law. It is as if here he had become momentarily seized with the chilling thought that he had been coddling a monster'). If ever there was an intellectual reversal, however, it was to be Professor Joffe, himself: see Horwitz, 237–40 (noting that 'history had made the New Deal era behind and made the Landis model obsolete': 240). Landis was also exceptionally critical of Frankfurter's tenure of the bench, see Landis above n 2, 96 (reflecting that '[I]t is so easy in this life to associate with people who have prestige and money and so on and you become a little loose in your thinking. The kind of things that you sweated for when you were twenty and thirty and forty, they get a little dim and you start to compromise. Now I suppose that's alright for anybody that's just looking at the dollar, trying to make a living, but when you have responsibilities with regards the destiny of the United States, it's a different story').

[28] Landis, above n 15, 6.

[29] Somewhat surprisingly Louis Jaffe ascribed this failure to Landis' idealism. Landis was a lot of things but he was not an idealist. He always recognized that regulatory authority required political authority: see L Jaffe, 'The Effective Limits of the Administrative Process' (1973) 67 *Harvard Law Review* 704, 713 (noting 'industry-orientation' was inevitably a condition endemic in any agency). The possibility of corruption was certainly canvassed by Landis but he found resolution a consequence of political will. Jaffe, in effect, had given up.

characterized the Bureau of the Budget's attitude towards the various agencies.'[30] In part, however, this also reflected a failure of ambition and political acquiescence on behalf of the agencies themselves who 'presumably under the general direction of the Executive Office of the President, curtailed their requests despite the growing pressure of the business pending before them for disposition.'[31] A further cause of delay, linked to increasing costs, was the increasing complexity of cases brought for adjudication. While this was inevitable, for Landis 'measures to make less rather than more complex what is an inherently complex problem, must be devised.'[32] Landis, therefore, was not suggesting the aggressive expansion of regulatory authority. Nor did he recommend resolution by a stroke of the legislative pen. Prescription and proscription were not, in his mind, the answers. Instead, he wanted to extract from the regulated entities a warranted commitment in stated promises to act in good faith, something he saw little evidence of.

The situation was exacerbated by the rapid expansion of organized lobbying in Washington, DC. The 'resort to public relations techniques to create a national atmosphere congenial to the position of a particular petitioner or intervener—and expensive operation—in the hope that such an atmosphere will produce a decision favorable to the applicant,' emasculated administrative capacity he warned.[33] Effective lobbying, social gatherings and provision of gifts all combined to cloud decision-making. Landis himself saw little problems with the provision of small gifts, such as a case of liquor. 'If you could be bought for a case of liquor you shouldn't be there in the first place.'[34] The primary problem was the closed nature of regulatory deliberation, in which the public interest was neither adequately defined nor taken into account.[35] He also identified, however, a much deeper problem, which reflected the advent of managerial politics devoid of underpinning vision. In the 1930s government service provided a source of employment as well as venue for policy entrepreneurship. By 1960, the lack of political vision, aligned with increased salary gaps between the agencies and remuneration available in private practice, made Washington if not irrelevant then certainly unattractive. In sharp distinction to the optimism that accom-

---

[30] Landis, above n 15, 6–7.

[31] Ibid, 7.

[32] Ibid, 8.

[33] Ibid, 9.

[34] See Landis, above n 2, 562. For Landis, the main problem was the revolving door. 'The kind of thing that occurs is frequently people, even at the high level of administrative agencies and more often at the low level or lower levels, knowing that their chance of advancement are limited and their chances of tenure are always coming to an end, are sort of given the indication that if they want it there would be a good job for them in this company or that company. That is not infrequent and if you trace the history of many individual that is what happened to them, that they have gone with a company': 564.

[35] Landis, above n 2, 574–75 ('The people who walk into your office are the people you are regulating. You see them all of the time. ... And they're not unintelligent. They're really intelligent people. And there's a tendency that that point of view, like the rat-tat-tat of machine gun fire, just keeps beating on you, and you tend to have that point of view. For example, take the SEC. Talk about the protection of investors. The investor never walks in. If he does he's not an investor, he's a speculator and he's the kind of son-of-a-bitch you don't want to protect anyway').

panied the New Deal, the 'fires that then fed a passion for public service have burned low.'[36] Urgent action was required because 'the spark, the desire of public service, has failed of re-ignition.'[37] Complaining of sinecures and the power of practitioners to gain privileged off-the-record access to senior commission staff, he foreshadowed many of the recurrent problems associated with the regulatory capture literature.[38] He also complained bitterly about the failure of the agencies themselves to address known problems. These problems, however, are never capable of resolution by administrative means alone if there is contestation over common propose. The result, as Landis identified but hoped to resolve, was political paralysis. As Landis puts it, 'where, however, the greatest gaps exist are in the planning for foreseeable problems. Absent such planning the need for *ad hoc* solutions to the particular manifestations of the problem precede and, indeed, may preclude any basic policy formulation.'[39] Resolving these issues was, ultimately, a question of political will, a fact Landis always recognized but ultimately could not make happen.[40]

The initial report to the president-elect was designed to provide a rationale for change. At its core was the proposed creation of an overarching coordinating body based in the executive. This, he argued, would provide coherence in policy and cohesion in strategy.[41] Following Kennedy's inauguration, Landis was provided an office at the White House to put in place a fundamental reorganization of what was plainly dysfunctional. As he explained retrospectively:

> [T]here's really no criteria upon which the independent agencies can act, and if there are criteria, they may be the criteria of two or three decades ago, rather than the criteria of today. It seems to be that there is a field, for example, where you have administration policy, rather than a policy that is handled by independent regulatory agencies. ... The problem, for example, of how much subsidy should be given to local

---

[36] Landis, above n 15, 9.

[37] Ibid, 10.

[38] The concern about moral rectitude of regulatory authorities pre-dated the passage of the Exchange Act: see J Seligman, *The Transformation of Wall Street: A History of the Securities and Exchange Commission and Corporate Finance* (New York, Wolters Kluwer, 2003) 100 (quoting Ferdinand Pecora, who ran the hearings into Wall Street abuse, saying the legislation to create a specialist agency to monitor the securities market would 'be a good or bad law depending upon the men who administer it'). Seligman was exceptionally critical of the Landis report, arguing that his proposal for a 'White House "agency czar" proposal presaged the considerable difficulties the SEC would have initiating new legislation on its own during the Kennedy administration': 291. Seligman's antipathy towards Landis is unfortunate, and derives largely from appreciation of the more swashbuckling approach adopted by William O Douglas, who succeeded Landis as chairman of the SEC in 1937. Just as Douglas could not have achieved what he did at the SEC without the groundwork laid by Kennedy and Landis, neither could William Cary (or indeed Landis) do much because of congressional opposition to effective operation of the administrative process. Seligman himself concedes this, noting that with the loss of 20 liberal Democrats in the 1960 election, the House of Representatives was much more conservative than the White House: 292. Equally the personal problems afflicting Landis, outlined below, robbed the SEC and indeed other regulatory agencies of professional political support at a critical juncture.

[39] Ibid, 16.

[40] Landis, above n 2, 648.

[41] See Ritchie, above n 10, 181.

airlines is a political problem, basically a political problem. And yet that isn't in the hands of the Executive. It's in the hands of an independent regulatory agency. They have a lot of trouble with that.[42]

Just as *The Administrative Process* was a pamphlet for the New Deal, so now the 1960 report was a manifesto for change at the New Frontier. The years spent in the political wilderness had not dented the capacity of the philosopher of regulation to identify through empirical study the source of the problem. Equally, his thinking continued to be animated by a belief that social progress could be achieved through more effective administration.[43] In an analogy with house building, the Landis report in 1960 was sufficient to secure planning approval. [44] Implementing the design required the building of coalitions. By working alone in preparing the design Landis had managed to avoid political compromises. Securing congressional assent, and indeed agency acquiescence, was another matter entirely. The proposed creation of an overarching body threatened congressional power, something it jealously guarded.[45] Likewise, notwithstanding the dialog Landis had engaged in in order to outline the problems, the lack of consultation prior to the unveiling of the blueprint to resolve these issue robbed the administration of unequivocal support from the agencies themselves. The battles associated with the reorganizational plan, an executive strategy but one presented in Congress by Landis as an advisor, were bruising. They reflected a combination of poor preparation, weak strategy and effective lobbying by well-funded opponents. In part the problem could be traced back to abrasive personality clashes between Landis and the new generation of regulators. The strategy adopted cemented accusations of aloofness and arrogance. It was symptomatic that Landis first moved to secure the program for change by concentrating on the SEC. He had recommended Columbia law academic William Cary for the SEC chairmanship. Tellingly, he did not share the blueprint with him in sufficient time to secure full backing for implementation. This needlessly complicated the challenge in transferring the ideal into practical outcomes.

The telegenic and charismatic president found in Congress suspicion and fear, particularly from southern Democrats. As with Roosevelt, the battle for administrative reform provided a cover for broader questions of race and politics in a still segregated society. It also reflected ongoing lack of political agreement on the legitimacy of the administrative process itself, something that the passage

---

[42] Landis, above n 2, 643.

[43] See C Koch, 'James Landis: The Administrative Process' (1996) 48 *Administrative Law Review* 419, 421 (noting Landis' 'faithfulness to an American approach to social problems and its overarching organizational pragmatism').

[44] For its political usefulness, see Kennedy's response: 'This is a most important and impressive analysis of the regulatory agencies which deserves the attention of the members of Congress as well as the agencies themselves,' cited in Ritchie, above n 10, 178; see also Editorial, 'Dean Landis Reports,' *New York Times*, 28 December 1960, 26 (noting 'If president-elect Kennedy is to breach any new frontiers, or even to repair old fortifications, this is a good place to begin'). For criticism of the proposed expansion of executive authority, see A Krock, 'Powers for Kennedy that Congress Denied FDR,' *New York Times*, 29 December 1960, 24

[45] Landis, above n 2, 642.

of the Administrative Procedure Act (1946) had papered over.[46] The battles over implementation gave truth to the adage that it is sometimes not politically possible to achieve the economically rational. There was no question, however, that Landis had with Kennedy, as with Roosevelt, the backing for transformative action. This was manifest in a presidential message to Congress in April 1961.[47] In retrospect, it represents the high-water mark in executive support for administrative legitimacy.

The message began with an attempt to mollify congressional unease by emphasizing its own power. Behind the faint praise was a challenge for Capitol Hill to use its oversight constructively. Kennedy advanced a partnership model to achieve societal progress, which he deemed to be in the public interest.[48] Administrative governance in this formulation was not an end in itself but a means to an end. Kennedy set out an integrated framework to balance responsibilities. This was designed to provide a more stable compact, thus transcending political gridlock and ongoing contestation. Congress, he argued, had an obligation to ensure that the underpinning statutes specified the goals that the agencies must follow. 'These statutes should neither place responsibilities upon agencies beyond the practical limits of administrative action, nor couch their objectives in such indecisive terms as to leave vast areas open for the free play of agency discretion.'[49] Moreover, according to the president, it was appropriate for Congress to determine the influence and ambit of regulatory authority through the hearings process. The presidency, however, had the task of determining how and whether the agencies applied their mandate as part of its responsibility to uphold all the laws of the land, including those that empowered agency independence.

> In short, the President's responsibilities require him to know and evaluate how efficiently these agencies dispatch their business, including any lack of prompt decision of the thousands of cases which they are called upon to decide, any failure to evolve policy in areas where they have been charged by the Congress to do so, or any other difficulties that militate against the performance of their statutory duties.[50]

Kennedy was at pains to point out that this more expansive executive oversight did not mean direct political interference:

> This does not mean that either the President or the Congress should intrude or seek

---

[46] For background on the political debates, see the definitive account in G Shephard, 'Fierce Compromise: The Administrative Procedure Act Emerges from New Deal Politics' (1996) 90 *Northwestern University Law Review* 1557.

[47] See JF Kennedy, 'Special Message to the Congress on the Regulatory Agencies,' 13 April 1961 ('the capacity of these regulatory agencies to meet their responsibilities, and the efficiency with which they dispatch their business, become a subject of tremendous significance to the entire nation'); for the importance of Landis as the intellectual author of the report, see J Grisinger, *The Unwieldy American State: Administrative Politics Since the New Deal* (New York, Cambridge University Press) 247–50.

[48] See Koch, above n 43, 423.

[49] Kennedy, above n 47.

[50] Ibid.

to intervene in those matters which by law these agencies have to decide on the basis of open and recorded evidence, where they, like the judiciary, must determine independently what conclusion will best serve the public interest as that interest may be defined by law. Intervention, if it be deemed desirable by the Executive or the Congress in any such matter, must be as a party or an intervenor in the particular proceeding; and such intervention should be accorded no special preference or influence.[51]

There was, however, a pressing need to improve operational efficiency and effectiveness:

I have long felt that too little attention has been given to the overall operation of these agencies by the President, and that too little cooperation between the Congress and the President has characterized the discharge—each in their respective roles—of their appropriate responsibilities with regard to the operation of these agencies. This cannot continue. For it is now clear that some advance in the methods by which the regulatory agencies dispatch their business is essential if they are to become, as Congress originally intended, effective aids to the growth of our private enterprise system. For these agencies are not merely regulatory: they are designed to further the expansion of certain facets of our economy, as well as the basic tenets that underlie our system of private enterprise. Delays in the disposition of agency business, and the failure to evolve, other than by a slow case-by-case method, policies essential for our national growth seriously handicap their effectiveness in meeting this function.[52]

In both content and tone, the message bore the indelible imprint of Landis' long-standing view that the agencies were not merely technocratic administrators. They were entrusted to advance societal preferences by engaging in effective partnership with given industries.[53] Administrative governance, as noted above, was conceived, therefore, as a means to an end. To confuse ends and means was, according to the president, a category error:

In the banning of unfair labor practices or the designation of employee representatives, the National Labor Relations Board seeks to uphold the right of collective bargaining—a right upon which we, as a nation, base our hopes for peaceful and satisfactory labor–management relationships. In the banning of practices that characterized our security markets in the nineteen twenties, the Securities and Exchange Commission is more than merely regulatory; it seeks, by its emphasis upon fair dealing, to achieve a saner and sounder outflow of savings into investment. In the banning of monopolistic and unfair trade practices, the Federal Trade Commission seeks to defend those fair trade practices which are necessary for the promotion of our system of private competitive enterprise.[54]

As well as the philosophical grounding, the transmittal message reiterated Landis'

[51] Ibid.

[52] Ibid. In his taped interviews with the Columbia Oral History Project, Landis made the same point with force: 'The President's duty, under the constitution, [is] to see the laws are faithfully executed extends to all laws, even laws that are being executed by independent agencies, and he has a responsibility in that connection, that he should not forget, and too often that is forgotten': see Landis, above n 2, 572–73.

[53] See JM Landis, *The Administrative Process* (New Haven, Yale University Press, 1938) 25–26.

[54] Kennedy, above n 47.

critique of the quality of personnel, particularly at the level of chair. Administrative oversight required drive, skill, judgment and integrity in equal measure, qualities that were lacking in many of the political appointments following the initial reforming zeal of agency creation and their expansion. Much more seriously, the lack of coordination between agencies, a consequence of the ad hoc nature of their establishment, had generated conflicting dynamics that led to dysfunctional outcomes:

> This history has in many instances resulted in a compartmentalization of regulatory activities—the tendency of each agency to consider only a single industry, or even a single part of an industry. This is wrong. The emphasis must now in the national interest be placed upon the health and the practices of a series of industries, rightfully competitive but which—from a national standpoint—must be viewed as a whole. ... In broad areas where the interdependence of industries is apparent, and where we have assumed regulatory functions over all or a portion of them, new and careful articulation of our regulatory efforts is essential. [55]

To do otherwise would, in the president's view, preordain fragmentation, incoherence and ongoing regulatory turf-wars;

> Iron curtains are drawn between agencies operating in the same general area. Their concern is only with the particular segment of the industry over which they have been given jurisdiction, rather than its inter-relation to the whole. Indeed, a lack of cooperative effort often characterizes divisional efforts within a single agency. To correct these regulatory imbalances calls for the shaping of attainable goals and the cessation within agencies and among agencies of jurisdictional strife.[56]

Kennedy proposed to address this on Landis' recommendation by augmenting the position of the chairman. The administration, however, wanted to go much further, extending direct accountability to individual commissioners. This reform had tactical and strategic value. First, the formulation of the rationale for action (or inaction) would be rendered transparent. Second, it could be traced to individual preferences:

> The practice of rendering anonymous decisions, which has hitherto generally prevailed, has served as a means of escaping precision and responsibility. When the actual source of the opinion is unknown save only that it is issued in the name of the agency, it not only impairs its value as a precedent, but also makes for that very dissipation of responsibility that we are trying to reduce in our administrative action.[57]

There were also sound strategic reasons for such an approach. It would, reasoned the president, allow for the building of precedent and finally put administra-

---

[55] Ibid. Landis was convinced that the independent model was superior but only if there was effective political support: see Landis, above n 2, 571–72 (noting that Congress wants 'the agencies to be independent form the standpoint of judgment. And I would too, just as you want your courts to be independent of the executive. On the other hand, from the standpoint of administration, and to a degree policymaking you want them to follow along with the general policies of the President of the United States').

[56] Ibid.

[57] Ibid. The origin of this can be traced to Landis, above n 15, 28.

tive determinations on the same standing as court precedent. In so doing it rendered operational Landis' prediction in *The Administrative Process* that the rise of the regulatory state would have as profound an impact on legal development as that of equity:

> Fortunately, from the beginning of American law, our judges assumed an individual responsibility for uttering the bases which underlay their decisions. This practice has made not only for conscientiousness in undergoing the travail of decision, but has invited examination of each proffered brick that would seek a place in the structure of our law. The adoption of this practice by the regulatory agencies would, in my opinion, tend to develop the law that they administer, as well as be a continual challenge to each agency member to make his contribution to the advancement of administrative justice. I am requesting a wider adoption of this practice.[58]

What was required, therefore, in regulatory decision-making was the display of judgment and integrity, professionalism and insulation from short-term political considerations, themes that animated Landis' classic theoretical work[59] as well as practical experience as a hearing examiner in the controversial Bridges deportation proceedings.[60] In his evidence to the Senate on the reorganizational plans, Landis was reprising arguments made to the House the previous month in which he had argued that the role of a regulatory chairman was akin to that of a Supreme Court Justice:

> My experience indicates one of the great things that a chairman should be able to do, just as a chief justice of the court, is to try and command, as well as he can, generally a majority of his colleagues. Failing that, he is not likely to be able to handle the managerial functions that attach to his position adequately and if he abuses those things he is likely no longer to command a majority of his colleagues.[61]

The unresolved question was now to ensure ongoing coherence in the building of precedent. Mindful of the lack of political support to centralize administrative oversight, Kennedy put forward a compromise solution. Administrative legitimacy was to be based on rigorous research into practice through the establishment of an administrative conference. It would guide practice through ongoing evaluation of the operation of the Administrative Procedure Act:[62]

> That Act sought to achieve standards of due process and fairness in the handling of controversies before the regulatory agencies both with respect to adjudication and the issuance of regulations. That aim naturally should be maintained and refined. A large amount of work pointed toward objectives of this nature has been undertaken by the legal profession and by various commissions, as well as by committees of the Congress. The process of modernizing and reforming administrative procedures is not an easy

---

[58] Kennedy, above n 47.

[59] See Landis, above n 53, 113–14.

[60] See Chapter 4.

[61] 'Reorganization Plans re SEC, FCC,' Hearings before a Subcommittee of the Interstate and Foreign Commerce, House of Representatives, US Congress, Washington, DC, 11, 16, 17 May 1961, 16.

[62] Executive Order 10934, 26 FR 3233; see also Landis, above n 2, 675–81.

one. It requires both research and understanding. Moreover, it must be a continuing process, critical of its own achievements and striving always for improvement. Judicialization—the method of determining the content of a controversy by processes akin to those followed by the judiciary—may well be the answer in many cases. But new procedures for the analysis of facts, based upon more informal methods and mobilizing the techniques of other disciplines, can be the answer in other cases, provided always that the fundamentals of due process of law are maintained. There can be no single set of conclusive and abiding formulas appropriate for the effective dispatch of all the diverse and ever-changing issues that these agencies are called upon to resolve.[63]

According to Kennedy,

[T]he results of such an Administrative Conference will not be immediate but properly pursued they can be enduring. As the Judicial Conference did for the courts, it can bring a sense of unity to our administrative agencies and a desirable degree of uniformity in their procedures. The interchange of ideas and techniques that can ensue from working together on problems that upon analysis may prove to be common ones, the exchanges of experience, and the recognition of advances achieved as well as solutions found impractical, can give new life and new efficiency to the work of our administrative agencies.[64]

This was to be one of the abiding legacies of the Kennedy administration, not least because its establishment was not subject to Congressional approval. The reorganizational plans, however, were not so fortunate. They faced sustained criticism from both the commissions themselves and from members of Congress, although for very different reasons. Both, however, were piqued at the lack of prior consultation. Consultation after the event was insufficient to mollify bruised egos. While opposition from the Republicans in both Houses was to be expected, the critical problem arose from the Democrats themselves.[65] The problem was a lack of faith in intentions and the unintended consequences of potential expansive interpretation of mandate.

While the creation of an oversight body for the commissions, which had informed the original Landis report, was dropped in substance, the plans allowed

---

[63] Ibid.

[64] Kennedy, above n 47.

[65] Plan 1 Securities and Exchange Commission, disapproval passed by the House of Representatives (15 June 1961) 212–176; rejected by the Senate (21 June 1961) 52–38. Plan 2 Federal Communications Commission, rejected by House of Representatives (15 June 1961) 323–77 (a much more restrictive version was passed by Senate (27 July 1961) and endorsed by House (3 August 1961). Plan 3 Civil Aeronautics Board, passed by rejection of motions of disapproval in House (20 June 1961) 178–213 and Senate (29 June 1961) 33–38. Plan 4 Federal Trade Commission, passed by rejection of disapproval in House (20 June 1961) 188–221 and Senate (29 June 1961) 31–47. Plan 5 National Labor Relations Board, killed by House (20 July 1961) 231–179; Plan 6 Federal Home Loan Bank Board, no attempt to veto because had support of member banks; Plan 7, calling for abolition of the Federal Maritime Board, passed through default by House not taking up disapproval option (20 July 1961) 184–218 and Senate (10 August 1961) 35–60. For details of the congressional disputes, see 'Reorganization of Regulatory Agencies' *CQ Almanac* (Washington DC, Congressional Quarterly, 1961) 352–56. For discussion of how presidential action could compromise regulatory capacity, see W Cary, *Politics and the Regulatory Agencies* (New York, McGraw-Hill, 1967) 19 (citing President Johnson's call in 1964 to regulatory chairmen not to rock the boat in an election year).

too much executive discretion and arguably, if applied by the agencies themselves, too much power to shape discourse and practice. The chair of the Federal
Communications Commission, for example, had used the hearings to decry the
state of American television, describing it as a cultural wasteland. Lobbyists went
into overdrive, securing the defection of a majority of Democrat representation
in the House.[66] Having failed to secure the mandate for change, the Kennedy
administration appeared to lose interest beyond the operation of the Administrative Conference, which convened for the first time in May 1961.[67] For Landis,
playing the role of architect, the conference should be conceived, primarily, as
'a source for ideas.'[68] From the start, tactical considerations were at play. In
Landis' estimation, the conference should not have final power to determine
mandate or purpose.[69] The aim was one of nudging administrative agencies to
achieve appropriately ordered and governed executive decision-making, itself a
proxy for democratic will.[70] Effectiveness, however, required ongoing external
evaluation, which in the absence of an overarching coordinating body needed a
secretariat that functioned as a 'continuing entity.'[71] Speaking before the Senate
Committee on Government Relations, Landis argued that the real danger facing
the commissions was political bias, not on party lines, rather social and philosophical bias.[72] In the absence of a public interest counsel within the regulatory
agency the research capacity of the Administrative Conference created a resource
to provide evidence of best-practice, challenge emergent orthodoxies, facilitate
contrarian thinking and justify administrative action where considered appropriate. The strategy was so successful that the Administrative Conference was
placed on a permanent footing in 1964.

[66] T McCraw, *Prophets of Regulation* (Cambridge, MA, Harvard University Press, 1984) 220–21.

[67] The conference was upgraded and given public standing with the passage of the Administrative Conference Act in 1964, 5 USC 591. Celebrating its 50th anniversary in 2014 (although the
Conference itself only came into operation in 1968), the conference website includes prominent
endorsements by two serving Supreme Court Justices. 'The ACUS is one the federal governments
best bargains for the buck,' according to Justice Antonin Scalia, who served as the ACUS chair from
1972 to 1974 and remains affiliated as a Senior Fellow. Fellow Supreme Court Justice Stephen Breyer
notes that the ACUS is 'a unique organization, carrying out work that is important and beneficial to
the average American, at low cost,' see www.acus.gov/sites/default/files/documents/ACUS-50th-an-
niversary-fact-sheet.pdf.

[68] Minutes of the Administrative Conference of the United States, United States Courthouse,
Washington DC, 8–9 May 1961, 8, https://bulk.resource.org/acus.gov/raw_scans/gov.acus.1961.
min.1.pdf.

[69] Ibid, 12.

[70] It was indicative that Landis ensured the involvement of Walter Gelhorn from Columbia, a
long-time associate, and Earl Latham, the eminent political scientist, whose main contribution to
the Conference was to emphasize that 'if this Conference is to surmount previous efforts and if it is
to develop proposals for administrative order through continuing review, it must avoid preoccupation with detail and must develop a conceptual basis for it undertakings,' ibid, 4; see also E Latham,
'The Group Basis of Politics: Notes for a Theory' (1952) 46 *American Political Science Review* 376.

[71] Landis, above n 2, 676–77 (with Landis noting that the conference 'did a lot of useful, very
useful work. I think more significant work was done in the year and a half during which that Conference functioned than has ever occurred within a similar period': 677).

[72] Hearings before the Committee on Government Relations, US Senate, 6–7 June 1961 (JM
Landis) 34.

Landis was also correct in noting that the planned reorganizations of the SEC and the FCC, for example, were later approved by the passage of legislation. 'Actually you had substantially 95% victory in that connection,' he argued. There was, however, little appetite in further directing the agencies following the resignation of Landis from government in September 1961. The emphasis on research did, however, galvanize some regulatory agencies, most notably the SEC, notwithstanding the failure of the original reorganizational plans. The agency could not secure White House backing for plans to extend the reach of the Securities Act.[73] Having lost the initiative for change, the agencies were left, as Cary memorably put it in reference to the SEC, as

> a [stepchild] whose custody is contested by both Congress and the Executive, but without much affection from either one. ... Without the cooperation of both Congress and the Executive, little constructive can be achieved. To reemphasize the point, an agency is literally helpless if either branch is uninterested or unwilling to lend support.[74]

Through careful stewardship the SEC did secure an evidential basis for internal policy calibration to escape the straitjacket caused by the lack of political support. A case in point was the SEC's monumental *Special Study on the Securities Industry*. As the leading historian of the SEC, Joel Seligman has pointed out, while

> Cary's transmittal letters and the Report itself repeatedly stated a 'continued belief in self-regulation as an ingredient in the protection of the investor,' the Report's findings illustrated that without the 'pointed stimuli' of the SEC, securities industry self-regulation consistently had been self-interested and self-protective, often failing to produce standards of conduct superior to those that existed before the enactment of the securities laws. ... Significantly, in most of the principal areas covered by the report—for example, entry requirements, selling practices, back-office problems, exchange floor members, fixed commission rates, mutual fund selling practices, and exchange disciplinary procedures—similar disadvantages of securities industry self-regulation were found. In several instances, like floor trading regulation, the SEC's postwar passivity had, in fact, permitted a deterioration of standards.[75]

The SEC study highlighted a lack of training and an unwillingness to police conduct. It was symptomatic that the failure rate for the entrance test was less than 2 percent. This failure by industry to advance consumer, and by extension societal, protection was a central feature of the Landis critique, which was intensified by the distance between the investor who required protection and the

---

[73] Cary, above n 65, 69 ('Even as to rule-making, if none of the industry's spokesmen feel there is a need and complaints mount, congressmen are likely to intervene and commence inquiry, and a committee may either stall the proposal or kill it').

[74] See J Seligman, 'Memories of Bill Cary,' *Columbia Law School Blue Sky Blog*, 13 January 2013, http://clsbluesky.law.columbia.edu/2013/01/24/memories-of-bill-cary/comment-page-1/ (noting that Cary never once met Kennedy on official business throughout his tenure at the SEC; see also SEC, *Special Study of the Securities Markets 1961–63* (Washington, DC, SEC, 1963); for discussion, see Seligman above n 38, 298–99.

[75] Seligman, above n 38, 300

regulatory agency, and the proximity of the regulated to the regulator's office.[76] The approach reflected the importance of marshaling evidence that informed the Landis model of regulatory oversight. Moreover, the most important of the New Deal studies, now hopelessly out of date, may have been authored by Douglas, as Seligman accurately points out, but the design (and therefore the justification) were conceived by Landis (who also recruited Douglas to carry out the study). Seligman quotes favorably Cary's use of the aphorism used by Karl Llewellyn that 'technique without ideals is a menace, ideals with menace is a mess.'[77] It is an aphorism that more accurately reflected Landis' work as a legal scholar, regulatory practitioner and theorist.

In June 1963 Landis explained to the Senate he had simultaneously found himself in the position of being 'quite a protagonist of the administrative process and perhaps its severest critic too.' This he claimed was understandable:

> You look around you and you find again and again what I would call the material rights under which we live are guarded by the administrative process. The right of collective bargaining, the right to be assured of some degree of truth in the securities markets, the cost of electricity that is burning up here, the insurance of our savings bank deposits. Almost every facet of our life is tied up in some way with the administrative process.[78]

The significance of the interjection was that it was to be Landis' final pronouncement on the value of his life's work:

> I felt rather deeply at the start of this administration, even before the start of this administration, that generally, if we wanted to assure ourselves of economic growth such as we deserved, in large part the administrative process was the key to that growth.[79]

In theoretical and practical terms in regulation to securities regulation, this was the animating drive behind Landis' view of the potentiality of legal research and its capacity to drive administrative action. That belief and that certainty was to puncture with the spectacular news on 1 August 1963 that Landis was to plead guilty to tax avoidance. The news stunned America.[80]

The five-count charge accused Landis of failing to file returns from 1955 to 1960 on income calculated at $357,927. The *New York Times* placed prominently the fact that the taxes had been paid in full, citing the conclusion of the

---

[76] See also Landis, above n 2, 575; see also M Edelman, *The Symbolic Uses of Politics* (Urbana, University of Illinois Press, 1964).

[77] Seligman, above n 38, 293.

[78] Opening Statement, Hearings Before the Sub Committee on Administrative Practice and Procedure of the Committee on the Judiciary, US Senate, Washington, DC, 12–14 June 1963 (JM Landis) 34.

[79] Ibid; see also Cary, above n 65, 69 ('[N]o major step forward can be achieved by an old-line regulatory agency in the absence of support from some of the leaders of the industry it regulates').

[80] See L O'Kane, 'Landis Admits Guilt in US Tax Case,' *New York Times*, 3 August 1963, 1, 45; see also Associated Press syndicated coverage, A Everett, 'JM Landis, Former Presidential Adviser, Admits Tax Laxity,' *Schenectady Gazette*, 1 August 1963, 1, 2 (noting the fact that Landis was best regarded as an adviser on ethics in government).

prosecutor in the case, Robert Morgenthau.[81] In a statement issued on Landis' behalf, his lawyers claimed that:

[T]he failure to file timely income tax returns was initially due to the unavailability of information concerning the tax basis of certain securities inherited by the taxpayer some 30 years earlier, which he had sold in order to meet a pressing family need. Subsequently the taxpayer being deeply engrossed in public affairs and the affairs of clients, neglected his own personal matters, including the income tax returns.[82]

The statement continued:

[T]he taxpayer mistakenly delayed filing returns for any subsequent years until he could complete the return for the first delinquent year. The taxpayer did not use the money due to the Government for his own personal advantage. ... in fact he maintained bank deposits and liquid funds to make timely payment of the taxes had the returns been filed when due.[83]

An indication of the political if not judicial complexity of the case was provided when the prosecutor, Robert Morgenthau, refused to answer a question as to whether Landis had made the payment prior to the government investigation, saying 'I would rather not make a statement on that.'[84] Morgenthau added, rather cryptically, however, that Landis' tax affairs 'did not meet government standards of voluntary disclosure.'[85] Unpacking the backstory of the case provides telling evidence of why regulatory policy received such little backing after the initial reorganization plans were put forward to Congress two years earlier.

The failure to provide the returns was uncovered as a result of routine vetting by the FBI of all administration staff. An official at the Internal Revenue Service (IRS), Kenneth Moe, with connections to the Kennedy family, called Joe Kennedy, who immediately made contact with Justin Feldman to track Landis down.[86] Landis confessed that he had not made the returns and worked for the next month with a tax accountant provided by Kennedy to pay the arrears, with some additional funding provided by Kennedy himself. The critical legal questions centered on whether the late filing was 'voluntary' or occurred as a consequence of departmental investigation. If the IRS determined that the filing was voluntary it would abide with long-standing precedent that payment was sufficient and would not prosecute.[87] The New York district office of the IRS, under the direction of Moe, accepted the voluntary nature of the filing but this was not to be the end of the matter. As the IRS in Washington investigated

---

[81] O'Kane, above n 80, 45. It is indicative of the interlinked world in which Landis operated that Morgenthau's father, Henry, served as Treasury Secretary in the Roosevelt administration and knew Landis well.

[82] Ibid.

[83] Ibid.

[84] Ibid.

[85] Everett, above n 80, 1.

[86] Feldman, above n 13, 76; see also V Navasky, *Kennedy Justice* [1971] (Lincoln, NE, Authors Guild Back in Print.Com, 2000) 431.

[87] Feldman, above n 13, 78; see also Navasky, above n 86, 432.

the circumstances surrounding the arrears, Landis was called into a meeting in New York. When asked why he made the return, he explained, naïvely, that he did so because Joe Kennedy had told him to.[88] It was a critical mistake. It took away any possibility that the return was voluntary. Still the IRS refused to make a final determination. The Tax Commissioner, Mortimer Caplin, refused to take direct action.[89] It turned the matter over to the Department of Justice. Turning the matter to Justice only heightened the conflicts, given Robert Kennedy's position as Attorney General. The case was first handed over to the head of the tax division, Louis Oberdorfer, who recused involvement on grounds that Landis had helped him through confirmation hearings.[90] Landis was now a direct political liability for both the administration as a whole and each of the Kennedy brothers. As the Department of Justice pondered its options, Landis found solace in alcohol and entered a period of deep depression.[91] By the summer of 1963 the trap began to close. The Department of Justice made the determination that the case could no longer be delayed.

The critical political dynamic in the case is revealed in an obscure recording held in the John F Kennedy presidential library in Boston. Just weeks before Landis' appearance in the Southern District, the president called his then Deputy Attorney General, Nicholas Katzenbach, to a meeting in the White House. Katzenbach had been given responsibility for managing the Landis affair given Robert Kennedy's need to recuse from determination. Katzenbach had labored to find a way to avoid taking the case to trial but came to the conclusion it was unavoidable. The recording provides direct evidence of the political calculation at play.

> JFK: If anybody ever gets the idea that the president's friends can get away with it … Gosh I think it would be an awful morale cracker to the internal revenue, to taxpayers, the next time that anyone got arrested they'd say well what the hell about Landis?

[88] Feldman, above n 13, 78; see also Navasky, above n 86, 433.

[89] A former academic at Virginia Law School, he was recommended for the job by Robert Kennedy, a former student. Caplin had made great play of the use of computers to streamline the submission process and detect evaders, prompting a front cover story in *Time*, see 'Tax Collector Mortimer Caplin,' *Time*, 1 February 1963 (Albert Einstein once admitted that figuring out his US income tax was beyond him—he had to go to a tax consultant. 'This is too difficult for a mathematician,' said Einstein, 'It takes a philosopher.' Most US taxpayers, being neither mathematicians nor philosophers, are baffled too by the intricacies of the income tax. Unless they take the straight and narrow path of the short form and the standard deduction, even conscientious taxpayers can never be really sure when they send off their returns whether they cheated themselves or their government. A philosopher fares no better than an Einstein.). The decision to pass the matter to the Department of Justice was rational but symptomatic of the conflicts of interest that dog the entire case. According to Navasky, the decision by the IRS left the Department of Justice exposed. He quotes Justin Feldman, quoting Robert Kennedy that 'son-of-a-bitch Caplin left us with no alternative': see Navasky, above n 86, 434.

[90] Ritchie, above n 10, 195.

[91] The official reason given for his departure from public affairs was that the immediate task was over. The resignation coincided with his naming in a divorce case, which the White House said played no role in the decision, see Associated Press, 'Landis Quits as Kennedy Aide,' *New York Times*, 8 September 1961, 1.

NDK: That's, right. That's right. I'm afraid that's right. But I don't think … I think we'd take it into court and it could be done quickly … and …

JFK: How quickly and quietly could it be done?

NDK: It can't be done absolutely quietly but I think that if Dean [William] Warren [of Columbia Law School] who's his counsel would cooperate, I think we could get it all over with maybe in one session.[92]

Katzenbach travelled to New York where he held a meeting with Landis' lawyers, including Dean Warren and Justin Feldman. They suggested to the Deputy Attorney General that they were determined to proceed to trial, citing psychological problems.[93] They had secured the services of a senior psychiatrist, Lawrence Kolb, whose diagnosis revealed a periodic over-reliance on alcohol linked to

> a long-standing, repetitive character-trait, which to my mind, explained his behavior. I pled with his legal friends to allow the case to be argued on these grounds, but they decided otherwise and exposed him to a legal situation which, in my opinion, eventually led to his demise.[94]

According to his psychiatrist, who had been treating him periodically since June 1962, following referral from Dean Warren, Landis was not in a position to make that call. He had initially presented with 'the symptoms of depression, difficulty in working, insomnia and suicidal ideation and excessive use of alcohol of approximately one year's duration.'[95] The psychiatrist concluded that Landis suffered from

> an underlying sense of pathological guilt which drives him to excel as a means of obtaining a sense of satisfaction and acceptance by others to cover a deep-seated insecurity and dependency. These drives and patterns of behavior spring from his strict and aspiring upbringing in an American missionary family, which also motivate him to repress underlying resentments. A major symptom expressive of the above conflict of drives is his longstanding procrastination which contains a magical wish to avoid unpleasantness by not confronting others and frankly discussing unpleasant problems.[96]

Kolb identified 'self-destruction' as the primary driver of this character trait, noting that 'the series of actions do not disclose a consistent pattern directed to acquisition of material goods or deceit of others for purposes of power.' He concluded his diagnosis with the opinion that 'the failure of Mr Landis to file his income tax return was the consequence of a longstanding personality distur-

---

[92] JF Kennedy, 'James Landis and the IRS,' JFK Presidential Library Telephone Recordings: Dictation Belt 23D.5, 25 July 1963, www.jfklibrary.org/Asset-Viewer/Archives/JFKPOF-TPH-23D-5.aspx.

[93] Feldman, above n 13, 79.

[94] Lawrence Kolb to Don Ritchie, 20 May 1975, 'Landis Psychiatric Papers,' *The Papers of Donald Ritchie*, Folder 1, Library of Congress.

[95] Lawrence Kolb to William Warren, 9 April 1963, 'Landis Psychiatric Papers,' *The Papers of Donald Ritchie*, Folder 1, Library of Congress.

[96] Ibid.

bance in a man of high intelligence and moral convictions which impaired his capacity to conform his behavior to the income tax law'.[97]

The reasoning was sound but the political implications of such a strategy were unpalatable. As Feldman explained, Katzenbach outlined the dilemma with brutal force:

> Justin, you're going to take the man who recommended to the President of the United States that he reorganize seven regulatory agencies, on the basis of whose recommendation the President has reorganized six regulatory agencies and you're going to tell a Grand Jury he was crazy? Jim will never do it. I know Jim better than you do ... Don't play God. Where's Jim. I want Jim to make that call in front of my face.[98]

Faced with the prospect that Kennedy had entrusted the sensitive task of regulatory reorganization to a person the media and opponents alike could now characterize as suffering from psychosis—a proposition put explicitly to him directly by Katzenbach—Landis acquiesced. Feldman recalled the encounter:

> Jim looked at me, and he said 'Justin, as well as you know me, Nick is right and nobody's going to say that any of those agencies were reorganized by a man who had psychiatric difficulty and didn't know what he was doing. So what do we do, Nick [asked Feldman] You say it could be handled.[99]

Neither the administration nor Landis could have anticipated what would happen next. It was agreed that the case would be heard in early August. The defense team was given the opportunity to choose the hearing date, which made it much more likely that a sympathetic judge would handle the case. In itself, this was an unusual concession.[100] The first stage went according to plan and media reporting highlighted the technical nature of the breach.[101] On the morning of the sentencing all were surprised when the Chief Justice of the Southern District, Sylvester Ryan, entered the room. He announced that the trial judge had recused himself and he would handle the case personally. Despite a perfunctory presentation of the case by the prosecution, Judge Ryan highlighted a significant problem with the defense strategy:

> [If] at all times he intended to file his returns and if because of incidents that occurred in his life, due to human weaknesses he omitted to file his returns, he is not guilty of a crime, He is charged here with willfully and knowingly failing to files these returns for those years ... to say that he at all times intended to file the return is

---

[97] Ibid.

[98] Feldman, above n 13, 80.

[99] Ibid; see also Lawrence Kolb to Donald Ritchie, 13 February 1981, 'Landis Psychiatric Papers,' *The Papers of Donald Ritchie*, Folder 1, Library of Congress ('Perhaps for him the shame of a psychiatric solution for his problem would have been greater than that of judgment by another lawyer. But it was a tragedy. I know he felt he deserved greater rewards than he had ever achieved for his enormously brilliant intellectual capacity and was also driven by compulsivity in all the efforts he ever made').

[100] Ritchie, above n 10, 198.

[101] It was indicative, for example that on the day of sentencing, media coverage privileged the fact that Landis was at best guilty of a minor infraction and the story was given little prominence: see Associated Press, 'Former Dean Landis Faces Sentencing,' *Lakeland Ledger*, 30 August 1963, 6.

substantially telling me that this defendant has pleaded guilty to a charge of which he is entirely innocent.[102]

He further wondered aloud why Landis had spent the previous month as an in-patient at the Columbia University Presbyterian Hospital. The judge appeared determined to humiliate the former Dean of Harvard Law School. That suspicion hardened when he sentenced Landis to one month's imprisonment, commuted to forced hospitalization in order to treat an undisclosed addiction.[103] The public humiliation was complete in an extraordinary ruling that left little to the imagination:[104]

> It is not a pleasant thing for me to try to pass judgment on you. You in your long career in public service have also been confronted with tasks that are not pleasant and yet as a public official, as the good public official that you were, you had to measure up to what came before you in the line of duty and pray to God for guidance and do what you felt was just and proper. That is what my government expects of me and that is what I expect of myself. Sometimes it is difficult but by the grace of God we continue and do the best we can. ... The Lord was good to you; you were blessed with a keen intellect, good family background and moral training and the ability to see and analyze problems but you, like all men, were born of flesh and blood, and in that flesh and blood there are certain human weaknesses and you have one of those weaknesses which through the years has been giving you trouble. I think that is the cause of your difficulty. It has interfered with the life of many, many brilliant men, particularly men of my heritage, brilliant men who had brilliant careers before them and let it go by the board by their own actions, because such a weakness, when you yield to it, dulls your moral values which you would otherwise would have and which were put in you as a young boy, and it interferes with the performance of your work and while you have done great work for your government, you might still have done greater. Well, it no sense in talking. I have given you a sermon—you could give me a sermon and I could give you a sermon and maybe we would both me right. ... I can't let you go today. I have to impose some penalty. I feel I have to do that in fairness and in justice. My purpose would be to give you a time for reflection, not so much

---

[102] Quoted in Navasky, above n 86, 435.

[103] E Ranzal, 'Landis Jailed for Tax Delays,' *New York Times*, 31 August 1963, 1, 6. The coverage from the wire agencies was much more graphic: see eg R Evans, 'Tardy Tax Returns Costs Thirty Days,' *Lodi New Sentinel*, 31 August 1963, 1 (Evans, a correspondent for UPI, reported that 'Landis, 63, who has been a voluntary patient in a neurological institution was shaking head to foot as the sentence was imposed ... slumped at the defense table, his spasmodically trembling hands clasped before his face'). One of the most astute analyses was published by a syndicated Scripps-Howard columnist: see R Ruark, '30 Days Hath Jim Landis,' *Victoria Sun*, 21 September 1963, 4 ('Jim Landis was a hard-driving, hard-working brilliant man. I have sat with him in a friend's house on occasion, when he passed out in his own chair from sheer combat fatigue. ... One does not "reform" or "punish" a man like Jim Landis by sending him to jail for 30 days, like some common disturber of the peace. If he is worthy of punishment he should have been hit with the book. If the man was sick, overworked, overwrought there should have been no jail sentence at all. I am glad I do not know the inside story of the Landis case because I do not care to think of its implications. But I do say that the sentence imposed by Judge Sylvester Ryan was a complete travesty, either in one direction or the other').

[104] See eg Associated Press, 'Harvard Ex-Dean Handed 30 Day Sentence on Income Tax Charges,' *Lewiston Daily Sun*, 31 August 1963, 1, 6.

by way of punishment, so that you may perhaps appraise yourself in quietness and perhaps make some resolutions that would strengthen your will to carry you on in the future to have a useful life.[105]

Judge Ryan closed by telling the crestfallen Landis that 'I give you my sincere prayer that God will give you the strength of character to help you overcome your weakness.'[106] The conviction was not only a personal tragedy for Landis. It contributed to an incremental erosion of the credibility and legitimacy of the administrative process, in the service of which Landis had dedicated his life as an academic, regulator and political adviser. As with Icarus in Greek legend, Landis had flown too close to the sun in pursuit of ambition.[107] The severity of the sentence has long perplexed scholars.[108] Victor Navasky's classic examination of Robert Kennedy's tenure as Attorney General provides the most in-depth evaluation of the case.[109] He viewed Landis exceptionally sympathetically and the psychiatric records put on the public record by Don Ritchie appear to confirm the initial evaluation. It is also the case that the prosecution regarded the case as a necessary evil.[110] The Deputy Attorney General, Nicholas Katzenbach, for example, described Judge Ryan's ruling as an example of 'monstrous legal egoism.'[111] Following the direct intervention of Justin Feldman to Robert Kennedy, Landis was transferred to the Columbia University facility.[112] If prosecution could not be avoided, then the ignominy of incarceration could be spared. Judge Ryan himself rejected the proposition put to him that the verdict was cruel in an account published in 1981.

What was so cruel? Here is a man who has enjoyed every advantage life can offer; while poor Irish and Jewish and Italian and colored kids were clawing their way out of the gutter, this guy was getting every break. Now, when he has been caught, the Government slobbers over him, the Dean of Columbia Law [lead defense attorney William Warren] slobbers over him and everybody in the courthouse is falling over

---

[105] *United States of America v James McCauley Landis*, 63 CR 654 (30 August) 33.

[106] Ibid, 37.

[107] Ranzal, above n 103, 1.

[108] See P Edson, 'Landis Tax Case Brings Enforcement Under Scrutiny,' *Sarasota Sun*, 16 September 1963, 7.

[109] Navasky, above n 86, 427–41; see also Ritchie, above n 10, 189–202. Both rely heavily on Feldman's account, which was placed on the record in the 2004 interview with the SEC Historical Society, see Feldman, above n 13.

[110] The political problem was intensified because of Landis' failure to file state-level taxes in New York, which opened the possibility of separate proceedings in the event that the federal government did not proceed: see Ritchie, above n 10, 196; Navasky, above n 86, 432.

[111] N Katzenbach, *Some of It Was Fun: Working With RFK and LBJ* (New York, WW Norton & Co, 2008) 102 (describing the case as one of the hardest things had to do in the Department of Justice. In a promotional interview for the book Katzenbach describes it as 'something that had to be done [which he argued Landis himself was aware of and accepted] but which did not amount to a row of beans,' http://bigthink.com/users/nicholaskatzenbach#!video_idea_id=5612. Katzenbach's video account, much more forceful and remorseful than the written version, is predicated on the belief that politics can and does result in brutal outcomes.

[112] Feldman, above n 13, 81–82.

himself to make it easy for him. I had to do my duty and my duty was to show that Landis was no better than anyone else. [113]

The actual prosecutor, Robert Morgenthau, the last surviving participant, now equates the case to a 'Greek tragedy.'[114] While the Landis prosecution was inextricably linked to political exigency, the severity of the sentence was also informed by what can now be revealed as inappropriate and clumsy attempts to influence the outcome of the case by those who counted themselves as friends. Landis' fate, apparently, was sealed when Thomas Corcoran went to the sentencing judge after the initial hearing to argue that the administration expected leniency. This deliberate and inexcusable attempt to influence the outcome by Corcoran, an exceptionally senior lawyer and close confidante of Oliver Wendell Holmes, for whom he clerked, and presidents Roosevelt and Lyndon B Johnson, was communicated directly to Judge Ryan.[115] The Chief Justice, already personally slighted because the Kennedy administration had passed him over for a vacancy in the Court of Appeals, was furious that the integrity of the Southern District could be so traduced by political factors. He determined to send a coded if unambiguous message to the Kennedy family. Landis was to become collateral damage.

On one level, it is not surprising that Corcoran would have adopted such an approach. He had form as one of the most successful if increasingly controversial lobbyists in Washington, where had made his name working with Landis in selling the Securities Act and Securities Exchange Act.[116] It was to be the most counterproductive and damaging intervention in his long and colorful lobbying history. What remains unclear is the extent to which Landis' defense team knew of Tommy Corcoran's intervention in advance. It goes a long way to explaining, however, why appeals to service fell on the deaf ears of Justice Ryan. As Landis pointed out in his own assessment of Corcoran in the Roosevelt administration:

[A] man of that type, besides making friends, he also makes enemies and sometimes in his enthusiasm I think he tends to overshoot the mark, in the sense that he would take in upon himself to represent the President's position without being authorized to do it. There were occasions when he tried to swing his weight around a little too much.'[117]

The problems did not end for Landis with the conviction. Now came an inev-

---

[113] M Gould, 'Landis: Classic Case of Hubris,' *New York Law Journal*, December 14, 1981, 1, 6–9, 28.

[114] Robert Morgenthau, interview with the author, New York City, 24 January 2013.

[115] Ibid.

[116] Corcoran had been under investigation since 1947, and subject to unlawful wiretapping because President Truman resented the strength of his political networks: see K Bird and M Holland, 'Truman and Corcoran: The Tapping of "Tommy the Cork",' *The Nation*, 8 February 1986; for Corcoran's attempts to influence judicial direction, see L Kalman, *Abe Fortas: a Biography* (New Haven, Yale University Press, 1992) 115 (describing Corcoran as someone who considered himself 'head of a government in exile' who attempted to secure Fortas' elevation to the DC Circuit Court of Appeals so that he could temper criticism of administrative agencies. Although the attempt failed it demonstrated the power that Corcoran had in influencing agendas); see also D McKean, *Peddling Influence: Thomas 'Tommy the Cork' Corcoran and the Birth of Modern Lobbying* (Hanover, NH, Steerforth, 2005).

[117] Landis, above n 2, 256.

itable ethics hearing to determine whether to bar him from practicing law. Feldman, once again, handled the proceedings. He recruited the psychiatrist Lawrence Kolb to provide a rationale for the failure to pay the income tax. In a staging of the arguments that could have been raised at trial, the rationale was accepted by a referee report provided by Justice Nolan:

> I am convinced, after consideration of the evidence that respondent was not guilty of fraud or deceit and find that although he failed to make and file his income tax returns for the five years referred to in the information filed against him, he had no intention of deceiving the government, or evading the payment of income taxes for the years in question.[118]

Judge Nolan further found that there was no question of dishonesty and went on to suggest that:

> [The] only possible explanation for his delinquency is that given on the hearing. He was during the period involved carrying a heavy professional workload and apparently never refused any request for the performance of public service, in many instances without compensation. ... I accept, without reservation, Dr Kolb's diagnosis as to the respondent's condition and his opinion as to the part which it played in respondent's failure to file his income tax returns and its probable effect on his future personal and professional activities. I have no doubt that respondent's professional engagements, his public service, and his personal troubles and worries all combined to cause him to put aside his personal obligations with respect to the tax returns, and other personal matters during the years in question; and I have no doubt, as I have stated, that what the respondent did was without fraudulent or deceitful intent. Neither do I have any doubt as to his fitness to continue as a member of the Bar.[119]

Writing to Kolb, Landis was rueful:

> Strangely enough, I have no feeling of a sense of personal relief as a result of these findings. The scars that this episode has inflicted upon me are too deep to be readily healed. My own image of myself, in which I took some pride, is marked pretty deeply by these scars, not to mention problems of economic and social rehabilitation.[120]

The recommendations, however, were not enough to stave off suspension of the right to practice.[121]

On 30 July 1964 James M Landis entered the outdoor pool at his home in Harrison, Westchester County, NY. Some hours later he was discovered floating face down in the water by neighborhood boys who had an open invitation to use the facility.[122] Paramedics pronounced Landis dead at the scene. Did the 64-year-

---

[118] *In the Matter of James McCauley Landis*, Supreme Court of the State of New York, 5 May 1964.

[119] Ibid, 7–8.

[120] James Landis to Lawrence Kolb, 13 May 1964, 'Landis Psychiatric Papers,' *The Papers of Donald Ritchie*, Folder 1, Library of Congress.

[121] 'Landis is Suspended for Year as Lawyer,' *New York Times*, 10 July 1964, 26 (noting the Appellate Division's reference to Landis' 'brilliant career' but requirement to suspend in order to uphold the 'dignity' of the profession).

[122] 'James M Landis Found Dead in Swimming Pool of Home,' *New York Times*, 31 July 1964, 1, 21 at 21.

old keen yachtsman and strong swimmer die of natural causes or was it suicide? If not suicide, were the strain and stress associated with a three-year investigation into his tax affairs contributing factors? The toxicology reports, while inconclusive, suggested the presence of alcohol.[123] The issue of alcohol and accusations of over-reliance on it had dogged Landis' life. Landis had won a number of battles and had fought valiantly. His vision of an American politics built on common purpose and delivered through impartial experts was to be destroyed by the compromises that placed intolerable and insurmountable pressures on regulatory governance. The failure to resolve these deep-seated political questions continues to haunt American politics and the regulation of its securities markets. The mere fact of prosecution was enough to distance previous supporters of this driven if volatile public intellectual. The Kennedy family showed no such fear. Having been forced to prosecute, Robert Kennedy had shown mercy in allowing Landis to serve the forced hospitalization in a private facility at Columbia University. Nor would he forsake the troubled former Dean in death. Robert Kennedy represented the family at the funeral service, where he openly wept.[124] More seriously, the circumstances of the fall robbed the academic, practitioner and policy communities of the most gifted, if strident, advocate of the role of the administrate state. His forced retirement from public life left a vacuum that none was able to fill. No other academic had quite the unique combination of experience, intellectual ability and, critically, access to the highest echelons of power.[125] In a eulogy, Louis Jaffe captured the verve and dynamism of this master of regulation when he wrote, 'throughout the last thirty years there has been a remarkable flow of constructive criticism and administrative creativity. Landis was in the forefront of those whose intellect and vigor were committed to the task of continuous regeneration.'[126] His fall from grace, the result of an inexplicable disregard for his personal affairs, was a tragic story of hubris and political expediency. It should not, however, distract from the fact that in Landis one finds the rationale and normative underpinning for regulatory intervention. It is this lost legacy that this book has sought to capture and restore to its rightful place.

---

[123] 'Landis Autopsy', Office of the Medical Examiner, Westchester County, New York, Case No 20935, Autopsy No 6186, 31 July 1964 (noting the cause of death as accidental drowning). Although the autopsy showed the presence of alcohol and 'a fatty liver' which evidences extensive use of alcohol, at the time of his death Landis had not consumed enough to be over the then drink-driving limit. The autopsy is contained in *The Papers of Donald Ritchie*, Library of Congress, Washington DC.

[124] Feldman, above n 13, 91; see also 'Kennedy Attends Landis's Funeral', *New York Times*, 3 August 1964, 25 (noting that Thomas Corcoran attended the funeral).

[125] M Katz, 'James M Landis' (1964) 78 *Harvard Law Review* 317 (noting that Landis never lost himself in the intricacies of disputes but saw in law a creative process); see also L Jaffe, 'James Landis and the Administrative Process' (1964) 78 *Harvard Law Review* 319, 320 ('Landis spoke for all of us who had been deeply committed to the New Deal and who had been intimately associated with the administrative process.').

[126] Jaffe, above n 125, 328.

Conclusion

The Lost Legacy: James M Landis and the Future of Regulatory Capitalism

The financial services industry has the potential to contribute significantly to wellbeing through the effective and responsible stewardship of savings and investments. In order to do so, it must conduct its affairs within an overarching framework capable of securing societal consent and support. Policymaking at its best is both sensitive to political interests and attentive to moral or ethical considerations.[1] Experience has taught us that the required framework for the financial services industry cannot be imposed by rules alone. Top-down command-and-control regulation has demonstrably failed in a range of domains. This includes financial services, which appears embroiled in a series of scandals that come round with increasing frequency. The ongoing investigations and potential future prosecutions by competition authorities invoking cartel-breaking provisions surrounding systematic manipulation of the London Interbank Offered Rate (Libor) and other key benchmarks, including the Australian Bank Bill Swap Rate, by some of the world's largest and most influential banks are just recent examples.[2]

The net result is to undercut, incrementally but decisively, a regulatory philosophy that, in more stable times, relies on the stated benefits of self-regulation. The central weakness of this framework is that it infers but does not impose binding obligations. The capacity to transact around legal obligation is dispiritingly familiar to students of financial regulation. Equally, a reliance on stated commitment to principles-based regulation has been shown to be a chimera. Given freedom to set and administer conduct, the values trumpeted by industry were not lived and regulators proved incapable or unwilling to keep up with

---

[1] See *Final Report of the National Commission on the Causes of the Financial and Economic Crisis in the United States* (New York, Public Affairs, 2011) xxii–xxiii; for failure of codes of conduct, see Parliamentary Commission on Banking Standards, *Changing Banking for Good* (Westminster, HM Parliament, 18 June 2013) 298–310 (suggesting that the transfer of responsibility to ensure market conduct within banking to a professional body would be mistaken).

[2] See eg Department of Justice, 'UBS Securities Japan Co Ltd to Plead Guilty to Felony Wire Fraud for Long-running Manipulation of LIBOR Benchmark Interest Rates' (press release, Washington, DC, 19 December 2012), www.justice.gov/opa/pr/2012/December/12-ag-1522.html; see also European Union Competition Directorate, 'Antitrust: Commission Fines Banks €1.71 billion for Participating in Cartels in the Interest Rate Derivatives Industry' (press release, Brussels, 7 December 2013); Australian Securities and Exchange Commission, 'ASIC Accepts Enforceable Undertaking from BNP Paribas' (press release, Sydney, 28 January 2014; 'ASIC Accepts Enforceable Undertaking from UBS' (press release, Sydney 23 December 2013).

innovation.[3] Crucially, absent from regulatory design and theory was sufficient emphasis on the role of culture in facilitating behavior.[4] The challenge, therefore, is to design and implement an institutional architecture that has sufficient flexibility to withstand future pressures. It must be guided by experience rather than hope, aspiration or continued belief in a paradigm that has lost legitimacy. For this to occur we must focus on the personal responsibility of individuals, institutions and sectors to uphold the integrity of the financial system and provide concrete mechanisms to operationalize it. In this we have no better guide than the New Deal blueprint. The answers to contemporary problems can be, as this book has suggested, found in a close reading of history. Rather than illuminating the archives, we seem paralyzed by a belief that somehow greed is new. Transpose state–federal relations with international negotiations and one can find the need to build coordinated political alliances. Similarly at the national level, resolving the notoriously complex question of too big to fail can be found in the application of a 'death sentence'. No culture or corporate form is inviolable. Similarly, one cannot take at face value the stated commitment of industry to change. Commitment to enhance professional standards by coopting the regulator onto a professional body can be a recipe for stasis, as Landis discovered and fought against in relation to the Investment Banking Association to huge political cost.

Seven years on from its August 2007 onset with the vaporization of the securitization market, regulatory authorities remain mired in crisis rather than strategic management. Within that timeframe, we have moved progressively from a rubric of 'too big to fail' to a dawning recognition that systemically important financial firms are not only too big to manage, to regulate, but also too big to litigate effectively against and arguably too complex to insure. Crucially, the malign manifestations are as apparent in systems that apply principles rather than rules in guiding market conduct. At the same time, the global investigation into the manipulation of Libor and other key benchmarks suggests the problem

---

[3] Treasury Select Committee, *Fixing Libor: Some Preliminary Findings* (Westminster, HM Parliament, 22 August 2012); see also Financial Services Authority, *Internal Audit Report: A Review of the Extent of Awareness Within the FSA of Inappropriate Libor Submissions* (London, FSA, March 2013), www.fsa.gov.uk/static/pubs/other/ia-libor.pdf ('The FSA's focus on dealing with the implications of the financial crisis for the capital and liquidity positions of individual firms, together with the fact that contributing to or administering LIBOR were not "regulated activities", led to the FSA being too narrowly focused in its handling of LIBOR-related information. This was both in terms of challenging and inquiring about that information, and considering its conduct responsibilities in relation to the Principles for Businesses and any potential for consumer or market detriment': 9). This criticism of the FSA's emphasis on technical compliance is even more pronounced in the findings of the Parliamentary Commission on Banking Standards as evidenced in its coruscating report of the FSA's failure to regulate HBOS, see *HBOS: An Accident Waiting to Happen*, (Westminster, HM Stationary Office, 2013) 28 (noting 'The FSA's approach also encouraged the Board of HBOS to believe that they could treat the regulator as a source of interference to be pushed back, rather than an independent source of guidance and, latterly, a necessary constraint upon the company's mistaken courses of action').

[4] See G Morgenson, 'Geithner, Staying on Script,' *New York Times*, 19 May 2014, B1, B6 (quoting Geithner as writing in his new book 'I did not view Wall Street as a cabal of idiots or crooks. My jobs mostly exposed me to talented senior bankers, and selection bias probably gave me an impression that the US financial sector was more capable and ethical than it really was': B6).

is systemic.[5] As the influential United Kingdom Treasury Select Committee reported in August 2012, '[T]he standards and culture of Barclays [the first bank to agree to a settlement in relation to Libor], and banking more widely, are in a poor state. Urgent reform, by both regulators and banks, is needed to prevent such misconduct flourishing.'[6] The Libor investigation, which remains at an early stage, has exposed systematic and pervasive corruption in the rate-setting process, as noted by the Financial Stability Oversight Council in the United States:

> Recent investigations uncovered *systematic false reporting and manipulations* of reference rate submissions dating back many years. This *misconduct* was designed to either increase the potential profit of the submitting firms or to convey a misleading picture of the relative health of the submitting banks. These actions were *pervasive, occurred in multiple bank locations around the world, involved senior bank officials at several banks, and affected multiple benchmark rates and currencies*, including LIBOR, EURIBOR, and the Tokyo Interbank Offered Rate (TIBOR). Each of the banks that faced charges engaged in a *multi-year pattern of misconduct that involved collusion* with other banks. These revelations have undermined the public's confidence in these benchmarks.[7]

The influential Parliamentary Banking Standards Commission in the United Kingdom has expressed similar concern at the failure of restraining forces. 'Prolonged and blatant misconduct' as evidenced in the Libor and associated scandals, was a result of a 'dismal' and 'striking limitation on the sense of personal responsibility and accountability,' it concludes.[8] The paucity of institutional memory in leading banks, the fact that such manipulative activities continued even after bailouts and a baleful reality of continued compartmentalized responsibility has made business ethics appear little more than an oxymoron.[9] Compliance failures, regulatory gaming and poor risk management have been revealed in sanctions violations and defective anti-money-laundering controls[10] and irresponsible derivative trading.[11] Taken together, they point to

---

[5] For an overview of the scandal and its impact, see J O'Brien and G Gilligan (eds), *Integrity, Risk and Accountability in Capital Markets: Regulating Culture* (Oxford, Hart Publishing, 2013).

[6] Treasury Select Committee, *Fixing Libor: Some Preliminary Findings* (Westminster, HM Parliament, 22 August 2012).

[7] Financial Stability Oversight Council, *Annual Report* (Washington DC: Department of Treasury, 25 April 2013) 137 (emphasis added).

[8] Parliamentary Commission on Banking Standards, *Changing Banking for Good*, above n 1, 16.

[9] A MacIntyre, 'Why Are the Problems of Business Ethics Insoluble,' in B. Baumin and B. Friedman (eds), *Moral Responsibility and the Professions* (New York, Haven Publishing, 1982) 358 ('Effectiveness in organizations is often both the product and the producer of an intense focus on a narrow range of specialized tasks which has as its counterpart blindness to other aspects of one's activity'); see also A MacIntyre, 'Social Structures and their Threats to Moral Agency' (1999) 74 *Philosophy* 311 ('Compartmentalization occurs when a 'distinct sphere of social activity comes to have its own role structure governed by its own specific norms in relative independence of other such spheres. Within each sphere those norms dictate which kinds of consideration are to be treated as relevant to decision-making and which are to be excluded': 322).

[10] See J O'Brien, 'Where the Buck Stops,' *Australian Financial Review*, 27 July 2012, R1, 10–11; see also J O'Brien, 'The Sword of Damocles: Who Really Controls HSBC in the Aftermath of its Deferred Prosecution Agreement with the US Department of Justice' (2012) 63 *Northern Ireland Legal Quarterly* 533.

[11] For discussion of systemic problems associated with incomplete disclosure in relation to the

patterns of conduct that embed recklessness and result in inefficient and unfair markets, not least because the time lag between implementation of the strategy and detection could lull investors into false confidence in probity and prudence.[12] Moreover, the nascent investigation by European competition regulators into benchmark manipulation suggests that collusion is widespread. By default, lack of oversight both at the level of the firm and incomplete regulatory supervision has allowed cartels to operate at the heart of global finance. The result, as the chairman of the Hong Kong Securities and Futures Commission observes, is the elevation of the superficial over the substantive. 'I think a lot has changed superficially. Deep down within particular financial institutions the reality is that not much has changed and that is the central dilemma with which many regulators around the globe are now struggling.'[13]

The facilitation of what end up becoming diametrically opposed outcomes to the purpose of market conduct and competition regulation makes it unsurprising that both the agencies themselves and the disclosure paradigm they operate under should come under sharp critique.[14] It is equally unsurprising that these attacks should be focused on the SEC in the United States. First, it is the archetype independent regulatory commission in this space and oversees the largest market. Second, given the implosion of the principles-based approach adopted by the UK Financial Services Authority, it remains the most visible regulator, with huge capacity to shape or thwart national and global agendas. Influencing SEC agendas and capacity still necessitates the prodigious reserves of Wall Street, mediated in lobbying terms by K Street, its ideational knowledge broker inside the Washington beltway. Third, the agency is engaged in a rearguard action to retain its authority. It is challenged through implementation battles, rising judicial skepticism about the efficacy of its enforcement agenda, and a degree of congressional populism. This criticism can be transcended, however, if one recalls that the original emphasis on disclosure is not a technical question. At its core, disclosure is a normative demand, a point explicitly made by its original framers. Demanding truth in securities is a moral claim. Seen from this perspective, what is required is not the retirement of the paradigm but its rejuvenation.

Building on this insight, we need to understand systematically how culture

---

risks associated with derivatives, see Permanent Sub-Committee on Investigations, 'JP Morgan Chase Whale Trades: A Case History of Derivatives Risks and Abuses' (US Senate, Washington, DC, 15 March 2013).

[12] European Union Competition Directorate, above n 2.

[13] A Alder, Chair of the Hong Kong Securities and Futures Commission, Interview, Madrid, 24 June 2014; see also M Edelman, *The Symbolic Uses of Politics* (Urbana, University of Illinois Press, 1964).

[14] See H Hu, 'Too Complex to Depict? Innovation, Pure Information and the SEC Disclosure Paradigm' (2012) 90 *Texas Law Review* 1601 ('[T]o remain vital, the SEC disclosure paradigm must be able to encompass in a meaningful and systematic way the vast complexities of modern markets and institutions': 1715); J O'Brien, 'The Façade of Enforcement: Goldman Sachs, Negotiated Prosecution and the Politics of Blame', in S Will, D Brotherton and S Handelman (eds), *How They Got Away With It: Lessons from the Financial Meltdown* (New York, Columbia University Press, 2012); S Schwarcz, 'Disclosure's Failure in the Subprime Mortgage Crisis' (2008) 1 *Utah Law Review* 1109.

plays out within individual institutions and across the sectors that make up the financial services industry. It is a, if not the, critical driver of behavior.[15] Culture can facilitate, embed or restrain conduct. Importantly, culture cannot simply be regulated into existence. Rather it depends on institutional actors internalizing ethically appropriate and sustainable organizational and occupational purposes. It is the guiding principle behind the agenda developed by the International Organization of Securities Commissions (IOSCO), currently chaired by the Australian Securities and Investments Commission chief, Greg Medcraft. 'You have got to think about what is driving behavior and generally what is driving it is the culture of an organization. If we look at what is happening with the manipulation of benchmarks, the culture was not right.'[16] It has not been right for some time. Reforming the ethos of banking and broader capital market govern-ance was at the heart of the New Deal. Take, for example, the first speech made by Joe Kennedy following his unexpected appointment as chairman of the SEC.

> We are seeking to recreate, rebuild, restore confidence. Confidence is an outgrowth of character. We believe that character exists strongly in the financial world, so we do not have to compel virtue; we seek to prevent vice. Our whole formula is to bar wrongdoers from operating under the aegis of those who feel a sense of ethical respon-sibility. We are eager to see finance as self-contained as it deserves to be when ruled by Honor and Responsibility. ... When abuses occur, checks and corrections arise. But the application of these processes is not the death hand that some proclaim it to be. Instead, it is the assurance of Life and Strength when Honesty and Intelligence are present. We have been brought into being to help you as part of the public, which erects government for its service. But you best can help yourselves. You can make the investing of money honest. Then you will truly become brother's keeper. And to me that is to acquire merit.[17]

It is precisely the failure of the industry to take advantage of this repositioning that necessitates a reconfigured normative account of institutional purpose, indeed, purposes. The need for such an approach can no longer be denied.[18]

---

[15] See O'Brien and Gilligan, above n 5; see also N Morris and D Vines (eds), *Capital Failure* (Oxford, Oxford University Press, 2014). For a more practitioner focus, see Economist Intelligence Unit, *A Crisis of Culture: Valuing Ethics and Knowledge in Financial Services* (London, EUI, 2013).

[16] G Medcraft, Chair of the Australian Securities and Investments Commission, Interview, Madrid, 24 June 2014.

[17] J Kennedy, 'Securities and Exchange Commission,' *Certified Public Accountant*, December, 1934, 722–36 (reprinting an address at Boston Chamber of Commerce, 15 November 1934).

[18] In evidence before the UK Treasury Select Committee on 9 January 2013, the head of invest-ment banking at UBS, Andrea Arcel, conceded: '[T]hese are industry-wide problems. We all got probably too arrogant, too self-convinced that things were correct the way they were. I think the industry needs to change,' see M Scott, 'UBS Executives Questioned by Parliament over Rate-Rigging Case,' *New York Times*, 9 January 2013'; see also M Carney, 'Rebuilding Trust in Global Banking' (speech delivered at Western University School of Business, London, Ontario, 25 February 2013), in the which the incoming Governor of the Bank of England noted that: '[O]ver the past year, the questions of competence have been supplanted by questions of conduct. Several major foreign banks and their employees have been charged with criminal activity, including the manipulation of finan-cial benchmarks, such as LIBOR, money laundering, unlawful foreclosure and the unauthorized use of client funds. These abuses have raised fundamental doubts about the core values of financial institutions.'

Trust in our corporations and in our institutions, both secular and religious, is at an all time low. Across myriad domains and jurisdictions—from policing to the media, faith-based schooling to banking—governance failures have blighted individual lives, ruined reputations and, in the case of the global financial crisis, threatened social cohesion.[19] Mark Carney, the Governor of the Bank of England put it well in an incisive speech in May 2014:

> My core point is this. Just as any revolution eats its children, unchecked market funda-mentalism can devour the social capital essential for the long-term dynamism of capitalism itself. To counteract this tendency, individuals and their firms must have a sense of their responsibilities for the broader system. All ideologies are prone to extremes. Capitalism loses its sense of moderation when the belief in the power of the market enters the realm of faith. In the decades prior to the crisis, such radicalism came to dominate economic ideas and became a pattern of social behaviour.[20]

How and why this occurred remains one of the pivotal questions facing contem-porary society. For academics, it requires excavating past practice. For the leaders of financial institutions, it necessitates creating and maintaining ethical cultures. For regulators, it necessitates effective and, where necessary, robust supervision. For the political establishment, what is required is the will to calibrate govern-ance and legislative frameworks that transcend short-term imperatives. The Secretary General of IOSCO, David Wright, neatly summarized the scale of the tasks in an interview with the author:

> We can heap blame all round for what has happened. I think it is primarily a failure of the industry. This is an industry of immense sophistication we were told but it clearly an industry in which parts of the industry and certain banks simply didn't manage their risks properly, or understand the risks or their boards didn't understand the risk. Regulators didn't understand the risk in the system either. Let us not forget the IMF was telling us in 2007 that never had the world better distributed risk in the financial system.[21]

Irrespective of domain, corporate culpability for individual ethical failures is invariably informed by the relative strength or weakness of organizational culture (ie the degree to which egregious conduct is informed by a disconnect

---

[19] See MD Higgins, 'President's Remarks at the Launch of Up The Republic' (speech delivered at the Royal Irish Academy, Dublin, 14 November 2012). For a recent report highlighting failure of the press in Britain to uphold their own codes of conduct, see B Leveson, *An Inquiry into the Culture, Practices and Ethics of the Press* (London, HM Stationary Office, 29 November 2012) 4 ('There have been too many times when, chasing the story, parts of the press have acted as if its own code, which it wrote, simply did not exist. This has caused real hardship and, on occasion, wreaked havoc with the lives of innocent people whose rights and liberties have been disdained. This is not just the famous but ordinary members of the public, caught up in events (many of them, truly tragic) far larger than they could cope with but made much, much worse by press behavior that, at times, can only be described as outrageous').

[20] M Carney, 'Inclusive Capitalism: Creating a Sense of the Systemic' (speech delivered at the Inclusive Capitalism Conference, The Mansion House, London, 27 May 2014) 2.

[21] D Wright, Secretary General, International Organization of Securities Commissions, Interview, Madrid, 23 June 2014.

between stated and lived values).[22] The disjunction can lie along a continuum. It ranges from unthinking or willful neglect, through reliance on formal but trans-acted-around compliance programs to misaligned incentives that privilege, and indeed reward, deviance.[23] It is equally dispiriting but nonetheless inescapable that within the financial sector neither commitments to enhanced self-regulation nor strengthened external oversight have proved capable of arresting a decline in its trustworthiness.[24] This is the case irrespective of whether rules or principles-based approaches to regulatory design are privileged.[25] Indeed, recent legislative innovations, particularly in the United States, have resulted in the design of suboptimal regulatory structures; suboptimal, that is, to society if not the finan-cial sector itself, ostensibly the target but ultimately the beneficiary of flawed implementation.[26] The societal cost of the bifurcation between stated and lived values raises a series of fundamental questions. Does this reflect regulatory incompetence, capture or the lack of political will? Can corporate culture be regulated? If so, should it and who should have carriage? Relatedly, how does one ensure the ongoing accountability of regulatory intervention to reduce the risk that shifts in the electoral calendar create imperatives that privilege fundraising over security? What is clear is that, given the financial costs, such a conversa-tion can no longer be held at rarefied self-referential levels.

The extent to which capital markets have departed from ostensible purpose—the efficient allocation of capital—has prompted public disquiet from civic society, including religious leaders. In complaining of the 'cult of money,' Pope Francis consciously replicated the language of the 1930s, most notably President Roosevelt's inaugural address.[27] For the pontiff this state of affairs has practical ideational roots. It derives from corruption, fiscal tax evasion and

---

[22] J Sorensen, 'The Strength of Corporate Culture and the Reliability of Firm Performance' (2002) 47 *Administrative Science Quarterly* 70 (defining culture narrowly as a system of shared values (that define what is important) and norms that define appropriate attitudes and behaviors for organi-zational members (how to feel and behave): 72); see also L Smircich, 'Concepts of Culture and Organizational Analysis' (1983) 28 *Administrative Science Quarterly* 339 (noting that research into corporate culture is an inquiry into the social order: 341).

[23] G Rossouw and L van Vuuren, 'Modes of Managing Morality: A Descriptive Model of Strate-gies for Managing Ethics' (2003) 46 *Journal of Business Ethics* 389 (noting a five stage process in which corporate activity moves from '(1) immorality; (2) reactivity; (3) compliance; (4) integrity; (5) total alignment': 391).

[24] J O'Brien, 'Re-Regulating Wall Street: Substantive Change or the Politics of Symbolism Revis-ited,' in I MacNeil and J O'Brien (eds), *The Future of Financial Regulation* (Oxford, Hart Publishing, 2010).

[25] K Keasey, H Short and M Wright, 'The Development of Corporate Governance Codes in the United Kingdom,' in K Keasey, S Thompson and M Wright (eds), *Corporate Governance: Account-ability, Enterprise and International Comparisons* (Chichester, John Wiley & Sons, 2005) 21 (noting that reform impulses are driven by scandal rather than acquired insight).

[26] See A Haldane, 'The Dog and the Frisbee' (speech delivered at Federal Reserve Bank of Kansas Annual Symposium, Jackson's Hole, 31 August 2012), www.bankofengland.co.uk/publications/Docu-ments/speeches/2012/speech596.pdf; see also D Gallagher, 'Remarks at the SEC Speaks in 2013' (speech delivered in Washington, DC, 22 February 2013).

[27] Pope Francis, 'Address of Pope Francis to the New Non-Resident Ambassadors to the Holy See' (speech delivered at Clementine Hall, The Vatican, Vatican City, 16 May 2013), www.vatican.va/holy_father/francesco/speeches/2013/may/documents/papa-francesco_20130516_nuovi-ambasci-

ideologies which uphold the absolute autonomy of markets and financial speculation, and thus deny the right of control to States, which are themselves charged with
providing for the common good. A new, invisible and at times virtual, tyranny is
established, one which unilaterally and irremediably imposes its own laws and rules.[28]

For the pontiff the situation is rendered unsustainable if those responsible are
not held to account and the systems put in place in the aftermath of crisis paper
over the cracks rather than address the structural dynamics that inform the
operation of a given regulatory regime. These include which institutional actors
have voice, authority and legitimacy and how given preferences are mediated,
evaluated and made manifest. These issues were fully developed in a November
2013 policy document that cast significant doubt on trickledown economics
as anything other than an elaborate public-relations exercise.[29] The delicate
balancing act advanced by the Vatican, and endorsed by leading regulators,
most notably the speeches by Mark Carney and Christine Lagarde at the inclusive capitalism conference, are not in themselves novel. They informed Landis'
action as a practitioner, most notably after the initial wave of enthusiasm for
regulatory intervention subsided. How to achieve forward momentum informed,
for example, his devastating report to Senator Kennedy in 1960 on the risks of
regulatory capture. It remains an essential guide to map regulatory battlefields
precisely because it focuses primarily on ideational factors and the impact they
have on framing discourse.

Critically, most regulatory battles occur at the crucial implementation stage,
which is largely but erroneously conducted on a technical basis, generally without
sustained public scrutiny, and informed by a remarkable degree of consensus

---

atori_en.html. Similar unease has been expressed by the Anglican community: see 'Statement By
Archbishops and Bishops Ahead of G8 Summit in County Fermanagh' (press release, Dublin, 6
June 2013), noting: 'The equitable management of economic affairs has the potential to bring many
benefits to a de–moralised world. ... It is perhaps one of the strangest and saddest aspects of the
world post 2008 that governments, especially governments of wealthy countries, have not promoted
serious discussion of alternative economic models beyond those of a particular form of financial
capitalism. The levels of youth unemployment in wealthy countries is not only an economic disaster,
it is also a moral tragedy', http://ireland.anglican.org/news/4618.

[28] Pope Francis, ibid. For positive political reaction to the speech, see 'Pope Francis Gets Merkel's
Ear on Financial Reforms,' *Deutsche Welle*, 18 May 2013 (quoting the German Chancellor after
meeting with the Pope as saying that '[I]t is true that economies are there to serve the people and
that has by no means the case in recent years', www.dw.de/pope-francis-gets-merkels-ear-on-finan-
cial-reforms/a-16822799).

[29] Pope Francis, *Evangelii Gaudium: Apostolic Exhortation on the Proclamation of the Gospel in
Today's World* (Vatican City, 24 November 2013) para 46 ('Some people continue to defend trickledown theories which assume that economic growth, encouraged by a free market, will inevitably
succeed in bringing about greater justice and inclusiveness in the world. This opinion, which has
never been confirmed by the facts, expresses a crude and naïve trust in the goodness of those
wielding economic power and in the sacralized workings of the prevailing economic system,' http://
w2.vatican.va/content/francesco/en/apost_exhortations/documents/papa-francesco_esortazione-
ap_20131124_evangelii-gaudium.html). The approach has been picked up and endorsed by the
Managing Director of the International Monetary Fund: see C Lagarde, 'Economic Inclusion and
Financial Integrity' (speech delivered at the Inclusive Capitalism Conference, The Mansion House,
London, 27 May 2014); see also Carney above n 20.

among participants. The effect can be to hollow out legislative intention (or more accurately the impression of legislative certainty). Nowhere is this more apparent than in the United States, a point made with great erudition by Paul Volcker, the legendary former chairman of the Federal Reserve in May 2013. Volcker was speaking at the Economic Club of New York, where he received a lifetime achievement award, only the second recipient to be so recognized. For Volcker, the regulatory architecture in the United States is a 'recipe for indecision, neglect and stalemate, adding up to ineffectiveness. The time has come for change.'[30]

This inevitably raises the question of whether the system as designed by Landis is irretrievably broken or has failed because it had already been dismantled, with political acquiescence and complicity, leaving behind an outer shell incapable of withstanding the combination of endogenous and exogenous shocks that brought the global economy to the precipice. We are, as at the time of the initial New Deal construction, therefore, living at a moment of potential paradigmatic change. The dominant conception of corporate governance and financial regulation, based on rational actors operating within efficient markets, is losing (or more accurately, has already lost) coherence, legitimacy and authority (at least insofar as public confidence can be deployed as a proxy for effectiveness).[31] Effective governmental control through dominant shareholdings in major banks has, as a consequence, forced unresolved reflection on what constitutes or should constitute optimal corporate governance and regulatory oversight. The global financial crisis has unleashed an avalanche of reform initiatives.[32] It is unclear, however, to what

---

[30] See P Volcker, 'Central Banking at a Crossroads' (speech delivered at the Economic Club of New York, 29 May 2013) 8–9. Critical in this process is the cost of campaign finance: see M Gilens, *Affluence and Influence: Economic Inequality and Political Power in America* (Princeton, Princeton University Press, 2012); for broader discussion of regulatory decline in the United States, see C Carrigan and C Coglianese, 'Oversight and Hindsight: Assessing the US Regulatory System in the Wake of Calamity,' in C Coglianese (ed), *Regulatory Breakdown: The Crisis of Confidence in US Regulation* (Philadelphia, University of Pennsylvania Press, 2012) 1–20 (suggesting 'the anemic pace of economic recovery following the Great Recession has generally made regulation a matter of great political contestation': 3).

[31] Lord A Turner, 'Reforming Finance: Are We Being Radical Enough?' (speech delivered at Clare College, University of Cambridge, 18 February 2011) 3 (noting 'we must understand' the crisis as one of markets and systems rather than of specific institutions); see also A Sen, 'Introduction', in A Smith, *The Theory of Moral Sentiments* [1759] (London, Penguin, 2009) vii–xxiv (noting that neglect of Smith's opus has led to stunted appreciation of the complexity and 'plurality of human motivations, the connections between ethics and economics and the co-dependent—rather than free-standing—role of institutions in general and free markets in particular in the functioning of the economy': viii); see also J Cassidy, *How Markets Fail: The Logic of Economic Calamities* (London, Allen Lane, 2009) 337 ('Between the collapse of communism and the outbreak of the subprime crisis, an understandable and justified respect for market forces mutated into a rigid and unquestioning devotion to a particular, and blatantly unrealistic, adaptation of Adam Smith's invisible hand').

[32] The Financial Stability Board has provided a critical coordinating role in implementing the architectural design mandated by the G20. This has buttressed the work of pre-existing sector-specific supranational regulatory groupings, including the Basel Committee on Banking Supervision, the International Organization of Securities Commissions (IOSCO) and the International Association of Insurance Superintendents (IAIS). Global trends and the domestic regulatory responses have, in turn, been tracked by the Organization for Economic Cooperation and Development (OECD) and the International Monetary Fund (IMF).

extent this will lead to convergence or facilitate ongoing arbitrage.[33] Implementation carries real risks that national systems will develop frameworks that preserve short-term competitiveness but do little to improve either the quality of oversight or shift the dynamics of financial regulation. More problematically they may not reduce the transmission of national or cross-border contagion. In a remarkably candid assessment the Secretary General of IOSCO told this author that divine intervention is probably the most effective restraining mechanism.

> Right now the global financial system and its regulators or its regulatory bodies have three tools in which to ensure implementation of principles. The first one is colored diagrams, the second one is peer pressure and the third one is prayer. And prayer is probably the strongest of the three. We have no binding institutions. We have no binding dispute settlement system like the WTO. The problem today is just about manageable because we have really two big jurisdictions, the EU and the US. Everybody else is caught between those two big institutions. But in ten or twenty years time we are going to have many more big capital markets, so what is everybody going to do just apply the rules as they see fit. That is a recipe for fragmentation.[34]

Undoubtedly, any successful proposal to extend responsibility and accountability to those involved in product design rather than clarifying the enabling conditions governing marketing and sale would constitute a seismic shift in the structure of the financial services industry. Specifically, it would breach the self-referential logic of private law. The integration of more interventionist normative objectives with enabling ones may also significantly change the ethical boundaries of global finance. It necessitates, however, political will. Paradoxically, notwithstanding early commitments to advance meaningful change, there has been a marked deterioration in political commitment.[35] All of this poses a critical question. What happened to the New Deal paradigm?

---

[33] Financial Stability Board, *Overview of Progress in the Implementation of the G20 Recommendations for Strengthening Financial Stability* (Basel, FSB, 4 November 2011) 2 (noting that '[M]uch work remains to establish legal frameworks for effective intervention in failing firms. ... Many jurisdictions need to address weaknesses in the supervisors' mandates, to ensure sufficient independence to act, appropriate resources, and a full suite of powers to proactively identify and address risks. ... Few jurisdictions have the necessary legislation or regulations in place [for implementing the G20 commitments on OTC derivatives reform]. ... International accounting standards will not have converged' [by end of 2012]'). By early January 2013 the US Federal Reserve was warning the implementation delays had reached crisis dimensions: see Tom Braithwaite et al, 'Fed Warns on Lack of Unity Among Regulators,' *Financial Times*, 28 January 2013, 1. In September 2013 the chairman of the Financial Stability Board warned in St Petersburg that insufficient progress had been made to deal with 'too big to fail', the regulation of derivatives or the oversight of shadow banking: see M Carney, 'Chairman's Letter' (Basel, Financial Stability Board, 5 September 2013), www.financialstabilityboard.org/publications/r_130905.pdf. At the time of writing the Bank for International Settlements warned that financial crisis remains a distinct possibility, see J Caruana, 'Stepping Out of the Shadows of the Crisis: Three Transitions for the World Economy' (speech delivered in Basel, 29 June 2014.

[34] Wright, above n 21.

[35] See eg Parliamentary Commission on Banking Standards, above n 1, para 273 ('If the arguments for complacency and inaction are heeded now, when the crisis in banking standards has been laid bare, they are yet more certain to be heeded when memories have faded. If politicians allow the necessary reforms to fall at one of the first hurdles, then the next crisis in banking standards and culture may come sooner, and be more severe').

The short answer is changed definitions of expertise along with a lack of meaningful acceptance by industry of the moral obligations associated with the disclosure paradigm and a progressive shortening of political horizons. Three intersecting trends were essential in contributing to the embedding of exceptionally narrow terms of reference within political and academic debate: liberalization, globalization and financialization. Each was vital in generating and legitimating the contours of the political debate limiting regulatory intervention.[36] The combination of mechanisms, processes and principles governing corporate governance and financial regulatory reform agendas generated what political scientists term a 'structured action field' (SAF).[37] Power within a SAF is determined by the salience of the ideational terms of reference, the coherence of the underpinning vision, values and norms, and the degree to which the interaction between both appear to provide beneficial outcomes. Once established, such a field is remarkably resilient, particularly if framed by the inculcation of a 'shared mental model.'[38] Inefficiencies (or indeed illegalities) can be—and often are—ignored, downplayed or addressed by the application of what appear to be more stringent rules or the more granular articulation of overarching principles. This dynamic is particularly apparent in corporate governance and financial regulation reform.[39] More often than not, however, these same initiatives tend to privilege the politics of symbolism.[40] By 2007 the ideational structure had not only become merely embedded but almost impervious to challenge, points retrospectively made public by practitioner[41] and academic[42] economists. It was

---

[36] For sociolegal exploration of this process, see S Picciotto, *Regulating Global Corporate Capitalism* (Cambridge, Cambridge University Press, 2011); see more generally T Porter and K Ronit, 'Self-Regulation as Policy Process: The Multiple and Criss-Crossing Stages of Private Rule Making' (2006) 39 *Policy Sciences* 41.

[37] N Fligstein and L Dauter, 'The Sociology of Markets' (2007) 33 *Annual Review of Sociology* 21; see more generally P Bourdieu, *The Logic of Practice* (London, Polity Press, 1990). Bourdieu refers to the importance of mapping the *habitus*—the complex social and physical institutional geography in which communities of practice assimilate and constantly adjust practice.

[38] A Denzau and D North, 'Shared Mental Models: Ideologies and Institutions' (1994) 47 *Kyklos* 3; for application of the model to neoliberalism, see R Roy, A Denzau and T Willet (eds), *Neo-liberalism: National and Regional Experiments with Global Ideas* (London, Routledge, 2007).

[39] See J Hill, 'Evolving "Rules of the Game" in Corporate Governance Reform', in J O'Brien (ed), *Private Equity, Corporate Governance and the Dynamics of Capital Market Regulation* (London, World Scientific Press, 2007) 29–54.

[40] A case in point is Sarbanes–Oxley, the Public Company Accounting and Investor Protection Act (2002). Introduced in the aftermath of the Enron and conflicts of interest in analyst research scandals, it privileged a rules-based approach to regulation. Rather than being seen as an early warning sign, the travails facing the US system were themselves arbitraged. The City of London exploited the unease of business, additional audit costs and litigation risk costs by suggesting an alternative framework based on the articulation of principles. Both practitioners and regulatory officials argued that the model could provide and did offer alternative and better oversight. The primary supporting evidence proffered for this derived from positive testing but the absence of an accounting scandal in the United Kingdom: see David Kershaw, 'Evading Enron: Taking Principles Too Seriously in Accounting Regulation' (2005) 68 *Modern Law Review* 594.

[41] C Borio, 'The Financial Crisis of 2007–? Macroeconomic and Policy Lessons' (speech delivered to the G20 Workshop on the Global Economy, Mumbai, 24–26 May 2009) 13

[42] R Rajan, *Faultines: How Hidden Fractures Still Threaten the World Economy* (Princeton, Princeton University Press, 2010) 3; see also E Dash and J Creswell, 'Citigroup Saw No Red Flags

only in the aftermath of catastrophic failure that these challenges received political attention.

The testimony provided by Alan Greenspan in 2008 of a flaw in his 'ideological reasoning' punctured the self-referential belief in the power of free-markets to self-correct.[43] It did not result, however, in a rapid deflation. This, in turn, can be traced to the abiding strength of the social norms that inform the operation of global capital markets and their regulation. It is not altogether waspish to conclude that the ethical deficit engendered by the global financial crisis reflected the triumph rather than the failure of banking culture and its narrow articulation of what constituted obligation. The externalities associated with introducing the austerity agenda to bail out large swathes of the financial sector in many developed countries demonstrate the bankruptcy of unthinking belief in the market's capacity to self-correct. It also demonstrates the need to resolve the existential conflict between enabling and communitarian approaches to corporate law and financial regulation.[44] The claim by the Goldman Sachs chief executive, for example, that the bank was doing 'God's work' is a carefully circumscribed one.[45] Apparent success was measured by short-term *efficiency* criteria (eg lower transaction costs, expansion of corporate profits, increased shareholder returns). These retrospectively justified and legitimated the innovation. The potential negative externalities were glossed over or ignored. The fallout impacted negatively the *responsibility* and *legitimacy* as well as longer-term *efficiency* dimensions.

Throughout the crisis and beyond, as we moved from the great moderation to the institutionalization of the politics of austerity, senior bankers expressed carefully couched regret. At no stage did they accept responsibility.[46] Instead a narrow technical defense was proffered. As the immediate crisis facing the banks receded, the strategies were framed even more aggressively. To preserve the sanctity of contract, there was a stated need to uphold terms entered into

---

Even As It Made Bolder Bets,' *New York Times*, 23 November 2008, A1 (quoting an April 2008 interview in which Rubin argued: 'In hindsight, there are a lot of things we'd do differently. But in the context of the facts as I knew them and my role, I'm inclined to think probably not'). This reprised an argument made in his autobiography on the financial reporting scandals at the turn of the millennium: see R Rubin, *In An Uncertain World* (New York, Random House, 2003) 337 ('The great bull market masked many sins, or created powerful incentives not to dwell on problems when all seemed to be going well—a natural human inclination').

[43] Evidence to the House Committee on Oversight and Government Reform, Washington, DC, 23 October 2008 (A Greenspan).

[44] See E Orts, 'The Complexity and Legitimacy of Corporate Law' (1993) 50 *Washington & Lee Law Review* 1565 (noting that: '[C]orporate law involves the simultaneous pursuit and coexistence of a number of ends or purposes, with the mix a preponderance of different values depending on particular legal context').

[45] J Arlidge, '"I'm Doing God's Work." Meet Mr Goldman Sachs,' *Sunday Times*, 8 November 2009, 4.

[46] See eg A Hornby and Lord Stevenson, 'Memo to Treasury Select Committee,' Westminster, 10 February 2009, 38 (in a joint statement the CEO and Chairman of HBOS stated they were 'profoundly sorry' but claimed 'unprecedented global circumstances affected virtually all the top banks in the world but HBOS specifically').

freely (if misguidedly). Moreover, a similar rationale justified the payments of market-determined bonuses to executives then working in de facto nationalized institutions. Second, the privileging of caveat emptor facilitated the transference of responsibility. Equally understandably, both sets of strategies fueled public resentment. This prompted, in turn, political recognition of the need for substantive reform to safeguard legitimacy. The fundamental problem, however, was that so much was left to agencies such as the SEC to implement through prescriptive rulemaking processes. These limit capacity to exercise discretion. Moreover, the DC Circuit, the premier venue for adjudication of administrative law, has been at best lukewarm about the utility of regulatory intervention without detailed cost–benefit analysis, irrespective of demonstrable evidence of market failure.[47] Such an approach is eerily reminiscent of the battles over the legitimacy of the New Deal itself, battles in which Landis played such a pivotal force as academic, practitioner, theoretician and advocate. As he put it in a famous address in Chicago at the height of the court-stacking scandal, the dispute centered on the apparent willingness of Supreme Court judges

> to insist upon writing their own individual economic prejudices and predilections into the fabric of constitutional law. … It means today an attitude towards constitutional law which incites to litigation, incites to defiance of government, and too frequently leads to the paralysis of a program before it even has a chance of initiation.[48]

The assessment gives particular resonance to Karr's famous French epigram, *plus ça change, plus c'est la même chose*. It is not simply a question of political or judicial sensibilities. More perniciously, it is an entire worldview that is informed by the elevation of trading mores over relational banking.

No sector has proved as incapable of institutionalizing memory of what happens when incentives become skewed as the major banks, which, internationally, increasingly became governed by trading imperatives.[49] Those imperatives privileged a very circumscribed worldview. Consider, for example, evidence

---

[47] See Gallagher, above n 26 ('I worry about the limits placed on the Commission's ability independently to apply its expertise and judgment under the paradigm established by the Dodd–Frank Act. The Act contains approximately 400 specific mandates to be implemented through agency rulemaking, around 100 of which apply directly to the SEC. Many of these mandates are highly prescriptive, and instead of directing the Commission to regulate in an area after studying the relevant issues, compiling data, and determining what, if any, regulatory action may be appropriate, they require the Commission to issue strictly prescribed and often highly technical rules under short deadlines. Unfortunately, although the Commission always has some degree of discretion when implementing a Congressional mandate, these more prescriptive rules limit the Commission's flexibility in the rulemaking process while occupying time and resources that could be better spent fulfilling the Commission's other important responsibilities. If one of the duties of an independent agency is to work proactively with Congress to ensure that statutes do not impose unnecessary or inappropriate mandates, then on that front the Commission unfortunately came up short with respect to many Dodd–Frank mandates').

[48] JM Landis, 'The Power the Court has Appropriated' (speech delivered at Fourth Annual Women's Conference, Chicago, 10 March 1937).

[49] See B Diamond, *Today Business Lecture* (2011), http://news.bbc.co.uk/today/hi/today/newsid_9630000/9630673.stm. For failure of this strategy, see M Arnold and A Sharman, 'Barclays Moves to Cut 7,000 Jobs in Retreat from Investment Banking,' *Financial Times*, 8 May 2014.

provided to the British Parliamentary Commission on Banking Standards. The extraordinary testimony provided by senior bankers at RBS in February 2013 offers, however, an opportunity, if acted upon, to regulate culture. Following a standard script, the banking executives were, in turn, shocked at the crookedness involved in the manipulation of Libor; dismayed at the lack of moral restraint; and keen to differentiate between ethical bankers and amoral traders. The class system that has always informed City mores was at the fore. As the elite blamed the collusion that undermined Libor on the traders—a different breed altogether it appeared, governed (if at all) by elastic conceptions of probity—a familiar refrain was evident. If the bankers, ostensibly in control, were guilty of anything it was, according to the serving head of investment banking, John Hourican, 'excessive trust.'[50] So what, if anything have the bankers remembered? It would appear not a lot, other than self-pity and special pleading.

'I have told people who are prepared to listen that they shouldn't waste my death,' Mr Hourican told the Commission; he had resigned to take 'ultimate responsibility' for the failing exposed in the Libor rigging scandal. The issue was not a core concern given the fact that 'we [presumably meaning the board and senior executives] had to deal with an existential threat to the bank.' Instead of dealing with misaligned incentives, the bank had (it was inferred himself included) exhibited 'blind faith' in the actions of traders. It was message repeated by the bank's chief executive, Stephen Hester, who (temporarily) kept his job if not his bonus. The scale of the abuse was, Mr Hester intoned, 'too readily redolent of a selfish and self-serving culture in banking which I think needs to be addressed and is exactly the reason for this commission's existence.' Nodding to the authority of the Commission is not, however, the same as abiding by its recommendations. The scale of the crisis was such that, according to the bank's chairman, Sir Philip Hampton, no useful purpose could to be served by 'a mass series of assassinations.' The forced departure of Mr Hourican would suffice. But this left many uncomfortable questions, most forcibly articulated by the Archbishop of Canterbury, himself a former corporate executive. How many whistleblowers had come forward in advance of regulatory inquiries?, asked the Archbishop, to which Mr Hourican and his colleagues could provide only one answer. None. The Archbishop was incredulous. 'Why? Was there not one person anywhere who thought this is not the right way to behave? So how do you, in the future, set a culture?'

The manner in which the RBS staff reacted to this line of questioning speaks volumes about the malaise facing the capital markets. Mr Hourican cautioned that he wanted to have a culture of calling people to attention rather than using a whistleblowing channel. Having lots of whistleblowing in a company is almost as bad,' he declared, without explaining what he meant by either statement. Attempts to elucidate meaning became harder as he sought to justify the unjus-

---

[50] H Ebrahimi and H Wilson, 'RBS Executive John Hourican Tells Colleagues "Not to Waste my Death"', *Daily Telegraph*, 11 February 2013.

tifiable. 'We want a culture where people hold each other to a high level of moral account,' he argued. He boasted that 1,000 graduates had been appointed, without explaining how these junior-level appointments could either 'stand up and feel the anger that exists around the issue, the industry and our company,' exert control or be protected from contamination by a pervasive culture that the executive admitted the bank's senior leadership was shocked by. Ignorance is, however, a shocking abdication of reasonability. Hourican's colleague, Johnny Cameron, was asked directly how to test for the moral culture of a trading floor. His answer, as reported by the *Daily Telegraph*, was instructive: 'That's straying into philosophical territory. I do think that traders have a particular approach to life and need much tighter controls.'[51] By inference, bankers were, and remain, a different breed, which could be trusted by the establishment, including the Church of England, formally represented in the Commission by the Archbishop of Canterbury. Indeed, at a global level the emphasis on the creation of safety nets for systemically important financial institutions risks creating a foundation for misplaced trust. As one senior market conduct regulator puts it:

> [W]e also have this perverse thing happening which is the safety nets that have been put in place have favored the growth of large institutions. [As a consequence] they get even bigger. [The argument runs that] they should not fail or there is a fear about them failing. So you end up with an ecology that is conducive to anti competitive conduct. It must do, if you have a regulatory system that favors the large and favors the few.[52]

The global financial crisis and its aftermath demonstrate, therefore, that much more holistic approaches to risk management are required that link private rights to public duties, precisely because the regulatory system privileges concentration.

The problem is exacerbated by ongoing disputation about the relative merits of innovation, security, performance and conformance. Many innovations in finance by their very nature operate outside the regulatory perimeter. Moreover, their legitimacy and utility are informed by an ethic of obedience. This approach privileges technical compliance. It facilitates courses of action that can undermine the underpinning spirit of the law, a move that now animates the Financial Conduct Authority in the United Kingdom.

> I think the old model, the ethic of obedience was, as long as we're compliant with a set of rules, then we're doing the right thing. Our view is that rules never quite keep up with what actually happens in markets. You can still be delivering bad outcomes for consumers even though the rules seem to allow you to do that. You disclose lots of information because the rules say you should but then you sell people the wrong product. If you have an ethic of care, you really care about people getting their needs met, not your needs met, not your sales processes.[53]

The integration of more interventionist normative objectives with enabling

---

[51] Ibid.

[52] Alder, above n 13.

[53] M Wheatley, Chief Executive Officer, Financial Conduct Authority, Interview, Madrid, 24 June 2014.

ones may significantly change the ethical boundaries of global finance, through demonstration effect and active leadership in inculcating cultural change. What consitutes or should constitute optimal cultural traits necessitates going beyond *efficiency* criteria (ie lower transaction costs) or relying, erroneously, on disclosure as an effective proxy for *consumer protection*. Three additional distinct but overlapping subjective normative dimensions must be applied: (i) *permissibility* (ie whether a particular product can be sold and if so to whom and on what basis); (ii) *responsibility* (ie who carries the risk if the investment sours and on what terms); and (iii) *legitimacy* (ie does the product serve a legitimate purpose). This, in turn, suggests the need for the dynamic integration of rules, principles and social norms within an interlocking responsive framework. There is significant international evidence to support such a proposition. As John Kay has persuasively argued in the UK, sustainable reform must be predicated on capability to 'restore relationships of trust and confidence in the investment chain, underpinned by the application of fiduciary standards of care by all those who manage or advise on the investments of others.'[54]

The Kay formulation builds on an insight first advanced in 2009 by the then managing director of the FSA, Hector Sants. Sants had famously complained that it was impossible for principles-based regulation to work when those charged with informal authority to maintain the integrity of the system had no principles.[55] This was not simply a particularly memorable aside. It reflected cognizance of the importance of what Oliver Williamson has termed the 'non-calculative social contract,'[56] which received twentieth-century articulation in the first keynote address delivered by Joe Kennedy as head of the SEC.[57] This social contract was, however, replaced by an agenda that suggested, without evidence, that the management of risk is best left in the hands of market actors. The invocation of the 'do no harm' principle, linked in part to a slavish definition of cost–benefit analysis, privileged inaction. The bifurcation between performance (unleashing competitive forces to drive innovation) and conformance (subservience to regulatory red-tape) reflects a battle for the maintenance of authority within a bounded system. In this context, the emphasis on market

---

[54] See J Kay, *The Kay Review of Equity Markets* (London, HM Stationary Office, July 2012) 9. According to Professor Kay, this necessitates a move away from short-termism, as 'trust and confidence are the product of long-term commercial and personal relationships: trust and confidence are not generally created by trading between anonymous agents attempting to make short term gains at each other's expense': 5.

[55] H Sants, 'Delivering Intensive Supervision and Credible Deterrence' (speech delivered at the Reuters Newsmaker Event, London, 12 March 2009) 2 ('The limitation of a pure principles-based regime have to be recognized. I continue to believe the majority of market participants are decent people; however a principles-based approach does not work with people who have no principles').

[56] O Williamson, 'The New Institutional Economics: Taking Stock, Looking Ahead' (2000) 38 *Journal of Economic Literature* 595, 597. Williamson notes that analysis of this 'level one' component of social theory is conspicuous by its absence with regulatory studies. The other three levels comprise institutional arrangements viewed primarily through property rights and positive political theory; governance mechanisms through transaction cost economics; and resource allocation frameworks generally examined through agency theory.

[57] Kennedy, above n 17.

ordering privileges one form of authority over another.[58] The emphasis is embedded through an ideational belief in the 'efficient market hypothesis'.[59] A partial reading of Adam Smith provides a cover of philosophical grounding.[60] In particular, it fails to take into consideration how informational asymmetry can, if unchecked, distort markets. Although the effect of this asymmetry is often assessed in the context of depositors being unable to determine whether or not a bank is solvent, asymmetry also applies to the regulator. To some extent, this has driven the regulatory approach. The international evidence is that in highly developed markets, neither the banks nor the supervisors knew or could explain the functioning of complex financial instruments released to the market. In cases where these issues have been litigated to a judicial conclusion, ignorance or incomplete understanding of products and product risk pertain. In this context it is valuable to explore the judicial reasoning of one of those few cases, a class action taken on behalf of a number of local councils against Grange Securities, a subsidiary of Lehman Brothers Australia.

In a landmark ruling, the Australian Federal Court found that 'the improvidence, and commercial naivety, of Grange's Council clients in entering into these transactions that were highly advantageous to Grange'[61] could only have occurred because the financial services firm was dealing with individual officials variously described as 'financially quite unsophisticated and completely out of his depth',[62] 'uninformed'[63] and 'careless'.[64] Notwithstanding the carelessness, the Federal Court did not find grounds to reduce liability through contributory negligence. It did so because Rares J held that the financial services firm had used a deliberate strategy to take advantage of its asymmetrical knowledge of product and regulatory complexity.[65] That it could do so necessitated capacity

---

[58] This, in turn, can be traced to the progressive rise to dominance of neoliberalism, which traces its roots to an earlier ideational battle, initially lost by the libertarians: see F Hayek, *The Road to Serfdom* (London, Routledge Press, 1944) 29 ('To create conditions in which competition will be as effective as possible, to supplement it where it cannot be made effective … provide indeed a wide and unquestioning field for state activity. In no system that could be rationally defended would the state just do nothing. An effective competitive system needs an intelligently designed and continuously adjusted legal framework as much as any other'). Contrast this certainty with other seminal, but progressively ignored texts from the period: see J Schumpeter, *Capitalism, Socialism and Democracy* (London, Routledge, 1943) 137 ('No social system can work in which everyone is supposed to be guided by nothing except his short-term utilitarian ends … the stock market is a poor substitute for the Holy Grail'); see also K Polanyi, *The Great Transformation* (New York, Farrar & Reinhart, 1944) 171 ('The principle of freedom to contract … is … merely the expression of an ingrained prejudice in favour of a definite kind of interference, namely such as would destroy non-contractual relations').

[59] E Fama, 'Efficient Capital Markets: A Review of Theory and Empirical Work' (1970) 25 *Journal of Finance* 383.

[60] A Smith, *The Wealth of Nations: Books 1–3* [1776] (Harmondsworth, Penguin Classics, 1982); see also, however, A Smith, *The Theory of Moral Sentiments* [1759] (Harmondsworth, Penguin Classics, 2010).

[61] *Wingecarribee Shire Council v Lehman Brothers Australia (in liq)* [2012] FCA 1028 at para 266.

[62] Ibid, 483.

[63] Ibid, 491.

[64] Ibid, 462.

[65] Ibid, 913 ('Grange was a person who, unlike each of the Council officers had the necessary financial acumen and expertise to be categorized as a "sophisticated investor" in the English ordinary

to circumvent the legal rules and failure of the audit process to ascertain the material risks of such a strategy.[66] As Rares noted:

> The contrast between the actual, and patent, lack of financial acumen of the various Council officers at each of Swan, Parkes and Wingecarribee [the local councils representing the class action] and the intelligent, shrewd and financially astute persons at Grange was striking.[67]

'Generally, risk-averse people do not take bets with substantial assets held for public purposes', he concluded.[68] That they did so could be rendered explainable by the fact that they were victims of an elaborate deception. This leaves open the question of whether Grange was an outlier, or its actions were symptomatic of a socially harmful worldview.

There are remarkable similarities between the Australian example and the case taken by the SEC in the United States against Goldman Sachs executive Fabrice Tourre for deception in the sale of CDOs to very sophisticated investors. A jury trial found Tourre guilty in August 2013, following on from an earlier settlement his employer reached with the SEC, involving a $454 million fine and commitment by Goldman to recalibrate its risk management and compliance programs.[69] The bank did so but in a very deterministic fashion following rather than challenging existing policy settings. Critically, the bank did not even acknowledge the fact that it was mandated to reform compliance regime as a consequence of the

usage of that expression. That is the capacity in which each Council engaged Grange to act on its behalf').

[66] This approach has come under significant attention both in Australia and in the United Kingdom: see eg Lateline Business, 'ASIC's Medcraft Outlines His Vision', *Australian Broadcasting Corporation*, 9 June 2011, in which the chairman of ASIC noted that '[W]e're focused on with particularly, say, investment bankers, the investment banks, we're really focused on them as product manufacturers. And in fact, when we undertake surveillance on the investment banks, we really focus on their new product approval procedures in terms of how they're bringing a product to market to make sure that they are focused on making sure that the products they're actually bringing to market are not inappropriate', www.abc.net.au/lateline/business/items/201106/s3240343.htm. In the United Kingdom the Financial Services Authority (FSA) initially privileged a similar approach: see H Sants, 'Annual Lubbock Lecture in Management Studies' (speech delivered at the Said Business School, 12 March 2010). Unfortunately the debate did not continue until relatively recently: see C Adamson, 'Journey Towards a Conduct Regulator' (speech delivered at Westminster Forum, London, 5 March 2013). Adamson noted that '[F]irms have designed, manufactured and sold products not always with the needs and interests of their customers in mind but instead, seeing the customer as somebody to maximize profit from. This has been accentuated by a view, and it has to be said encouraged by the FSA, that disclosure at the point of sale absolves the seller from a real responsibly of ensuring that the product or service represents a good outcome for the customer. This, in turn, has led in many cases to a tick-box and overly legalistic compliance culture within firms, encouraged by what has been seen as a tick-box regulatory approach. ... Where we believe cultural measures exposure the firm to a high level of risk in the context of our objectives, we will expect the firm to take account of it.' See also C Adamson, 'Regulation and Professionalism: The Importance of Culture in Driving Behaviours of Firms and How the FCA Will Assess This' (speech delivered at UK Professionalism Conference, London, 19 April 2013).

[67] *Wingecarribee Shire Council v Lehman Brothers Australia (in liq)* [2012] FCA 1028 at para. 752.

[68] Ibid, 895.

[69] See J O'Brien, 'Professional Obligation, Ethical Awareness and Capital Market Regulation' in Morris and Vines, above n 15, 209–33.

settlement agreement.[70] This leaves open the question of what else the regulatory agency, in this case the SEC, could have achieved? In current settings, the unsettling reality is very little. The Goldman Sachs case provides ample evidence that this is the case. This is no longer sustainable.[71] The critical policy question, then, is how to render an alternative framework operational in a systematic, dynamic and responsive way. To be successful, it needs to balance specific economic efficiency (ie benefits to business) and professional rights to self-governance with explicit requirements that society should not be held responsible (or liable) for the failures of the former.[72] This is not in itself a particularly novel insight. The problems were identified many years ago. Self-certified reform has always been problematic, as a reading of history demonstrates.

The manner in which codes of conduct were used to circumvent obligation was apparent from the very beginning of the New Deal, for example. This unease was captured by an internal report prepared for James Landis and the other members of the FTC on the workings of the NRA.[73] The internal report was forwarded to President Roosevelt, who in turn handed over responsibility for evaluation of code operation to the FTC, effectively limiting the power of the NRA long before the Supreme Court deemed it unconstitutional the following year. For Landis and the other designers of the disclosure paradigm, its power, first set out in the Securities Act (1933) and reinforced by the Securities Exchange Act the following year, lay primarily in the capacity to set and frame broader discourse. The aim was not to mandate organizational change as some early commentators, including William O Douglas, advocated.[74] Instead, disclosure and the development of codes of conduct were means to an end—a necessary response to societal obligation. It was the failure of industry to accept these restraints that undermined effectiveness. It remains the case, notwithstanding the evidence not just from the New Deal but also from the founding father of

---

[70] Ibid.

[71] See L Seabrooke, 'The Everyday Social Sources of Economic Crises: From "Great Frustrations" to "Great Revelations" in Interwar Britain' (2007) 51 *International Studies Quarterly* 795 (noting that 'ongoing processes of legitimation [reflect] two-way relationships between claims made by those who seek to govern by the rightfulness and fairness of their actions, and the conferral or rejection of such claims by those being governed': 796); for a similar (and failed) attempt to suggest common cause between regulator and regulated, see M Shapiro, 'Address to the Practising Law Institute' (speech delivered at PLI Securities Regulation Seminar, New York, 4 November 2009): 'We might sit on opposite sides of the table in any given matter, but I believe that all of us—regulators, attorneys, and business people alike—all share the common goal of ensuring that our capital markets work—and work fairly and effectively.'

[72] For application to business as an intangible asset, see J Petrick and J Quinn, 'The Challenge of Leadership Accountability for Integrity Capacity as a Strategic Asset' (2001) 34 *Journal of Business Ethics* 331; for original formulation of the model, see J Petrick and J Quinn, 'The Integrity Capacity Construct and Moral Progress in Business' (2000) 23 *Journal of Business Ethics* 3.

[73] Memorandum for the Federal Trade Commission provided by Millard E Hudson, 22 December 1933, *Papers of JM Landis*, Harvard Law School, Box 18-8.

[74] W Douglas and G Bates, 'The Federal Securities Act of 1933' (1933) 43 *Yale Law Journal* 171. Douglas and his co-author viewed the disclosure paradigm as insufficient. What was required, they argued, was a much more substantive reordering of relations between market participants.

economics.[75] This reality increasingly underpins market conduct if not banking regulation. Take, for example, the views of the head of the Swiss Financial Market Supervisory Authority, Ann Héritier Lachat. She argues that actual practice must be evaluated on an ongoing basis and subject to ongoing external validation.[76] She argues that it is insufficient to rely on stated commitment. 'You have to be more intrusive in your supervision meaning you send people to check what is really [being] done.'[77] This, however, cuts against the emergence of new and powerful orthodoxies. The challenge, therefore, is to maintain political support, an exceptionally difficult thing for market conduct regulators to achieve given the ideational and reputational risks associated with unpicking the regulatory agenda followed with increasing zeal since 2008. As Ashley Alder from the Hong Kong Securities and Futures Commission puts it, there are major risks associated with challenging emergent orthodoxies:

> If you address elephants in rooms, firstly once you have unveiled them you [find] they are usually too heavy to move and if you try to move them you are going to break lots of things. ... But if you really look at what is happening, we are deferring a problem. We are deferring a problem about debt, deferring a problem about credit and we are deferring a problem about the fact that financial institutions need intermediaries, have transformed their businesses to such an extent, in a political environment that has encouraged that, it is very hard to pull it all back from the brink. Just look at asset managers and the way in which they are effectively or many of them are divorced from and not interested in because there is no incentive to be [involved] in corporate governance. I don't think there's a political will to really tackle it head on.[78]

Absent that agreement, however, it is hard to see how a sustainable outcome can be achieved. At corporate, professional and regulatory levels the regulatory framework needs to be mutually reinforcing. It needs to be capable of evaluating the calculative, social and normative reasons for behaving in a more (or less) ethically responsible manner.[79] It also requires reciprocal obligation from

[75] A Smith, *The Theory of Moral Sentiments*, above n 60, 133 (arguing that '[W]e can never survey our own motives, we can never form any judgment concerning them, unless we remove ourselves, as it were, from our own natural station, and endeavour to view them as at a certain distance from us'). The political drivers of self-certification are, however, finely tuned: see M Granovetter, 'Economic Action and Social Structure: The Problem of Embeddedness' (1985) 91 *American Journal of Sociology* 481 ('Idealized markets of perfect competition have survived intellectual attack in part because self-regulating economic structures are politically attractive to many. Another reason for survival, less clearly understood, is that the elimination of social relations from economic analysis removes the problem of order for the intellectual agenda, at least in the economic sphere': 484).

[76] A Héritier Lachat, Chair of the Swiss Financial Market Supervisory Authority, Interview, Madrid, 24 June 2014.

[77] Ibid.

[78] Alder, above n 13.

[79] S Winter and P May, 'Motivation for Compliance with Environmental Regulations' (2001) 20 *Journal of Policy Analysis and Management* 675; see more generally I Ayres and J Braithwaite, *Responsive Regulation* (Oxford, Oxford University Press, 1992). For study suggesting the power of outsiders to frame the emphasis on effective internal controls only if there is a perception within the company that performance is being monitored, see C Parker and V Nielsen, 'To What Extent Do Third Parties Influence Business Behaviour' (2008) 35 *Journal of Law and Society* 309 (reporting survey evidence from 999 large Australian companies); for broader theoretical issues, see M Dubnick and

each institutional actor to maintaining (and certainly not contributing through omission or commission to the erosion of) the integrity of the governance arrangements. These must articulate common understandings of what constitutes the ethical problem. Moreover, it must generate a framework in which disputes over interpretation can and should be resolved in a manner that is proportionate, targeted and, ultimately, conducive to the building of warranted trust in the operation of the financial sector. Only government has the capacity to deliver these outcomes through creating a framework that specifies duties and obligations as well as rights, and providing incentives to participants in the form of directed self-regulation.

As John Kay has astutely noted,

> [T]he most powerful mechanism for establishing a culture of trust and respect is for intermediaries and market participants to impose it on each other. Conversely, the contagious effect of failure to observe these standards at any point in the investment chain undermines them at every point in the market chain.[80]

This signaling capacity takes us back to the critical question of culture.[81] The deception at the heart of the multifaceted Libor scandal, for example, points to patterns of conduct that embed inefficiency and unfairness. 'Here is the challenge with market manipulation', argues Howard Wetston, chair of the Ontario Securities Commission and Vice Chairman of IOSCO.

> There is a lot of smoke filled rooms in the world, there are a lot of places in which participants can get together to decide to agree to conspire, to collude and obviously that kind of collusion can reduce the integrity of a particular benchmark.[82]

As such, on both a descriptive and analytical level within individual entities and the broader regulatory 'regime',[83] the manipulation of benchmarks represents what Lawrence Lessig has termed 'institutional corruption' (ie 'an influence, financial or otherwise, within an economy of influence, that weakens the effectiveness of an institution, especially by weakening public trust in that institution').[84] This has profound implications for governmental as well as regu-

---

J O'Brien, 'Retrieving the Meaning of Accountability in Capital Market Regulation', in M Dubnick and G Fredrickson, *Accountable Governance* (Armonk, NY, ME Sharpe, 2011) 282–301.

[80] Kay, above n 54, 47.

[81] J Sorensen, 'The Strength of Corporate Culture and the Reliability of Firm Performance' (2002) 47 *Administrative Science Quarterly* 70 (defining culture narrowly as a system of shared values (that define what is important) and norms that define appropriate attitudes and behaviors for organizational members (how to feel and behave): 72); see also L Smircich, 'Concepts of Culture and Organizational Analysis' (1983) 28 *Administrative Science Quarterly* 339 (noting that research into corporate culture is an inquiry into the social order: 341).

[82] H Wetston, Chair, Ontario Securities Commission, Interview, Madrid, 24 June 2014.

[83] C Hood, H Rothstein and R Baldwin, *The Government of Risk* (Oxford, Oxford University Press, 2001) 8 (describing a regulatory regime as a 'complex of institutional [physical and social] geography, rules, practice and animating ideas that are associated with the regulation of a particular risk or hazard').

[84] L Lessig, 'Institutional Corruption' (speech delivered at Harvard Law School, Cambridge, MA, 12 October 2009), www.youtube.com/watch?v=0-lEDiUFXUk. See more generally, L Lessig, *Republic*

latory authority. Concern that authority has been traded for an inferior bargain informs the demands by figures as disparate as Pope Francis and Paul Volcker for a reimagined conception of responsibility and accountability. Much more holistic assessment of existing trust boundaries is required, as is evaluation of how codes of practice deviate from agreed institutional commitments and reinforce patterns that undermine stated adherence to integrity.[85] In the aftermath of the global financial crisis public trust in technical expertise is understandably unforthcoming. What is therefore required for regulator and regulated alike is an articulation of a renewed 'non-calculative social contract' capable of embedding ethical restraint.[86] Such an approach now animates the governance agenda being developed by Brazil. As Brazil's primary securities regulator put it to this author recently:

> [I]f you [want to have] have the right risk management framework, one of the things that you have to ensure is that you have the right corporate responsibility and transparency and the right levels of accountability in the market place so that's why I strongly believe that we have to work very hard in spreading risk management culture from a proactive point of view, both from the banks and also from the non-banks.[87]

Note that there is no reference to social responsibility, an intellectual cul de sac that has diverted attention for too long from the obligation that the state has the capacity to extract in return for the privilege of incorporation.

Creating or sustaining structures that facilitate the weakening of ethical obligation (or provide opportunities for gaming) are, by definition, self-defeating. This, in turn, necessitates a return to philosophical underpinnings of market regulation and articulation of its purpose. As the leading British philosopher Derek Parfit has pointed out, it is essential to integrate utilitarian and categorical imperatives: 'An act is wrong just when such acts are disallowed by the principles that are optimific, uniquely universally willable, and not reasonably rejectable.'[88] Parfit's formulation is highly abstract, and therefore in need of appro-

Lost: How Money Corrupts Congress and a Plan to Stop It (New York, Twelve Books, 2012). For analysis of interaction between legislative design and regulatory policy, see F McChesney, *Money for Nothing: Politicians, Rent Extraction and Political Extortion* (Cambridge, MA, Harvard University Press, 1987) 157 (characterizing politicians 'not as mere brokers redistributing wealth in response to competing private demands but as independent actors making their own demands to which private actors respond').

[85] For discussion of Libor reform, see J O'Brien, 'Singapore Sling: How Coercion May Cure the Hangover in Financial Benchmark Governance' (2014) 7 *Journal of Risk Management in Financial Institutions* 174.

[86] Williamson, above n 56; see also D Kingsford Smith, 'A Harder Nut to Crack: Responsive Regulation in the Financial Services Sector' (2011) 44 *University of British Columbia Law Review* 695 (noting the reputational damage associated with licensing as is 'gives an imprimatur of approval to the operating standards that the firm adopts ... When it becomes clear that this is not the case (as with the global financial crisis) the regulator and the regulated lose legitimacy and the investing public loses confidence in the safety and security of the market': 696).

[87] L Pereira, Chairman, Comissão de Valores Mobiliários, Brasil, interview, Madrid, 23 June 2014.

[88] D Parfit, *On What Matters* (Oxford, Oxford University Press, 2007) 25. This approach takes cognizance of the objection by Alaisdair MacIntyre that the 'elevation of the values of the market to a central social place' risks creating the circumstances in which 'the concept of the virtues might

priate contextualisation in terms of specific institutional purposes, standards and requirements. Nevertheless it does describe moral parameters, which are universally acknowledged to be fundamental to the design of morally acceptable and socially sustainable human institutions, including markets. Paradoxically it is this very imperative that underpinned the initial (but lost) normative basis of the disclosure paradigm. As one of its key architects, Baldwin Bane, pointed out 80 years ago the disclosure paradigm was 'informed by a moral idea.'[89]

It is, therefore, time to reimagine the lost normative impulses of financial regulation. Moreover this investigation necessitates evaluating whether compartmentalized conceptions of responsibility contribute to suboptimal outcomes. Why, for example, were the professions so close to the executive suites and trading floors, unwilling or incapable of exercising skepticism, the hallmark of expertise? This is an existential question for both the established professions and those who would like to see the establishment of a professional standards board for banking, an idea canvassed but viewed with extreme caution by the British Parliamentary Banking Standards Commission. Professionalizing finance is a laudable goal but it necessitates both cognizance and acceptance of broader obligations that inform the grant of professional status.

The specific duties that bind a professional are, therefore, defined by the expectations that the profession has itself created in the public mind. Necessarily, these extend beyond putting the interests of clients first. These expectations, however, become exceptionally problematic in environments such as capital markets, which are governed by specific cultural norms and mores and separated from broader society through (potentially) unbridgeable income disparities. The financial sector is one of the areas in which these regulatory source imbalances have been most pronounced over the years. Professional, structural and cultural embeddedness condition the interplay of regulatory authority and regulatory responses. These coalitions of embeddedness allow those players or firms with the requisite resources and interorganisational alliances to build up and legitimate their image of regulatory authority. If their regulatory authority is strong, then they can subsequently challenge and/or negotiate the rules of regulation. It is clearly in the self-interest of powerful actors within an industry such as financial services to be as reflexively influential as possible on current regulatory practice, so as to maintain or increase future levels of influence. The great challenge is achieving balance. It is now clear that balance had slipped too far in the years preceding the global financial crisis. The enormity of the global financial crisis has demonstrated just how misplaced confidence in market ordering was.[90] As such, it represents a *fin de siècle* moment. The material and ideational certainties associated with the privileging of financial capitalism have evaporated.

---

suffer at first attrition and then perhaps something near total effacement': see A MacIntyre, *After Virtue* (Notre Dame, University of Notre Dame Press, 1994) 196.

[89] BB Bane, 'The Securities Act of 1933' (1933) 1 *Certified Public Accountant* 587, 592 (reprinting address to Annual Meeting of the American Society, Milwaukee, WI, 19 September 1933).

[90] For discussion, see J O'Brien, G Gilligan and S Miller, 'Culture and the Future of Financial

The *Wingecarribee Shire Council v Lehman Brothers Australia* decision highlights the suboptimal effect of a retreat to technicalities in dealing with substantive ethical considerations. The critical issue is how to respond. As we have seen, rules are too easily transacted around and principles without external validation and oversight lack the granularity to be enforceable. Tackling ethical deficiencies requires we pay much more attention to the moral dimension of market conduct. It is essential to stress the ethical component of corporate and professional obligation. For the product manufacturer it demonstrates corporate responsibility, which can then be evaluated. For the regulator it offers an opportunity to engage in proactive strategies that prevent systemic risk from developing. Ultimately, for the consumer and the sophisticated investor alike it provides a basis for trust.

Corporate cultures do not exist in a vacuum; nor are they mere reactive responses to externally mandated rules. Instead they reflect the values of the organization. The emphasis on culture underpins an influential definition of corporate governance provided by the Australian jurist Justice Neville Owen. In his investigation into the collapse of HIH Insurance, Justice Owen maintained that he was 'not so much concerned with the content of a corporate governance model as with the culture of the organization to which it attaches.' For Justice Owen,

> [T]he key to good corporate governance lies in substance, not form. It is about the way the directors of a company create and develop a model to fit the circumstances of the company and then test it periodically for its practical effectiveness. It is about the directors taking control of a regime they have established and for which they are responsible.[91]

It is in this context that corporate culture plays an essential disseminating role. It informs employees of what the company stands for.[92] To be effective it must be informed by belief not prudence (ie the fear of detection) precisely because the risk of detection can be quite low and fines written off as part of the price

---

Regulation: How to Embed Restraint in the Interests of Systemic Stability' (2014) 8 *Law and Financial Markets Review* 115.

[91] Report of the HIH Royal Commission, *The Failure of HIH Insurance* (Canberra, Commonwealth of Australia, 2003) xxxii, www.hihroyalcom.gov.au/finalreport/index.htm. For rare recognition of failure to internalize responsibility from former head of compliance at British Bank HBOS, see P Moore, 'Memo to Treasury Select Committee,' Westminster, London, 10 February 2009 ('My personal experience of being on the inside as a risk and compliance manager has shown me is that, whatever the very specific, final and direct causes of the financial crisis, I strongly believe that the real underlying cause of all the problems was simply this—a total failure of all key aspects of governance. In my view and from my personal experience at HBOS, all the other specific failures stem from this one primary cause').

[92] See LS Paine, 'Managing for Organizational Integrity' (1994) 3 *Harvard Business Review* 106 (noting that '[T]he task of ethics management is to define and give life to an organization's guiding values, to create an environment that supports ethically sound behavior, and to instill a sense of shared accountability among employees.' As such, 'organizational ethics helps define what a company is and what it stands for': 111).

of doing business.[93] As Rose puts it, '[T]here is no escaping the fact that why one holds the required moral tastes matters as much as having the right kind of moral tastes.'[94] However, notions and practices of recurring routinization and neutralisation of deviance are well entrenched in the finance sector, as they are in some other industries, for example real estate, with its seemingly perennial problems of transparency and accountability in pricing and sales campaigns. Thus, the operational reality of financial services is that ignoring or abusing regulatory standards can be common practice and regulators have limited flexibility in instrumental approaches to sanction. For more conventional offences such as burglary and theft, it is easier to take an instrumental view because the law is fairly clear and rarely challenged on a moral basis. However, it is harder to do this in the financial services sector because ambiguity and moral contestation may be features of a range of market behaviours. A significant explanatory variable of widespread rule violations in the financial services sector is that many offenders feel relatively immune from conviction and imprisonment.

The book opened with a quotation from Landis' address to the Catholic University of America in 1937. In closing it is worth restating his rationale for academic research:

> One grasps for shadows the better to comprehend sunlight. One reaches into the past, more clearly to know today and tomorrow. It is the privilege of all who care about education to test the depth and quality of that shadow for there, perhaps more than anywhere, one must try to pierce the brilliance of continuing dawns.[95]

The lost legacy of the disclosure paradigm that Landis did so much to propagate was its moral foundation. For Landis, as with Adam Smith, moral sentiments are the drivers for social cohesion. Weakening those risks fraying the ties that bind. It is a lesson from history we ignore at our peril. We all need to make that journey back to the Sargasso of financial regulation. There is no better guide than Landis, who truly does provide 'the wisp, a wick that is its own taper and light through the weltering dark.'[96]

---

[93] The rise of class actions, however, may change this dynamic: see J Harris and M Legg, 'What Price Investor Protection: Class Actions vs Corporate Rescue' (2009) 17 *Insolvency Law Journal* 185. Recent litigation success (through settlements) in Australia has underscored the monetary pain—see eg the $200m settlement reached by Centro and its auditors PwC to end a class action: N Lenaghan and B Wilmont, 'Centro, PwC to Take Record $200m Hit,' *Australian Financial Review*, 9 May 2012, http://afr.com/p/national/centro_pwc_take_record_legal_hit_6CaSTKu6K1w7nJFFIZOxWL.

[94] D Rose, *The Moral Foundations of Economic Behavior* (Oxford, Oxford University Press, 2011) 188.

[95] JM Landis, 'Address to the Third Annual Eastern Students Conference' (speech delivered at the Catholic University of America, 20 March 1937).

[96] S Heaney, 'A Lough Neagh Sequence,' in *A Door Into the Dark* (London, Faber & Faber, 1969).

INDEX

accountancy profession 37–9, 40–1
Administrative Conference 149–50
administrative development/enforcement *see under* Securities Exchange Act 1934
administrative law debate 24–5
Administrative Procedure Act 1946 (APA) 129–32, 136, 144–5, 148
Administrative Procedure, Attorney-General's Special Committee on 128, 129
Administrative Process, The 9–10, 60, 78, 113, 144
administrative state
    acceptance of 78–9
    engagement with 100–1
    initial grant of authority 75
    isolation from administrative processes 76–8
    and JML's fall from grace 158, 161
    judiciary limitations 76
    legitimacy 74
    see also Public Utility Holding Company Act (PUHCA); regulatory state
Agius, Marcus vii–viii
Agricultural Adjustment Agency 23, 70
Alder, Ashley 182
Alien Registration Act 1940 90
American Bar Association (ABA) 98
    campaign against administrative burns 121–3, 124–5, 127, 131
    as knowledge broker 113, 119
American Law Institute 115
American Scholar Journal 100
Anstee, Nick vii
Australia
    global financial crisis (2007 onwards) (GFC) 96
    policy reform 61
Australian Bank Bill Swap Rate 163
Australian Federal Court ruling 179–80, 186

Bane, Baldwin 32, 38, 39, 185
bank sector, institutionalizing memory 175–8
Banks and Currency, 1912 House Committee (Pujo Hearings) 26–7
Barclays vii–viii, x
Beaman, Middleton 33
Berle, Adolf 17–19, 21, 46, 49, 74

Biddle, Francis 90
Black, Hugo 68, 114–15
Boston Law Review 48
Brains Trust approach 16–17, 49
Brandeis, Louis 8, 103–4
Bridges deportation hearings case, as hearings examiner 9–10
    administrative/judicial methods, combination 91–2
    circumstantial evidence 85–6
    conclusion reached 81
    critique of government's case 88
    further hearings 90–1
    hearings process 84–5
    nature of case 81, 83–4
    official investigations 86–7
    praise/opprobrium 82, 85, 88–9
    regulatory purpose, conception 81
    response of administration 89–90
    witch-hunt nature of case 82
Bridges, Harry R
    arrest/hearings process 84–5
    communist affiliation 83, 85
    HML's view of 87
    nature of case against him 82, 83–4, 85
    response to critique of case 90
    as union power broker 81, 83
Bridges v Wixon 9n 10
Burns, John 69
Business Standards Committee Impact Report (Goldman Sachs) 93–7, 110–11

Canterbury, Archbishop of 176–7
Caplin, Mortimer 154
Carney, Mark 62, 168, 170
Cary, William 144, 151, 152
Catholic University of America 1, 187
Central Intelligence Agency (CIA) 138
Chicago Tribune 89
Christie, Robert 54
Citigroup Capital Markets 94
Civil Aeronautics Board (CAB), chair 10–11, 135–6
    not reappointed 136–7
Clark, Charles 10
Code of Fair Competition for Investment Bankers 44, 47, 54

codes of conduct debate 54–6, 57–8
Cohen, Benjamin 23, 29, 31, 33, 52, 56, 66, 79–80, 127
  Bridges deportation hearings case, reaction to 82
Columbia University
  New Deal involvement 17, 20, 23, 49, 101, 144
  Oral History Project 5, 12
  Presbyterian Hospital 157, 158
Companies Act (British) 45
Constitutional Convention (1787) 72–3
Corcoran, Thomas 23, 29, 31, 52, 56, 66, 79, 137
  Bridges deportation hearings case, reaction to 82
  intervention in JML trial 159
corporate responsibility vii–viii
Coughlin, Father Charles 85, 116
CPA (Certified Public Accountants), New York State Society of 39–40
  partnership with NRA 40–1
Cummings, Homer 28

Daily Telegraph 177
Davidson, Henry 44
Dean, Arthur 44–5
disclosure paradigm 3, 11, 181, 187
Douglas, William O 1, 20, 49, 50–1, 116–17, 152, 181
Doyle, Stanley 86
Dudley, William 63

Economic Club of New York 171
Ehrlichmann, Ben 40–1
Electric Bond & Share case 69–70, 79
electricity/gase sectors *see* Public Utility Holding Company Act (PUHCA)
Elihu Root Special Collection Room 11
Encyclopedia Britannica 53

fall from grace, JML's 11, 152–61
  and administrative state/process 158, 161
  drinking/personal depression 154, 161
  payment of arrears 153–4
  as political problem 154–5, 156, 159
  psychological problems 155–6
  sentencing trial 156–9
  suspension from right to practice 159–60
  tax returns filing, charge 152–3
Federal Bar Association 118–19
Federal Communications Commission (FCC), planned reorganization 151
Federal Reserve Bank of New York 63
Federal Reserve Board, creation 56
Federal Trade Commission (FTC) 28, 31
  Commissioner, HML as 37, 38, 41–2
  consultant, HML as 35–6
  enrollment of professions 37–9

  NRA relationship 40–1, 42, 43–5, 46–8, 51–2, 181
  regulatory intervention, HML approach 41
Feldman, George 35, 44
Feldman, Justin 3, 138, 155, 158
Financial Conduct Authority (UK) 177–8
financial sector, institutionalizing memory 175–8
Financial Stability Board (FSB) 62
Financial Stability Oversight Council 165
Financial Times vii
Fortune magazine 2, 45, 53
Francis, Pope 169–70
Frankfurter, Felix
  advises JML 46, 50, 52–3
  holding company model 64–5
  initial link with JML 7–8, 9
  post-war education 107
  presidential advisor 21–3, 24–5, 29, 30, 33
  public utilities legislation compromise 68
  and Supreme Court 116, 117, 138–9
Freund, Paul 108
Fuller, Lon 107–8

G20 Summit (St Petersburg) 62
Gannett, Frank 119
Gay, Charles 120
Gelhorn, Walter 101, 123, 131
global financial crisis (2007 onwards) (GFC)
  aftermath vii–viii
  business ethics and accountability 93–7, 109–11
  contrast with New deal 13
  erosion of trust 108–9
  institutions too big to fail 61
  reform progress and risks 62–3
  social mores of global finance viii–ix
  systemic ethical deficit 37
  systemically important institutions 62
Goldman Sachs
  apparent success 174
  Business Standards Committee Impact Report 93–7, 110–11
  Tourre prosecution 180
Grange Securities 179
Greenspan, Alan 174
Griswold, Erwin 5, 100, 107

Hampton, Sir Philip 176
Hanes, James 120
Harvard Law Review 3
Harvard Law School Dean
  administrative state, engagement with 100–1
  appointment 9
  Bridges deportation hearings case, as hearings examiner 81, 82, 84, 85, 92
  critical knowledge broker, role 101–2

difference with predecessor 121–2
evidence presentation, scientific method
  advocacy 103–5
lack of public recognition 11, 12
leaving post 108, 157
post-war education 107–8
previous teaching career 1, 7–9
primary attraction of position 97–8
prior academic ability, as entry
  qualification 99
professional responsibility to society 105–8
research enhancement 99–100
statement of approach 102–6
strategic positioning of school 100
tripartite approach 98–9, 102–3
Harvard University, New Deal involvement 17,
  23
Hewart, Lord 118
HIH Insurance 186
holding company model 64–5
Holmes, Oliver Wendell 23, 73, 104, 159
Hong Kong Securities and Futures
  Commission 166, 182
Hoover Commission 132–3
Hoover, Herbert 14, 132
Hoover, J Edgar 138
Hourican, John 176–7
House of Truth 22
Hudson, Millard 47
Hughes, Charles Evans 115, 118–19

income tax, non-payment among law
  partners 2n
International Organization of Securities
  Commissions (IOSCO) 167, 168, 172
Investment Banking Association 54, 164
Iowa University 9
Irons, Peter 23

Jackson, Robert 79, 117–18
Japan 6
Johnson, Hugh 43, 47

Karr's epigram 175
Katz, Milton 24
Katzenbach, Nicholas 4, 154–6, 158
Katznelson, Ira 130–1
Kay, John 108, 178, 183
Keegan, John 86, 97
Kennedy administration 2
  epicentre of political life, JML at 135
Kennedy family 3, 135–6, 137–8, 161
Kennedy, Joe 3
  Hoover Commission 132
  public utilities legislation administration 67
  SEC chairman 59–60, 135, 167, 178
  tax returns filing, JML's 153–4
Kennedy, John F 3, 10
  Administrative Conference 149–50

and fall from grace of JML 154–5
family links 137–8
landis report *see* Landis report (to the
  President-Elect) 1960
partnership model 145–9
president-elect appointments 138–9
presidential library 154–5
Kennedy, Robert 4, 154, 158, 161
Klu Klux Klan 114
Knowles, Harper 86–7
Kolb, Lawrence 155–6, 160

La Follette, Senator 118
Lachat, Ann Héritier 182
Lagarde, Christine 170
Landell Hall library 11
Landis, James M
  belief system 5
  biographies of 3n
  birth 1, 5
  Bridges case *see Bridges* deportation
    hearings case
  death 2, 160–1
  disclosure paradigm 3, 11, 181, 187
  education achievements 5, 7
  fall *see* fall from grace
  father's influence 5–7
  final pronouncement on life's work 152
  Harvard *see* Harvard Law School Dean
  lack of public recognition for 11, 12
  mother's influence 6
  New Deal 2
  personal life 135–6
  personality clashes 144
  political damage to 10
  professional lobbying against 10–11
  prosecution/conviction/sentence 2, 4, 11
  realism towards Wall Street 30–1
  regulatory theorist/practitioner 4–5, 11
  religious faith 6–7
  report for president-elect 10
  social justice, integrated approach 8–9
  socially distant 2–3
  Supreme Court nomination 138–9
  teaching career 1, 7–9
  see also Administrative Process, The
Landis report (to the President-Elect)
  1960 139–44, 170
  Administrative Conference 149–50
  delegation of discretion 139–40
  implementation 144–52
  as manifesto for change 143–4
  organised lobbying 142–3
  partnership model 145–9
  regulatory commission model, operational
    failure 140–1
  structural problems 141–2
  warranted commitment 142
Lehman Brothers 179, 186

Lessig, Lawrence 183
Libor (London Interbank Offered Rate) viii, ix,
    x, 163, 164
Lippman, Walter 54–5
Llewellyn, Karl 152
Logan, Mills 130
Long, Huey 16, 114, 115
Los Angeles Times 88–9

Mack, Judge Julian 70
Means, Gardiner 18, 74
Medcraft, Greg 167
Milner, Lawrence 86
Moe, Kenneth 153
Moley, Raymond 19, 29, 33–4, 35, 49, 59
Morgenthau, Robert 4, 153, 159
Murphy, Frank 115–16, 128

National Industrial Recovery Act 67
National Industrial Relations Agency 77
National Labor Relations Act 124–5, 130
National Labor Relations Board (NLRB) 23,
    73, 118, 119, 120, 146
National Recovery Administration Act 126–7
National Recovery Administration (NRA) 23
    codes of conduct proposals 54–6
    FTC relationship 40–1, 42, 43–5, 46–8,
        51–2, 181
    legal challenges to 70
Navasky, Victor 158
New Deal
    administrative law debate 24–5
    Brains Trust approach 16–17, 49
    conflicts/tensions 15
    contrast with GFC 13
    corporation governance/accountability
        issues 17–18
    critical objective 13–14
    current paradigm 172–4
    emphasis on action 14–15
    enlisted academics 17–20
    initial success ix–x
    international pressures 16
    lobbying battles 123
    regulatory agencies, challenges to 70–1
    union pressures 16
    Washington establishment/conflicts 20–4,
        25
New York Investment Bankers Conference 120
New York Stock Exchange 41–2
New York Times 2
Nolan, Judge 160
non-calculative social contract 178

Oberdorfer, Louis 154
Ontario Securities Commission 183
Owen, Neville 186

Parfit, Derek 184–5

Parliamentary Banking Standards Commission
    (UK) 165, 176, 185
partnership model 145–9
Pecora, Ferdinand 59
Pecora hearings 32
Perkins, Frances 83, 90
Pound, Roscoe 9, 121–2
Presbyterian church 5, 6–7
professional responsibility
    alternative framework 109–10
    declining faith in 133
    Harvard Law School model 105–8, 111
    self-monitoring 108–9
Profiles in Courage 137–8
Public Utility Holding Company Act (PUHCA)
    background 63
    constitutionality ruling 69–70
    death sentence clause 66–8
    Electric Bond and Share case 69–70, 79
    holding company model 64–5
    interstate commerce 65–6
    national interest compromise 67–8
    purpose/goal 63–4
    SEC oversight 65–6, 67, 68–9
    Supreme Court judgment 79–80, 114
    see also administrative state

Rakoff, Judge Jed 94
Rares, Judge 179–80
Rayburn, Sam 28–9, 33, 34, 47, 49
RBS (Royal Bank of Scotland) 176–7, ix
Reed, Stanley 116
regulatory capitalism's future
    background 163
    disclosure paradigm 3, 11, 181, 187
    efficient market hypothesis 179
    ethical culture, role in behavior 164,
        166–9, 183–7
    institutionalizing memory 175–8
    investigations 163, 164–6
    non-calculative social contract 178
    patterns of conduct 165–6
    performance/conformance
        bifurcation 178–83
    potential change 170–2
    professional role 185
    prosecutions 163
    public disquiet from civic society 169–70
    self-regulation, reliance 163–4
    structured action field (SAF) 173–4
    technical defenses 174–5
regulatory state
    accountability 120–1, 132–3
    Administrative Conference 149–50
    Administrative Procedure Act 1946
        (APA) 129–32, 136, 144–5, 148
    advancement of goals, post-war 131–2
    critique by JML of attacks on 124–7
    exemptions 124–5, 132–3

fear of arbitrary power 118
judicial review process 129–31
legitimation compromises 113–14
partnership model 145–9
political factors 119–23, 127–9, 129–33
regulatory agencies, challenges to 70–1
rigorous analysis of practice 125–6
Supreme Court changes 114–19
see also administrative state
*Report on Regulatory Agencies to the President-
Elect* 10
Ritchie, Don 158
Roosevelt, Franklin D
bank regulation 28
court-packing controversy 71–4
election campaign rhetoric (1936) 70–3
emphasis on action 14–15, 18, 111
holding company model 64–5
interest group politics, opposition to 127–8
mentioned 5, 10, 21, 39, 42, 45, 46, 79,
132, 137, 144
political conflict on regulation 119–20
relationship with academics 17, 18, 19–20
Securities Exchange Bill 59–60
support for SEC 141
Supreme Court nominations 114–15, 138
Rose, D 187
Ryan, Chief Justice Sylvester 2, 4
Ryan, Sylvester 156–9

Sachs, Alexander 55–6
San Francisco News 88
Sants, Hector 178
Schlesinger, Arthur 4
Sears, Charles 90
Securities Act (1933) 181
delay/waiting period 31–2
drafting process 31, 32–4
enactment 35
evaluation panel 44
further powers requested 52–3
modification proposals 45–51
as moral instrument 32
progress through Congress 34–5
Wall Street reaction 35
Securities Exchange Act 1934
administrative development/
enforcement 56–7
disclosure paradigm 181
enactment 56
goals 56
restrictions on speculation 57
strengths/weaknesses 53
Securities and Exchange Commission (SEC) 1,
3, 4
aggressive enforcement 117
chairman, HML as 1, 8, 37, 59–60, 67, 69,
72, 97, 120
creation 56

current criticism of 166
eightieth anniversary 12
global financial crisis (2007 onwards)
(GFC) 94–5
planned reorganization 151–2
PUHCA oversight 65–6, 67, 68–9
Tourre prosecution 180–1
securities reform
critique of Thompson draft 29–30
implementation 35–6
initial responsibility 25–6
Pujo Committee 26–7
realism towards Wall Street, Landis,
James M 30–1
recruitment of JML 25, 29
Seligman, Joel 151
Shepherd, George 123, 129–30
Smith, Adam 108, 179, 187
social responsibility 184
Social Security Act 73
Social Union visit 8
Southern District of New York 69–70, 94
Stone, Harlan 78
structured action field (SAF) 173–4
Supreme Court 23
acceptance of the administrative 78
anti-semitism and 21
Bridges case appeal 90–1
challenge to SEC 1–2, 5
competence of administrative procedures,
ruling 126
court-packing controversy 71–4, 114, 123,
124, 175
evidence presentation in 103–5
political appointments 114–16
precedent, JML as student of 75–7
PUHCA judgment 79–80, 114
regulatory agencies, legal challenges
to 70–1
regulatory state 114, 116–19
Sutherland, Justice 115, 119
Swiss Financial Market Supervisory
Authority 182
systemic ethical deficit 37

Thompson, Houston 25–6, 32–3
Thompson, Hunter 28
Today journal 49
Tokyo 1, 5, 6
Tourre, Fabrice 180–1
Treasury Select Committee (UK) 165
Truman Administration 10–11, 136–7
Truman, Harry 129, 132–3, 141
Tugwell, Rexford 16–17, 20

United Kingdom
Financial Conduct Authority 177–8
global financial crisis (2007 onwards)
(GFC) 96

United Kingdom – *continued*
    Parliamentary Banking Standards
        Commission 165, 176
    Treasury Select Committee 165
Untermayer, Samuel 26, 27–8, 39–40

Valentine, Robert 22
Volcker, Paul 171
Volcker Proposal 61

Wang, Jessica 75
Warren, Dean William 155, 158
Washington DC 1
Washington DC
    and new Deal 20–4, 25

    and Wall Street 101
Welby, Justin *see* Canterbury, Archbishop of
Wetston, Howard 183
Whitney, Richard 42
Wilkie, Wendell 67
Williamson, Oliver 178
Wilson, James 72–3
World War One 5, 6–7, 21
Wright, David 168
Wzinski, Charles 82

Yale University 10
    New Deal involvement 17, 20, 23
YMCA 5

www.ingramcontent.com/pod-product-compliance
Lightning Source LLC
Chambersburg PA
CBHW061218220326
41599CB00025B/4681